AN INTRODUCTION TO MULTICULTURAL COUNSELING

AN INTRODUCTION TO MULTICULTURAL COUNSELING

Wanda M. L. Lee
San Francisco State University

USA	Publishing Office:	ACCELERATED DEVELOPMENT *A member of the Taylor & Francis Group* 325 Chestnut Street Philadelphia, PA 19106 Tel: (215) 625-8900 Fax: (215) 625-2940
	Distribution Center:	ACCELERATED DEVELOPMENT *A member of the Taylor & Francis Group* 47 Runway Road, Suite G Levittown, PA 19057-4700 Tel: (215) 269-0400 Fax: (215) 269-0363
UK		ACCELERATED DEVELOPMENT *A member of the Taylor & Francis Group* 1 Gunpowder Square London EC4A 3DE Tel: +44 171 583 0490 Fax: +44 171 583 0581

AN INTRODUCTION TO MULTICULTURAL COUNSELING

1 2 3 4 5 6 7 8 9 0

Printed by Edwards Brothers, Ann Arbor, MI, 1999.
Cover design by Joan Wendt

A CIP catalog record for this book is available from the British Library.
⊗ The paper in this publication meets the requirements of the ANSI Standard Z39.48-1984 (Permanence of Paper).

Library of Congress Cataloging-in-Publication Data

Lee, Wanda M. L.
    An introduction to multicultural counseling / Wanda M. L. Lee.
      p.   cm.
    Includes bibliographical references and index.
    ISBN 1-56032-567-4 (alk. paper). — ISBN 1-56032-568-2 (pbk. : alk. paper)
    1. Cross-cultural counseling.   I. Title.
  BF637.C6L415   1999
  158'.3—dc21   99–17941
                                                        CIP

ISBN 1-56032-567-4 (case)
ISBN 1-56032-568-2 (paper)

This book is dedicated to Ken, Malia, and Logan, my multicultural family, whose enduring love, support, and sacrifice made this work possible.

CONTENTS

Dedication   V
Preface   XI
Acknowledgments   XIII

1   **Multicultural Counseling: Past, Present, and Future**   1

Culture   2
Ethnicity   3
Minority Groups   3
Early Issues   3
Current Issues and Controversies   5
Future Needs   9

2   **Understanding and Appreciating Difference**   10

Racism   12
Barriers in Counseling   14
Developing Cultural Awareness   16
Counseling Clients Who Have Been Subject to Discrimination   19
Recommended Cultural Resources   21

3   **Cultural Aspects of Psychological Assessment**   22

Historical and Sociopolitical Influences on Testing   22
Bias in Testing   25
Culture-Specific Testing   30
Recommendations for Multicultural Assessment   32

4   Cultural Transition   36

   Culture Shock   38
   Counseling Individuals and Families in Cultural Transition   40
   Re-Entry Shock   44
   Generational Effects of Acculturation   46

5   Cultural Identity Development   48

   Racial–Ethnic Identity Development   49
   Other Dimensions of Minority Identity Development   54
   Counseling Implications   56
   Recommended Cultural Resources   56

6   Native Americans in Counseling   57

   Histories and Diversity   57
   Cultural Values   60
   Indigenous Treatment Methods   63
   Treatment Implications   65
   General Counseling Issues   68
   Recommended Cultural Resources   72

7   African Americans in Counseling   73

   Histories and Diversity   73
   Cultural Values   76
   Indigenous Treatment Methods   80
   Treatment Implications   82
   Recommended Cultural Resources   87

8   Latinos and Latinas in Counseling   88

   Histories and Diversity   89
   Cultural Values   92
   Indigenous Treatment Methods   95
   Counseling Issues   97
   Recommended Cultural Resources   101

9   Asian and Pacific Islander Americans in Counseling   102

Histories and Diversity   102
Cultural Values   104
Indigenous Treatment Methods   106
Counseling Issues   108
Recommended Cultural Resources   113

10   European Americans in Counseling   114

Within-Group Characteristics and Variability   115
Indigenous Treatment Methods   118
Counseling Issues   119
Recommended Cultural Resources   121

11   Counseling Women   123

Histories and Diversity   123
Cultural Values   126
Indigenous Treatment Methods   126
Counseling Issues   129
Recommended Cultural Resources   135

12   Counseling Men   136

Histories and Diversity   136
Cultural Values   138
Indigenous Treatment Methods   140
Counseling Issues   142
Recommended Cultural Resources   145

13   Counseling Gay Men and Lesbians   146

Histories and Diversity   146
Cultural Values   151
Indigenous Treatment Methods   151
Counseling Issues   152
Recommended Cultural Resources   158

14   **Counseling Older People**   **159**

Histories and Diversity   159
Cultural Values   163
Indigenous Treatment Methods   163
Counseling Issues   164
Other Counseling Implications   168
Recommended Cultural Resources   172

15   **Counseling People With Disabilities**   **174**

Histories and Diversity   175
Cultural Values   180
Counseling Issues   182
Treatment Implications   184
Recommended Cultural Resources   185

16   **Developing Multicultural Counseling Competency**   **186**

Multicultural Theory   187
Multicultural Competencies   188
Multicultural Training   190
Multiculturalism Within the Counseling Profession   197

Appendix A: Guidelines for Providers of Psychological
Services to Ethnic, Linguistic, and Culturally Diverse
Populations   201

Appendix B: Proposed Cross-Cultural Competencies
and Objectives   207

References   213
Index   239
About the Author   259

PREFACE

When culture-specific information is presented or discussed there is always the danger that the information will form the basis of stereotypes; in other words, making generalizations about any cultural group is potentially misleading. More accurate or positive stereotypes may replace those commonly held, but they are still stereotypes. This issue seems unavoidable when attempting to present cultural knowledge in the hopes that it will broaden the range of assessment and treatment planning considerations counselors make with respect to each individual client. It cannot be overstated that regardless of the general knowledge that is available regarding a particular cultural group, every counselor must be open to meeting each client as an individual whose background, values, and other characteristics may or may not be similar to those of others within their cultural group(s).

It was impossible to include all the relevant cultural groups in the United States, as the population continues to diversify. Many important specific ethnic groups have not been included or are included only within the context of a broader ethnic group, often due to a lack of research on these groups. The concerns of these groups are significant, but unfortunately there has been comparatively little research or writing available related to counseling these groups. In particular, Arab, Filipino, Pacific Islander, and Russian Americans are groups in need of additional research. The most coverage has been given to groups who are numerically and/or politically most salient and where there is substantial existing counseling or psychology literature.

This book is written with respect to information about ethnic and cultural minority groups within the United States. Many of the general issues and recommendations related to counseling may be applicable to counseling cultural minority populations in other countries; however, the reader is cautioned not to overgeneralize from the minority experiences in one country to members of the same cultural group in another country.

This book is part of the evolution of my teaching a course on multicultural counseling since 1981. Over the years, I became increasingly dissatisfied with existing books on the subject because they tended to focus only on ethnicity and there were several other dimensions of cultural diversity that were to be included in the class to meet curriculum and accreditation requirements, including gender, sexual orientation, physical disability, and aging. Eventually, I developed a course reader which sampled from existing texts and current journal articles. The drawback of this approach was that each writer had a different voice and often covered the material from a somewhat different approach, which was sometimes confusing to students new to the topic. In the end, it seemed that the best way to cover the topic of multicultural counseling, in the manner I felt it needed to be covered: with 1) a balance of etic and emic issues, 2) an emphasis on indigenous treatments, and 3) recognition of the complexity of multiple minority status (e.g., female and ethnic minority, ethnic minority person with a disability, etc.) was to write a book myself. Years later, you are now reading the results of this effort and it is my sincere hope that this book will be of some help to you along your own path to multicultural competence.

☐   A Note for Instructors

This book is planned as a primer, a general introduction to counseling issues. Ideally, students would read one chapter each week as an overview of background, cultural, and clinical issues of importance. Each topic can then be supplemented by current, much more specific readings either chosen by the instructor or the students themselves. Many of the chapters list recommended resources for further study. The book is tailored to a semester format, but can be adapted to a shorter term by either omitting selected chapters or assigning two chapters per week as needed.

ACKNOWLEDGMENTS

I would like to thank my students, whose interest and questions over the years motivated me to begin and continue developing this book. In particular, thanks to Sinead Smith, research assistant, who helped with library resources and provided valuable input and suggestions of her own. Thanks also go to former students Christa Siringo and Raphael Chang, who made contributions to the work as well.

Many thanks go to my friends and colleagues, Alvin Alvarez, Sal Chavez, Bob Chope, Doris Galvin, Andy Hogg, Alice Nemon, Jackie Reza, Mike Sullivan, Norm Sundberg, Patricia Walker, and Gerald West, for their thoughtful comments and helpful perspectives on portions of the manuscript. My special thanks to Joseph Hollis, Accelerated Development publisher for many years, whose support, patience, and guidance was instrumental throughout the initial phases of the publishing process.

This book was in part written with the institutional support of a San Francisco State University Faculty Affirmative Action Award and a San Francisco State University Presidential Award for Professional Development of Probationary Faculty.

Multicultural Counseling: Past, Present, and Future

Who decides what is margin and what is text? Who decides where the borders of the homeland run? Absences and silences are potent. It is the eloquent margins which frame the history of the land.

—Janette Turner Hospital (Biggs, 1996, p. 82)

The population of the United States is becoming more and more diverse. Twenty-four percent of the current population is African American, Chicano/Latino, Asian American, or Native American (U.S. Bureau of the Census, 1990a), yet the vast majority of counselors are European American by ethnicity, and all of the major theoretical approaches to counseling were developed by Europeans (Freud, Jung, Adler, Perls, etc.) or Americans of European descent (Rogers, Skinner, Ellis, etc.). The counseling profession is basically a product of European American culture (Das, 1995). As the field of counseling moves into the 21st century, cultural differences in addition to ethnicity have increasingly gained recognition as important considerations in the counseling process: gender roles, sexual orientation, aging, and physical disability. Understanding the complex social and cultural background of each client is integral to successful counseling. This book is written for beginning counselors and practicing counselors who have not had previous formal training in multicultural counseling.

☐ Culture

To begin the journey toward becoming a culturally competent counselor, you must first ask yourself "What is culture?" Haviland (1975) defined *culture* as "a set of shared assumptions where people can predict each others actions in a given circumstance and react accordingly" (p. 6). When the client and counselor come from different cultural backgrounds, whether in terms of ethnicity, sex, sexual orientation, disability, or age, they may not share the same assumptions about many things, including the counseling process. Counseling becomes an uncomfortable, unpredictable interaction for both parties, and the likelihood of a second session, let alone productive change, becomes low.

Webster's Seventh New Collegiate Dictionary (1969) defines *culture* as "behavior typical of a group or class" (p. 202). In this definition, what is typical or normative for a particular group is key. To understand a client's culture, the counselor must understand what is typical of that client's cultural group(s). In this context, the client's own behavior can then be evaluated as it compares to how others in his or her group would typically behave. Behavior that is abnormal in one culture may be adaptive in another.

There are many facets of culture, among them language, customs, values, beliefs, spirituality, sex roles, and sociopolitical history, and culture is important in counseling in many ways. First, counseling occurs in a cultural context, within an office, school, college, or other organization and, beyond this, within a larger community or society. If the client must seek treatment within an environment that is culturally foreign, he or she may be reluctant even to initiate counseling. Second, as briefly mentioned above, appropriate assessment of a client's problems should take into consideration the client's culture. Third, counseling itself is culturally based. Counseling as it has been traditionally taught in most English-speaking countries developed from historical and social influences most relevant to younger, White, heterosexual, able-bodied clients. There are many cultures that do not have a word for counseling, and the ways people ordinarily seek help within their culture may not include going to a counselor. Finally, culture itself may be the focus of counseling. When a client is going through cultural transition; when there are cultural differences within his or her intimate relationships; when a client has been the victim of cultural racism, sexism, homophobia, ablism, or ageism; when a client's personal culture is so different from that of the society around him or her that the stress is unbearable, then culture itself may become the center of the counseling process.

☐ Ethnicity

McGoldrick, Pearce, and Giordano (1982) described *ethnicity* as a sense of commonality that is more than race, religion, or national or geographic origin. Conscious and unconscious processes contribute to a sense of identity and historical continuity. Another way to look at ethnicity is as a perceived common ancestry, whether real or fictitious (Shibutani & Kwan, 1965). In this respect there are several broad ethnic groups within the United States: Native Americans, African Americans, Latinos and Latinas, Asian Americans, and European Americans. Some of these ethnic groups may have people of several races grouped within them—for example, Latinos. What is salient in the United States is that members of these groups are perceived by others as having a common ancestry even though there is much cultural diversity within each of these groups.

☐ Minority Groups

Corey, Corey, and Callanan (1988) defined a *minority group* as people who have been discriminated against or subjected to unequal treatment. All of the ethnic groups mentioned above are minority groups within the United States except some European American subgroups that have historically been afforded the political, social, and economic power to discriminate against others. Using this definition of minority group would also include women, gay men and lesbians, the elderly, and people with disabilities, because all these groups also have been subjected to unequal treatment in the history of this nation.

A broad view of cultural differences in counseling includes, therefore, many specific cultural groups that may differ from the counselor in a variety of ways that are not limited to ethnicity, sex, sexual orientation, age, or disability.

☐ Early Issues

Historically, there have been many ways of looking at cultural differences between people. How differences are viewed has been a reflection of the sociopolitical climate of the time. In the 1800s, England was at the height of its colonization of other lands. Sir Francis Galton, a member of the ruling class and a relative of Charles Darwin (who proposed the biological concept of natural selection), began to look at differences between people and concluded that these differences were a result of genetic deficiency. In this case, social science could help justify the social and economic policies that would keep the upper classes in a superior position. This sort of genetic interpretation of cultural differences is still held by more recent writers, such as Jensen (1969) in the 1960s, Shockley (1971) in the 1970s, and Herrnstein and Murray in the 1990s (Morganthau, 1994).

Another view of cultural differences is a more anthropological one. As anthropology developed into a social science, some researchers may have been drawn to studying different cultures as primitive and interesting scientific curiosities, while others may have wanted to observe and record other cultures before they were destroyed by modern influences. The term *cross-cultural* in psychological literature originally referred to comparisons of behavior in different cultures, particularly different countries.

The next view of cultural differences became popular in the 1960s along with government programs such as the Peace Corps and Vista. Although the people who selflessly volunteered in these programs brought increased goodwill and understanding between cultures, an implicit meta-message of these programs was that other cultures were in some ways deficient or deprived and in need of assistance. These sincere efforts should be viewed in contrast to the centuries of slavery, colonization, and commercial exploitation of non-European peoples that continue today.

In the 1960s people of color were described as "culturally disadvantaged" or "culturally different" (Jackson, 1995). Many sources of cultural deprivation were assumed. Nutritional deprivation (i.e., poor diet) contributed to mental retardation and physical susceptibility to illness. Environmental deprivation included crowding, noise, and lack of stimulation, all factors that have negative psychological effects. Sociocultural deprivation included factors such as a lack of role models or parental encouragement. Linguistic deprivation meant a lack of exposure to "proper" English. In many of these areas a person from a cultural minority background might be considered disadvantaged, and many social programs were funded to address these possible sources of deprivation. However, the underlying message was still the implication that a minority person's culture was in some way inferior to that of the majority.

The most recent approach to viewing cultural difference is to make the assumption that no culture is more desirable than another and to explore the legitimacy and benefits of any differences between cultures. This implies a valuing of diversity. This view of cultural differences is particularly timely in today's global economy, where countries and peoples must increasingly learn to understand and respect each other for their mutual survival. What this means for counseling is that cultural differences between counselor and client are potentially beneficial if accepted and included in the counseling process. This is the viewpoint from which the current field of multicultural counseling has developed.

The study of multiculturalism is a relatively new emphasis within the field of counseling. Much of the professional literature on the mental health needs of ethnic minorities has been written only in the last 30 years (Das, 1995). One of the first books on the subject was Paul Pedersen and colleagues' *Counseling Across Cultures* (Pedersen, Lonner, & Draguns), written in 1976 and now in its fourth edition (Pedersen, Draguns, Lonner, & Trimble, 1996). Another early contributor to the field was Clemmont Vontress. Articles about women and African Americans, in particular, have seen substantial growth over the years (Hoyt, 1989).

Some of the major theoretical developments in the field of multicultural counseling are (a) the triad model, (b) research on culture shock, and (c) multiple developmental stage approaches conceptualizing cultural identity development. The triad model was developed by Pedersen (1977) for use in training. The roles of counselor, client, and "anti-counselor," or embodiment of the problem, are used to simulate a counseling session and increase awareness and skills. Years of research on culture shock (Furnham & Bochner, 1986) have yielded models of cultural transition that can be applied to the experiences of international students, immigrants, refugees, and others in counseling. Also, several models of cultural identity development have been proposed and refined to apply to many specific ethnic and cultural groups (D.W. Sue & Sue, 1990). Each of these conceptual developments and models is discussed in detail in later chapters. Although the field of multicultural counseling is growing in maturity, and some substantial accomplishments have been made, there is still much room for theoretical development and later research substantiation.

☐ Current Issues and Controversies

Is Multiculturalism an Exclusive or an Inclusive Concept?

The issue here is whether multiculturalism should exclusively involve the study of ethnic differences as they affect the counseling process. Proponents of an exclusive viewpoint are concerned that the influence of racism will be ignored or diluted if other cultural differences, such as gender, age, sexual orientation, or disability, are also included (Jackson, 1995). Proponents of a more inclusive viewpoint recognize that discrimination and unequal treatment for reasons other than race are also widespread and affect clients, counselors, and the counseling process in important ways that should be studied. Like ethnic minorities, other cultural minorities experience discrimination based on a permanent aspect of themselves that cannot be changed. In this book, an inclusive view of multicultural counseling will be taken. Chapter 2, *Understanding and Appreciating Difference*, focuses on individual differences and prejudice from a broad psychological perspective as they affect all people, and other chapters emphasize the experiences of different ethnic and other cultural groups.

Do the Same Basic Counseling Principles and Techniques Apply to Everyone, Regardless of Cultural Background?

The controversy here is between taking an *etic* or an *emic* perspective (Berry, 1969). The etic approach emphasizes the universal elements of counseling that all cultural groups are assumed to share. Examples are discrimination, identity development, validation and empowerment, communication, social class differences, acculturation, and transference and countertransference (Das, 1995; C.C. Lee, 1994). The emic approach emphasizes the indigenous or specific characteristics of each cultural group that may have an impact on the counseling process. The comparison is between a group (in-depth coverage of specific cultures) versus a conceptual approach to multicultural counseling. Many books on multicultural counseling have tended to take a more emic perspective; however, the best approach is a blend of etic and emic perspectives (Das, 1995). This book adopts a blended approach. The first section covers etic themes that are more universal across cultures (e.g., discrimination, assessment, acculturation, identity development), and the next two sections focus on ethnic groupings (e.g., Native Americans, African Americans, Latinos and Latinas, Asian Americans, and European Americans) and some specific cultural minorities (e.g., women, gay men and lesbians, older people, and people with disabilities).

Should We Be Adapting Traditional Counseling to Meet the Needs of Nontraditional Clients or Examining Nontraditional Counseling to Enlighten Traditional Approaches?

Because traditional counseling developed from a European perspective for use with people of European cultural background, professionals should either match or modify traditional counseling techniques to fit people of various cultural backgrounds. One way to do this is to study traditional counseling skills and see how well they apply to each specific cultural group. Some research has been done in this area, but much more remains to be conducted, especially in light of the fact that there are myriad counseling techniques and specific cultural groups. Another approach is to study the indigenous helping traditions within a specific cultural group and either work concurrently with traditional healers or learn from them and develop new counseling techniques appropriate to the client's cultural group. This approach calls on the counselor to become somewhat of a cultural anthropologist, to learn about other cultures through travel, film, reading, and personal relationships. This approach is more challenging and requires the counselor to be continually open to new ways of viewing the world and new techniques. Eventually this approach should prove more successful as it makes use of the client's own worldview and values, but at present there is relatively little research that has examined indigenous counseling techniques. In this book, *indigenous counseling techniques* will refer to counseling methods that have been developed by and for the cultural group itself and, in some cases, these techniques will be described.

Should Multicultural Training Be Required for Licensure or Certification in Counseling?

At present there is no general requirement that a counselor be trained in multicultural counseling before becoming licensed or certified, although the state of Massachusetts requires some training in multicultural issues for psychologists (DeAngelis, 1994a). The American Psychological Association (APA) has adopted Guidelines for Providers of Psychological Services to Ethnic, Linguistic, and Culturally Diverse Populations (APA, 1991; see Appendix A). Also, the Ethical Principles of Psychologists and Code of Conduct (APA, 1992) explicitly includes cultural differences and calls for appropriate training (see box on page 8).

There are efforts to make multicultural training a necessary part of a counselor's expertise. The Council for Accreditation of Counseling and Related Educational Programs (CACREP) requires counselor education programs to include content on the social and cultural foundations of counseling within the counseling curriculum as an accreditation standard (CACREP, 1988). Ninety percent of counselor education programs include specific coursework on multicultural counseling (Das, 1995). In 1995 the Association for Multicultural Counseling and Development approved a document describing and explaining multicultural counseling competencies (D.W. Sue, Arredondo, & McDavis, 1992a; 1992b; see Appendix B).

Ethical Principles Related to Multiculturalism, from the American Psychological Association

Principle D: Respect for People's Rights and Dignity

Psychologists are aware of cultural, individual, and role differences, including those due to age, gender, race, ethnicity, national origin, religion, sexual orientation, disability, language, and socioeconomic status. Psychologists try to eliminate the effect on their work of biases based on those factors, and they do not knowingly participate in or condone unfair discriminatory practices.

Ethical Standard 1.08: Human Differences

Where differences of age, gender, race, ethnicity, national origin, religion, sexual orientation, disability, language, or socioeconomic status significantly affect psychologists' work concerning particular individuals or groups, psychologists obtain the training, experience, consultation, or supervision necessary to ensure the competence of their services, or they make appropriate referrals.

Ethical Standard 1.12: Other Harassment

Psychologists do not knowingly engage in behavior that is harassing or demeaning to persons with whom they interact in their work based on factors such as those persons' age, gender, race, ethnicity, national origin, religion, sexual orientation, disability, language, or socioeconomic status.

Ethical Standard 2.04.c: Use of Assessment in General and With Special Populations

Psychologists attempt to identify situations in which particular interventions or assessment techniques or norms may not be applicable or may require adjustment in administration or interpretation because of factors such as individuals' gender, age, race, ethnicity, national origin, religion, sexual orientation, disability, language, or socioeconomic status.

Competencies such as these may eventually become widely recognized standards for licensing or certification.

☐ Future Needs

There are substantial areas within the field of multicultural counseling that have received significant research interest and development, as noted earlier. However, there are several areas in need of much additional research. Primary is the need for a broad conceptual framework for the process of multicultural counseling itself that goes beyond training, identity development, or cultural adaptation. Such a framework would do well to take into account the counselor's own level of cultural awareness, an individually tailored assessment of the client's cultural background, the sociopolitical influences on both client and counselor, the use of both traditional and indigenous counseling techniques, and the complex interaction among client, counselor, and the societal context surrounding them. *A Theory of Multicultural Counseling and Therapy* (Sue, Ivey, & Pederson, 1996) attempts to address this need (see chapter 16).

Another area for further study is that of within-group differences. There has previously been much focus on differences between broad ethnic groups, particularly comparison of a certain minority group to the White, European American majority. Scholars in the field are now calling for more sophisticated analyses of variations within an ethnic group, for example, among Chinese, Japanese, Vietnamese, Koreans, and Filipinos or among Mexicanos, Puerto Ricans, and Cubans. Examining within-group differences would not only yield more specifically applicable knowledge, but it would also tend to counteract the tendency to stereotype people from a similar group.

Another area that has had little research to date is that of culture conflict resolution. In other words, how can the counselor address conflicts between cultures within the counseling setting? For example, physical punishment may be an acceptable form of discipline within the client's own culture, but this comes into conflict with the dominant culture when the behavior is labeled child abuse. Another example is that of counseling a couple who come from different cultural backgrounds.

Understanding and Appreciating Difference

In 12 step lingo, we are all recovering oppressors. (Sudbury, 1993, p. 47)

Counselors can begin to develop an understanding of the potential impact of cultural minority status on the psychological experience of their clients by turning to the work of social psychologists, who have long been interested in examining the roots of prejudice and the effects of discrimination, stereotyping, and racism on individuals.

The word *prejudice* comes from the Latin words *prae*, meaning before, and *judicium*, meaning judgment. In other words, prejudice occurs, for example, when someone is prejudged before any real knowledge of that person is known. Gordon Allport (1954) defined prejudice as a negative attitude or dislike based on faulty and inflexible generalization.

According to social comparison theory (Festinger, 1954), people tend to make judgments about themselves by comparing themselves to a similar group of people, or *reference group*. If the comparisons are positive, they feel better about themselves. *Prejudice* occurs when a person takes his or her own group as the positive reference point from which to judge other people negatively. *Discrimination* takes place when actions occur that favor one group at the expense of another group. An example of this would be if a person thinks of his or her own ethnic group as his or her primary reference group. To the extent that he or she feels he or she is succeeding, in comparison to others in the reference group, his or her self-esteem may increase. However, if he or she judges people from other groups as unfit or inadequate compared to his or her own ethnic group, he or she is exercising prejudice. If he or she then takes actions to favor his or her ethnic group at the expense of another group—for example, if he or she passes laws that do not allow members of another group to own property or vote—this constitutes discrimination.

One definition of a *stereotype* (L. Ho, 1990) is a generalized description of a group of people that has usually developed over time on the basis of cross-cultural interactions. In this media-rich age of television, video, and CD-ROM it is easy to take media exposure as true cross-cultural interaction. Someone who has never met another person from a particular ethnic background may have a stereotype of that culture based on what he or she has heard, seen, or read, but not based on real personal interaction with others of that ethnicity.

Stereotypes can be psychologically useful. They can assist memory by providing a device for chunking several pieces of information together under one label. This can seem helpful to an individual because it makes the world less complicated, more predictable and, as a result, more comfortable. When a counselor sees a client's age, sex, or ethnic background on an intake form, she or he may feel more at ease meeting a new client because she or he uses the information as a stereotype in recalling all her or his previous experience with people of a similar age, sex, or ethnicity. However, there are drawbacks to stereotypes. If counselors put too much emphasis on their stereotypes of a new client, they may assume that they already know a lot about the person and neglect to consider ways in which their client does not fit their stereotypes. This can result in faulty assessment and treatment planning.

There are also potential negative effects of a client's own stereotypes. Such stereotypes may contribute to increased mistrust and unwillingness to self-disclose to a counselor. If clients have incorporated negative stereotypes about themselves into their images of themselves, this may contribute to low self-esteem and limit optimism for change. This process has been called *internalized oppression*. For example, in one study, African American children pointed to a drawing of a White child more often than an African American child when asked which of the two was more beautiful or smarter (cited in Pine & Hilliard, 1990). One interpretation of the data is that the African American children had internalized the negative societal messages they had been exposed to regarding their ethnicity. A competing interpretation is that the children responded in what they might have perceived to be a socially desirable or "correct" manner and that they did not necessarily believe the negative stereotypes of African Americans.

Claude Steele has studied the concept of *stereotype vulnerability*, an effect that may occur when a person tries to do well in an atmosphere in which he or she is aware that others of a similar cultural background have had difficulty; this can detract from his or her performance ("How affirmative," 1995; Watters, 1995). Stereotype vulnerability operates as an extra burden on the person to disconfirm a negative stereotype. To date, evidence for this phenomenon has been found with African Americans tested with verbal Graduate Record Exam (GRE) questions and women tested with math problems (Watters, 1995).

☐ Racism

One definition of *racism* includes two components: first, the assumption that traits and abilities are biologically determined by race, and second, the belief in the inherent superiority of one race and its right to dominate other races (*Webster's Third New International Dictionary of the English Language*, 1981). Given this definition, which combines an assumption and an ensuing belief, it is not surprising that racism is so prevalent. The assumption that abilities are biologically determined is very controversial (see the discussion of IQ and culture in Chapter 3, Cultural Aspects of Psychological Assessment). However, even the concept of race is itself very questionable. Race is usually associated with physical features, especially skin color and type of hair (L. Ho, 1990), yet there is no anthropological standard as to the physical definition of one race versus another. Indeed, the American Association of Physical Anthropologists has asserted that race is not a legitimate, scientific concept, as genetically homogeneous populations do not exist in the human species (Scott-Jones, 1995). Zuckerman (1990) noted large amounts of variability within one race compared to the degree of variability between races when examining psychological traits, supporting the notion that the biological distinctiveness of various racial groups is also an illusion when it comes to examining traits and abilities. "The major component of genetic diversity is between individuals in the same tribe or nation" (Zuckerman, 1990, p. 1300), as this accounts for 84% of the total variance in a large, well-conducted, multicultural, multinational study.

Another definition of racism involves unjustified negative treatment resulting from individual prejudice and discrimination or institutional policies and procedures (Pine & Hilliard, 1990). This second definition includes *institutionalized racism*, or the use of established laws, customs, and practices or norms that produce racial inequities (Baratz & Baratz, 1970).

For example, several versions of potential institutionalized racism make equal access to college education more difficult for students of color.

School counselors may have a tendency to counsel ethnic minority students toward non-college–preparatory courses in high school, which then results in a disadvantage when the students apply to college. The use of written essays as a college admissions criterion can result in Asian Americans with equal grades and test scores being subsequently accepted at a lower rate than European Americans. The practice of using standardized test scores as a selection criterion for graduate admissions (when past grades or other factors may be a better predictor of graduate performance) works against students from many ethnic groups who tend to, as a group, score lower on either the verbal, quantitative, or both sections of the Graduate Record Exam.

Institutionalized racism can be very subtle and difficult to detect because it can be done under the guise of customs, norms, policies, or practices that are not illegal but do result in inequities. For example, locating a counseling center in an area that is inaccessible to public transportation, having neither evening hours nor a sliding fee scale, and staff who speak only English can easily contribute to a restricted ethnic diversity of clientele, even before a client ever meets a counselor. Note that none of these practices are illegal in that they do not exclude a specific ethnic group, yet they can result in inequitable service provision to ethnic minority clients.

Cultural racism occurs when one cultural group believes that another group is inferior in some way and posesses the power to impose its standards on the other group. This broadens the definition of racism beyond just ethnicity. If men believe that women are too emotional or fragile to hold positions of responsibility and have the power to make such judgments by not hiring women for managerial posts, cultural racism is occurring. A more specific term for this is *sexism.* When cultural racism is based on age, it might be called *ageism. Heterosexism* is cultural racism based on sexual orientation, and *ablism* is cultural racism based on physical disability. What all these cultural groups share is that they may experience discrimination based on an aspect of their culture that they cannot themselves change. A milder, but no less harmful, version of cultural racism is the assumption that there is no specific uniqueness to another culture. This failure to acknowledge the cultural differences of the group carries with it an implicit failure to acknowledge discrimination that the group may experience.

It may be very difficult for someone who is part of the cultural majority in power to acknowledge his or her cultural racism. According to psychologist Leon Festinger's *cognitive dissonance theory* (1957), when someone is confronted with a discrepancy between his or her own professed attitudes and his or her actual behavior, this creates an uncomfortable state of disequilibrium, or cognitive dissonance, which the person can resolve by rationalizing or justifying the discrepant behavior. A White person who does not believe others should be treated inequitably and who also receives benefits or privileges in a society that discriminates against ethnic minorities can rationalize the cognitive dissonance by denying his or her participation in a racist system by not perceiving him- or herself as "White" or not identifying with any ethnic group. Unfortunately, this denial of one's own ethnicity can by itself result in identity confusion and discomfort and can unconsciously perpetuate racism. If someone of European American ethnicity is not White, or European, or English, for example, then what is he or she, and with whom can he or she identify? And why are other people so overly focused on their ethnicity?

☐ Barriers in Counseling

From the first use of slaves during the early colonization of North America in the 1600s through modern legal battles over the use of affirmative action in educational and employment settings, racist beliefs have been ingrained in United States society. American psychologists, as a part of that society, have been greatly affected, either consciously or unconsciously, by racism and, through them, the field of psychology in general has been affected. Several fascinating examples of this have been documented by Leon Kamin in his book *The Science and Politics of I.Q.* (1974). Three eminent psychologists—Lewis Terman of Stanford University, Henry Goddard of the Vineland Training School, and Robert Yerkes of Harvard University—were responsible for developing the Army Alpha and Beta group intelligence tests. Both Terman and Yerkes served as president of the American Psychological Association at some time. Terman, Goddard, and Yerkes also were members of societies and organizations, such as the Eugenics Research Association and the Galton Society, that interpreted scientific data to promote political beliefs in the genetic inferiority of some races. These organizations supported practices such as the sterilization of prisoners and people on welfare and the limitation of immigration by people who were members of ethnic groups that were considered to be intellectually inferior. These psychologists' work assisted in the passage of a 1917 immigration law that severely restricted the number of immigrants from southern European countries. For example, Goddard, as described in *The Science and Politics of I.Q.*, tested immigrants at Ellis Island and found that 83% of the Jews, 80% of the Hungarians, 79% of the Italians, and 87% of the Russians were mentally retarded. Psychologists who were part of the movement to promote the testing of mental abilities "pressed upon the

Congress scientific I.Q. data to demonstrate the 'New Immigration' from southeastern Europe was genetically inferior. That contribution permanently transformed American society" (Kamin, 1974, p. 12). Issues of cultural bias in testing (to be discussed in Chapter 3), such as a lack of familiarity with the language in which the test is given, or a lack of comfort with the test administrator, were ignored. Another noted psychologist of the era, Carl Brigham, who is credited with the development of the Scholastic Aptitude Test (SAT), interpreted the relationship of length of time in the United States with higher IQ scores as supportive of the intellectual superiority of Nordic races, who had immigrated earlier, rather than the effect of acculturation.

Counselors are at great risk to behave in a racist manner without being aware of it. This problem was first described by Wrenn (1962) as the "culturally encapsulated counselor." It follows from Wrenn's prophetic entreaty that counselors be open to change that encapsulated counselors are so completely engrossed by the traditional approaches and attitudes of Western counselor training that they have no awareness that cultural differences might be important within the counseling process. These encapsulated counselors may be proud of the notion that they treat all their clients equally and that they are "color blind." They may assert that color makes no difference at all in assessment, goal setting, treatment planning, client communication, or selection of counseling skills. These counselors assume that cultural modifications are not needed, or they are unwilling or unable to make them. In practice, however, failure to acknowledge or appreciate differences may instead communicate disrespect for a client's cultural background and lead to inappropriate or ineffective treatment. These same counselors may be surprised if a client who is culturally different from themselves drops out of counseling, and they may attribute lack of progress as due to resistance or client unreadiness as opposed to a mismatch between their knowledge and skills and what the client actually needs.

Ridley (1989) expanded on the influence of racism in counseling to include seven counseling process qualities. In addition to (a) color blindness, (b) *color consciousness* involves attributing all of the client's problems to his or her cultural background. (c) *Color transference* refers to client reactions to the counselor that arise from the therapist's cultural background alone, whereas (d) *color countertransference* refers to counselor reactions toward the client based on the counselor's past experience with people of a cultural background similar to that of the client. (e) *Cultural ambivalence* is related to counselor paternalism, "the Great White Father Syndrome" (Vontress, 1981). (f) *Pseudotransference* involves labeling the client's defensive reactions to racist behavior by the counselor as pathology. Finally, (g) the counselor may misinterpret client nondisclosure as paranoid behavior rather than as healthy, cultural skepticism. These characteristics are indicative of unintentional covert racism on the counselor's part. Ridley asserted that unintentional racism is the most insidious form of racism because people are unaware of it.

From another perspective on cultural barriers in counseling, D. W. Sue and Sue (1990) grouped the generic aspects of counseling, developed from a European perspective, into three major categories that counselors need to consider. In the first category, culture-bound values include focusing on the individual; valuing client expressiveness toward the counselor; openness; a linear, cause-and-effect approach; and a mind–body dichotomy. The second category, class-bound values, includes adherence to time schedules; unstructured, exploratory problem solving; and long-term goals. Social class differences influence many aspects of clients' lives, including diet, discipline, and child-rearing practices (Havinghurst & Neugarten, 1968) as well as how counselors may react to the clients (Lorion, 1974). The third category, language variables, includes dependence on standard English and verbal communication skills. These values and communication styles differ among various ethnic groups within the United States, and in a multicultural counseling context many of these aspects may come into sharp contrast.

☐ Developing Cultural Awareness

Unlearning racism is the first step a counselor must take on the path of developing cultural awareness. This involves first acknowledging the prevalence of cultural racism in the United States and then beginning to understand one's own prejudices toward people who are in some way culturally different. Wilkins (1995) asserted that "Denial of racism is much like the denials that accompany addictions to alcohol, drugs or gambling" (p. 412). The first step is breaking through the denial. This is an emotional as well as a cognitive process and is often facilitated by experiential exercises to increase self-awareness. Several such exercises are included in this chapter to give you a sample from which to choose. Several handbooks are available that are collections of additional multicultural awareness exercises (L. Ho, 1990; J. H. Katz, 1989; P. McGrath & Axelson, 1993).

When counselors come face to face with their own cultural racism, it may be a very unsettling experience. Many people do not intentionally discriminate against others. Feelings of anger, guilt, sadness, or confusion about personal participation in cultural racism may be temporarily overwhelming. However, these feelings are a positive sign in many ways. First,

---

Exercise 1: *The Color of Fear*

Arrange to see the documentary film *The Color of Fear* (M. W. Lee, 1994). This is a 90-minute film about a weekend group experience about racism and how it affects the African American, Asian American, European American, and Latino men who are participants in the group. Viewing this film brings up many personal and emotional feelings for those watching it. Discuss the film afterward with others. DelVecchio (1995) reviewed the film.

---

they are an indication that the counselor is not in denial of the effects of cultural racism, that his or her learning includes his or her whole being, and that emotional as well as cognitive change is occurring. Second, the counselor may be able to use his or her own feelings as a source of new or renewed empathy for clients. Third, the effects of cultural racism are felt by the counselor in a more controlled setting, such as a workshop, class, or training session, outside of the counseling interaction, ensuring that the client is not burdened by having to deal with the counselor's own feelings.

The second step in developing cultural awareness is for the counselor to begin to increase his or her appreciation of cultural differences. Allport (1954) contended that contacts with members of minority groups that result in increased knowledge and understanding lead to more accurate and stable beliefs about minority groups and eventually reduce prejudice. Counselors may seek out people and experiences in their personal lives that increase their exposure to other cultures. This could involve a whole spectrum of behavior, such as going to movies and restaurants, reading novels, increasing travel, and developing new friendships. This is a time of personal change and exploration for the counselor, and care should be taken so that the counselor does not bring this newly awakened interest into his or her counseling sessions as countertransference in the form of cultural curiosity. The culturally different client is in counseling to receive help, not to increase the counselor's knowledge and experience. More appropriate at this time is for the counselor to seek out professional development activities, courses, and workshops with a cultural focus, and to consult colleagues with different cultural backgrounds for professional stimulation. A hallmark of a counselor engrossed with this level of cultural awareness is that multicultural experiences become welcomed as opposed to forced or merely tolerated.

Exercise 2: Questions About Culture

Answer the following questions for yourself:

- What are some of the prejudices of your ethnic group, your religion, your gender group, or other subcultures to which you belong?

- In what ways are these prejudices expressed?

- What are your personal prejudices?

- How does your socioeconomic level affect your attitude toward people of other economic groups?

- How might your cultural prejudice give you difficulty in connecting with others in your professional role?

- How would you describe your own state of mental health, culturally speaking?

- Have you ever gone through a period of confusion and uncertainty about any of the values and practices with which you were raised?

- Have you borrowed any other culture's ways to help you live a better life? List all of them. What have they done for you?

Note: Adapted from D. S. Murphy (1994) and L. Ho (1990).

☐ Counseling Clients Who Have Been Subject to Discrimination

Clients who become aware that they have been subjected to racial discrimination, sexual harassment, or cultural racism in other forms may be referred to or seek assistance from a counselor. Discrimination has many effects on individuals. The client may experience feelings of helplessness or anger. Sexual harassment is one example of discrimination and, because it is an abuse of power and humiliating, victims may tend not to report it (J. A. Hamilton, Alagna, King, & Lloyd, in press). The same may be true for other forms of discrimination. Koss (1985) reported that victims often do not perceive themselves as victims. They may not want to acknowledge the losses of control, self-esteem, and other negative experiences, and they may not want to compare themselves with other stigmatized individuals (Taylor, Wood, & Lichtman, 1983).

Recommendations for treating victims of discrimination may be generalized from those for treating women who have been sexually harassed, described by Koss (1990):

1. Validate the victim's feelings.

2. Provide information. Discrimination may be frequent given the current norms of American society and the distribution of power.

3. Express anger safely.

Exercise 3: Sharing About Culture

With a partner (preferably someone you do not know well, who is culturally different from you), spend about ten minutes sharing your ethnicity and social class and the advantages and disadvantages of each in your life. Then discuss your cultures and find some similarities and some differences between your experiences.

Exercise 4: Institutionalized Cultural Racism

In a small group, develop policies and procedures for your own counseling center. Pick a group you wish to discriminate against and build this legitimately into your plans. For example, it is illegal to put up a sign that says "No persons of X cultural group allowed," but it is easy to discourage clients from X cultural background by the office location, physical layout of the office, reading materials and decor of the waiting room, intake procedures, fee structure, availability of hours, languages of counseling available, choice of therapeutic orientations offered, and so on. When you are finished, share your plans with another group and see if the group can determine which cultural group you are trying to exclude. Discuss together how institutionalized cultural racism can be subtly and legally incorporated into counseling centers and other institutions.

---

4. Monitor the effects of discrimination, including maladaptive coping patterns by the victim or impact on his or her family.

5. Provide a place to mourn losses (e.g., loss of a belief in a fair world), build new beliefs, and develop support systems.

6. Offer hope. Filing a complaint with a pertinent agency or bureau may eventually have beneficial effects.

The counselor need not press for legal justice, but offering options, including legal remedies, helps empower the victim.

Even if a client is not aware that he or she has been subjected to discrimination, the results can have great psychological impact. Boden (1992) noted, in working with disabled lesbians, that "When difference is experienced as a defect, it results in shame, self-loathing, and fear of exposure. These shame-based feelings become the central themes that color self-organization" (p. 158). She asserted that it is crucial for the counselor to welcome and understand difference in order for shame-laden material to be revealed and worked through, leading to increased self-esteem. These considerations may be relevant for any client who experiences difference from any source, among them ethnicity, gender, sexual orientation, age, or disability.

☐ Recommended Cultural Resources

Print Media

Kamin, L. J. (1974). *The science and politics of I.Q.* New York: Wiley.

Katz, J. H. (1989). *White awareness* (6th ed.). Norman: University of Oklahoma Press.

McGrath, P., & Axelson, J. A. (1993). *Accessing awareness and developing knowledge: Foundations for skill in a multicultural society.* Pacific Grove, CA: Brooks/Cole.

McIntosh, P. (1988). *White privilege and male privilege.* (Working Paper No. 189). Wellesley, MA: Wellesley College Center for Research on Women.

Multimedia

Kasdan, L., Okun, C., & Grillo, M. (Producers). (1997). *Grand canyon.* [Videorecording]. Beverly Hills, CA: Twentieth-Century Fox Home Entertainment.

Lee, M. W. (Producer). (1994). *The color of fear* [Film]. Oakland, CA: Stir-Fry Productions.

Nozik, M., & Nair, M. (Producers). (1992). *Mississippi masala* [Videorecording]. Burbank, CA: Columbia Tri-Star Home Video.

3

CHAPTER

Cultural Aspects of Psychological Assessment

If we are to achieve a richer culture, rich in contrasting values, we must recognize the whole gamut of human potentialities, and so weave a less arbitrary social fabric, one in which each diverse human gift will find a fitting place.

—Margaret Mead, anthropologist (Bartlett, 1992, p. 707)

☐ Historical and Sociopolitical Influences on Testing

IQ and Culture

Almost from its inception, intelligence testing has had a long history of use as a pseudoscientific tool to promote cultural racism. The overlap between prominent psychologists in the development of intelligence testing and the membership of influential political organizations that supported social policies limiting immigration, sterilizing the "feebleminded," and other repressive practices in the 1910s was described in Chapter 2. In the 1960s, Jensen (1969) cited the lower average IQ scores of Negroes compared to

Whites as evidence that IQ is innate and cannot be altered by environmental enrichment and therefore that compensatory education programs are doomed to failure. In 1979, the Larry P. *v.* Riles class-action suit in the state of California banned the use of standardized intelligence tests as a primary selection criterion for placing children into classes for the mentally retarded because it erroneously overselected African American children (Lambert, 1981; White, 1984). The political forces behind the use of testing for discriminatory purposes were so potent that the suit took 7 years to litigate, and to the present day it continues to be challenged in the judicial appeals process. Herrnstein and Murray's (1994) book, *The Bell Curve*, which describes correlations between IQ, as a measure of intelligence, and many social problems, has again brought attention to the use of science to promote political agendas.

Objections to the use of intelligence testing have been made on both sociopolitical and scientific grounds. When used for selection purposes in educational programs, college admissions, and employment, intelligence or aptitude testing often has the prejudicial effect of putting more Blacks, Latinos, Native Americans, and other ethnic minority people into stigmatizing programs or denying them access to higher education or jobs. From a scientific standpoint, there is considerable controversy about what the tests really measure and how to control for the effects of social class and cultural differences. For example, social class is correlated with IQ in the .35–.40 range (Jensen, 1969). Zuckerman (1990) summed up the issue:

> Generalizations about the innate intelligence or social responsibility of large and genetically diverse segments of the species are open to criticism on the grounds that they serve no important scientific purpose, given the present ambiguities in definition of the independent variable and immense sampling problems. (p. 1301)

However, most states continue to use intelligence tests, perhaps in conjunction with other information, to make important decisions that affect the lives of ethnic minority people (Williams, 1987).

Affirmative Action and Testing

Affirmative action programs are aimed at making positive efforts to remedy past discrimination toward minority groups. Ever since the 1964 Civil Rights Act (see box on page 24 for a brief history of affirmative action), which outlawed disparate treatment of different racial groups, there has been continuing controversy over how to implement programs that seek to remedy past discrimination without in turn discriminating against any other groups (i.e., reverse discrimination).

However, the continuing need for affirmative action is unequivocal. Blacks and Latinos are still denied jobs that are offered to similarly qualified Whites 15%–20% of the time (Fendel, Hurtado, Long, & Giraldo, 1996). Asian Americans are admitted to top universities such as Harvard, Yale, Berkeley, Brown, and Princeton at a lower rate than Whites although their academic qualifications may not warrant lower admission rates (Raspberry, 1990).

A Brief History of Affirmative Action

1964 — Title VII of the Civil Rights Act outlaws disparate treatment based on race.

1970 — Federal regulations require that all government contractors implement written, result-oriented, affirmative action compliance programs with specific goals and timetables for minority hiring.

1971 — Griggs v. Duke Power Company Supreme Court ruling decrees that disparate effects are prima facie evidence of employment discrimination and that testing is deemed unlawful if it results in racial differences in selection and the test is not job related.

1978 — Federal guidelines establish the "four-fifths" rule: If the pass rate for any group is less than four-fifths of the group with the highest passing rate, then the test is regarded as having an adverse impact on a particular group.

1991 — Civil Rights Act outlaws race-norming (establishing separate normative groups for different races).

Note: Adapted from Gottfredson (1994) and Sackett and Wilk (1994).

Additional efforts to increase the employment of minority group members are generally accepted by the public, especially when this entails broadening the pool of applicants. Difficulties arise when affirmative action is applied to the use of tests for selecting one person over another and especially when used to screen out people at early stages of a selection process. Affirmative action selection procedures that have the appearance of giving minority group members preference over others are the center of controversy (Sackett & Wilk, 1994). There are many methods of using tests that take into consideration group membership. Some of these are assigning bonus points, developing separate within-group norms, establishing separate cutoff scores, creating separate rating lists, banding (treating as equal two individuals whose scores are not statistically significantly different), empirical keying by group, and eliminating test items. There are philosophical and scientific advantages and disadvantages to each of these methods, and no method has been established as widely acceptable. In fact, the use of separate within-group norms, often referred to as *race-norming*, as a means of affirmative action, was banned by Congress in 1991 (Gottfredson, 1994).

□ Bias in Testing

Using the same test with different cultural groups is problematic, because a test may be biased with respect to one of the groups. Test bias may occur when a test does not select the same proportion of the group that would be selected by the criterion—in other words, if fewer people pass the test than would be successful at the real task for which performance is estimated by the test. A test may be culturally biased in many ways. Some of these sources of bias have to do with the cultural nature of the testing process itself, and others have to do with aspects of test development such as item content, standardization sample, and issues of differential construct or predictive validity (Dent, 1995).

Use of a test often makes the implicit assumption that the person being tested understands the presuppositions of the testing situation itself as well as the language of testing (Rogoff & Chavajzy, 1995). With respect to cognitive testing, Rogoff and Chavajzy (1995), in their excellent review of the cultural issues involved, concluded that one cannot assume "that a cognitive test reveals a general ability across tasks unrelated to people's experience" (p. 863). A person growing up in a nonliterate culture may have different premises about his or her world and may refuse to answer hypothetical questions because his or her worldview is to interact with what he or she has directly experienced. For some recent Southeast Asian immigrants or refugees, many questions typically used for assessment of mental status and cognitive functioning are either inappropriate or senseless because they depend on either an understanding of abstract concepts or school learning. Some examples are: "What is the thing to do if you find an envelope on the street, that is sealed, addressed, and has a brand new stamp?" or "If you had three wishes, what would they be?" (W. M. Lee & Nakagawa, 1996). In addition, people without formal schooling have difficulty memorizing unrelated items and often do not use organizing strategies spontaneously (Rogoff & Chavajzy, 1995), and even a nonverbal task such as matching patterns may seem strange (W. M. Lee & Nakagawa, 1996). These difficulties with testing may also apply to people whose formal education experiences have been lacking in quality.

Many Western cultures value speed and associate intelligence with performing quickly (Rogoff & Chavajzy, 1995). Timed tests may place people from some cultural groups at a disadvantage. For example, the SAT performance of Latinos and Latinas has been shown to be negatively influenced by the demand for speed (Dent, 1995).

Language issues may make test scores unrepresentative of a person's performance. Instructions may be unclear to a person whose first language is not English. Immigrants to the United States have been inappropriately given intelligence and personality tests requiring familiarity with English (J. Vernon, 1995). Even among native speakers of English there are cultural differences. Some common words are known to have different meanings for Blacks than for Whites (Samuda, 1975). Some tests, such as the Vocabulary subtest of the Wechsler Adult Intelligence Scale (WAIS), tend to unwittingly stress how well a person can articulate his or her ideas regardless of his or her level of understanding. People from cultural backgrounds that do not stress oral dialogue, especially with people in positions of authority, may not elaborate on their answers sufficiently to attain full scoring credit.

Another source of potential bias is the lack of culturally representative standardization groups during test construction. Many frequently used tests have few ethnic minority people included in the standardization group.

In addition, the test administrator may be an unconscious source of cultural bias, although the research related to this issue is inconclusive. An individual's performance may differ when tested by someone with whom they feel more comfortable, perhaps someone from their own ethnic background. Similarly, the person administering a test to someone from a cultural background different from his or her own may not notice or may misinterpret nonverbal cues or respond differently to certain accents.

Given the many sources of potential test bias (see box below), some of which have been discussed above, it is not surprising that there are group differences on many well-known assessment devices. A review of the literature by Sackett and Wilk (1994) concluded that physical ability and personality test differences have been found to be related to gender, and cognitive and personality test differences have been found to be related to ethnicity.

The meaning of group differences in test performance may be linked to inequitable social and environmental conditions. Thus, group differences may be more reflective of systemic problems in U.S. society than of individual deficits. For example, standardized IQ measure scores for Black children tend to be 1 *SD* below those of White children, and similar differences have been found for Hispanic and American Indian groups. However, when samples are comparable in terms of age, educational level, socioeconomic status, and other demographics, differences between groups on personality and intellectual measures decrease (Suzuki & Kugler, 1995).

On the Minnesota Multiphasic Personality Inventory (MMPI), perhaps the most widely used and well-researched personality assessment test, and its revision, the MMPI-2, Blacks score differently on the Schizophrenia, Paranoia, Mania, and F subscales (Williams, 1987), whereas Asian Americans report more somatic complaints (S. Sue & Sue, 1974). These

---

Culturally Relevant Sources of Test Bias

1. Illiteracy

2. Language differences

3. Emic communication styles (e.g., somatization as an expression of psychological distress)

4. Unfamiliarity with testing procedures

5. Inappropriate item content or test tasks

6. Nondependence on abstract concepts or speed

7. Lack of appropriate normative data

8. Interpreter error

9. Test administrator variance

Note: Adapted from W. M. Lee and Nakagawa (1996).

group differences coincide with general differences in cultural values and experiences, supporting Dana's (1988) assertion that the MMPI/MMPI-2 is an emic instrument, relevant primarily to the one particular cultural group for which it was developed. Thus, the Black alienation syndrome that may turn up on the MMPI/MMPI-2 is not necessarily an indication of individual pathology but rather of cultural group alienation in the United States. One possibly ameliorating recommendation is to carefully explore the life situation of the person being tested whenever the MMPI profile is markedly deviant (Dahlstrom, Lachar, & Dahlstrom, 1986).

Differences among Native American, African American, Mexican American, and Caucasian groups on another widely used personality test, the Meyers–Briggs Type Indicator, also have been noted (Oxford & Nuby, 1998).

The Strong Interest Inventory, a widely used vocational interest test, also yields ethnic group differences. Blacks tend to score higher in business and social service occupations, lower in physical science occupations, lower on the Realistic scale, and higher on the Social and Conventional scales on earlier versions of the Strong (e.g., SVIB), and no studies have been reported on the current version of the test with any visibly racial–ethnic group members (Carter & Swanson, 1990). Carter and Swanson (1990) concluded that "little evidence exists for the psychometric validity of the Strong with Blacks" and that "this lack of research attention is appalling, particularly for an instrument with such widespread use" (p. 206). According to Carter and Swanson, in 1952 Strong himself, the developer of the test, concluded that there was a need for a Black norm group, but no such norms are as yet widely available. It is recommended that counselors explore with Black and other ethnic minority clients the extent to which various occupations may be open to them and the influence of cultural variables in the selection of their college majors and careers (Carter & Swanson, 1990). A more individualized test, such as Holland's Self-Directed Search (Sweetland & Keyser, 1983), may be more useful with ethnic minority clients.

One survey of 332 vocational rehabilitation counselors found that only 27% rated psychological and vocational evaluation results as often or almost always culturally relevant for Native American clients living on a reservation, and only 35% rated them as relevant for off-reservation clients (W. E. Martin, Frank, Minkler, & Johnson, 1988). Such results also suggest that, for ethnic minority clients, individualized work samples, situational assessment, and on-the-job evaluations should be weighted more heavily than standardized testing.

People with disabilities also may be misrepresented by traditional assessment devices. For example, deaf people in the early 1900s were given oral intelligence and personality tests, and even now there is a lack of appropriate instrumentation for properly assessing mental health, educational, and rehabilitation needs of people who are deaf (J. Vernon, 1995). Pollard (1996) noted that unusual diagnostic trends in samples of deaf people appear to be related to testing biases rather than clinical reality.

Older people are yet another group for whom appropriate testing is difficult. J. E. Myers and Schwiebert (1996) noted several specific concerns and recommendations relevant to the testing of older people:

1. Use short sessions, as older people may tire more easily.

2. Use of large type and double spacing is helpful.

3. Monitor the reading level demanded by instructions and items.

4. Timed tests may be frustrating and inaccurate because of slower reaction times.

5. Older people may be unfamiliar with standardized testing procedures and lack test-taking behaviors.

6. Guard against lower examiner expectations of test performance as well as low motivation to take tests on the part of the older person being tested.

Many attempts have been made to develop more appropriate, culture-fair tests that have content equally familiar or unfamiliar to all groups and minimize speed and verbal content. Cattell's Culture-Fair Series, Davis–Eells Games, Leiter's International Performance Scale, and Raven's Standard Progressive Matrices all de-emphasize verbal content (Sweetland & Keyser, 1983; Williams, 1987). The System of Multicultural Pluralistic Assessment incorporates the content of an intelligence test for children within a broader format that includes measures of health and adaptive functioning (Mercer, 1979).

The work of Reuven Feuerstein (Chance, 1981) is promising in that the Learning Potential Assessment Device (LPAD) does not depend on prior knowledge and focuses instead on finding out what a child can learn. Unfortunately, the LPAD may take from 9 to 15 hours to administer, much longer than conventional aptitude tests. Feuerstein's work has been translated into at least 17 languages and has been used in more than 30 countries.

The Joint Committee on Testing Practices (1988) developed a *Code of Fair Testing Practices in Education* that makes several excellent recommendations relevant to the multicultural use of testing in general (see box on page 31). All in all, however, it is important for counselors to remember that there is general agreement that no test is truly free of culture (Williams, 1987), because it is not possible to remove from a test all references to language, abstract concepts, and prior knowledge.

☐ Culture-Specific Testing

Tests have been developed that incorporate the influence of culture in three specific areas: worldview, acculturation, and identity development. Other tests, such as the Latin American Stress Inventory (Salgado de Snyder, 1987), have been developed to measure a psychological concept (e.g., stress) from a more emic perspective.

One measure developed to assess differences in worldview is the Scale to Assess World Views (Ibrahim & Kahn, 1984). This measure incorporates Kluckhohn and Strodtbeck's (1961) five dimensions of culture: the nature of humans (good–bad), the relationship of humans to nature (harmony with–power over–all powerful), time orientation (past–present–future), the essence of human activity (being–being in becoming–doing), and social relationships (hierarchical–mutual–individualistic). Research and utility in counseling for this instrument are as yet limited.

Measures of acculturation try to assess the extent to which the respondents retain their ethnic group behaviors, whereas measures of ethnic identity development assess the extent to which individuals perceive themselves to be part of their ethnic group and how positively this group membership is experienced. Dana (1993) suggested that to assess a client's degree of acculturation, the counselor may inquire about language preference, primary language spoken in the home, place of birth, community and social relationships, and food and clothing preferences. Even more important, but more difficult to assess, are the client's own values and level of comfort living in U.S. society. For example, Zuniga (1988) suggested asking a client with a Mexican American background to identify Mexican traits that he or she feels characterize his or her family lifestyle, if any, and how the client was affected by these traits. Discussing cultural role expectations and acknowledging cultural preferences also are recommended. Thus, acculturation assessment could be a means of addressing potential culture conflicts in a problem-solving fashion that the client can learn to apply to other situations as well.

It has been estimated that there are 50 specific measures that have been developed to examine either ethnic identity development or accul-

Code of Fair Testing Practices in Education

Recommendations relevant to the multicultural use of tests:

1. First define the purpose for testing and the population to be tested. Then, select a test for that purpose and that population based on a thorough review of the available information.

7. Ascertain whether the test content and norms group(s) or comparison group(s) are appropriate for the intended test takers.

10. Interpret scores taking into account any major differences between the norms or comparison groups and the actual test takers. Also take into account any differences in test administration practices or familiarity with the specific questions in the test.

14. Evaluate the procedures used by test developers to avoid potentially insensitive content or language.

15. Review the performance of test takers of different races, gender, and ethnic backgrounds when samples of sufficient size are available. Evaluate the extent to which performance differences may have been caused by inappropriate characteristics of the test.

16. When necessary and feasible, use appropriately modified forms of tests or administration procedures for test takers with handicapping conditions. Interpret standard norms with care in the light of the modifications that were made.

Note: Excerpted from *Code of Fair Testing Practices in Education.* (1988) Washington, D.C.: Joint Committee on Testing Practices. (Mailing Address: Joing Committee on Testing Practices, American Psychological Association, 1200 17th Street, NW, Washington, D.C. 20036.)

turation (Grieger & Ponterotto, 1995), and most of these focus on a specific cultural group (Lai & Sodowsky, 1992). Several examples are listed in the box on the facing page. These measures vary in terms of their reliability, validity, and how extensively they have been researched. Refer to Dana (1993) for an excellent review of many of these measures.

The White Racial Identity Attitude Scale (WRIAS; Helms & Carter, 1990) provides a good example of the issues involved. The WRIAS was developed to measure five different White racial identity ego statuses and has been widely used. This 5-point Likert scale, 50-item instrument reveals that men are more uncomfortable and confused about race than women are and are less accepting of racial differences (Pope-Davis & Ottavi, 1994). However, there has been considerable recent debate about the reliability and factorial aspects of the WRIAS (Behrens, 1997; Behrens & Rowe, 1997; Helms, 1997; Row, Behrens, & Leach, 1995).

The Multigroup Ethnic Identity Measure (MEIM; Phinney, 1992), which takes a broader, more etic view of ethnic identity, has reasonably high reported reliability: .81 and .90 in samples of high school and college students, respectively. The MEIM is a 20-item, 4-point Likert scale instrument that yields a single factor, Ethnic Identity. MEIM Ethnic Identity has a low positive correlation with self-esteem in the .25–.31 range.

☐ Recommendations for Multicultural Assessment

Given the many sources of bias in testing and difficulties in developing culture-fair tests, the use of standardized testing should be minimized unless the content is culturally appropriate and relevant norms are available. Even the use of translated tests is questionable, because there are many concerns about their validity and interpretive comparability, and there is no regulating body or ethical code regarding test translation (Suzuki & Kugler, 1995). If the purpose of testing is for selection or diagnostic purposes, testing should be scrutinized even more cautiously. Instead, counselors can allocate more time to idiographic and nontraditional assessment, using testing for exploration rather than decision making.

Clinical diagnosis of cultural minority clients is a difficult task. Interviewer bias is hard to avoid and may take many forms. Lopez (1988) noted that the client may be viewed as more disturbed than he or she truly is, some symptoms may be inappropriately viewed as normative for certain groups, and certain diagnostic categories may either be avoided or overapplied as a function of group membership. Another problem is the

Some Group Specific Measures of Acculturation or Ethnic Identity

- Native Americans

  Indian Assimilation Scale (Howe Chief, 1940)

  Native American Value–Attitude Scale (Plas & Bellet, 1983)

  Rosebud Personal Opinion Survey (T. Hoffman, Dana, & Bolton, 1985)

- Latinos/Latinas

  Acculturation Rating Scale for Mexican Americans (Cuellar, Harris, & Jasso, 1980)

  Acculturation Rating Scale for Puerto Ricans (Pomales & Williams, 1989)

  Bicultural–Multicultural Experience Inventory (Ramirez, 1984)

  Children's Hispanic Background Scale (Martinez, Norman, & Delaney, 1984)

  Cuban Behavioral Identity Questionnaire (Garcia & Lega, 1979)

  Hispanic Acculturation Scale (Marin, Sabogal, VanOss Marin, Otero-Sabogal, & Perez-Stable, 1987)

- African Americans

  African Self-Consciousness Scale (Baldwin & Bell, 1985)

  Developmental Inventory of Black Consciousness (Milliones, 1980)

  Black Racial Identity Attitude Scale (Parham & Helms, 1981)

- Asian Americans

  Ethnic Identity Questionnaire (Masuda, Matsumoto, & Meredith, 1970)

  Suinn–Lew Asian Self-Identity Acculturation Scale (Suinn, Rickard-Figueroa, Lew, & Vigil, 1987)

- European Americans

  White Racial Identity Attitude Scale (Helms & Carter, 1990)

diagnostic classification system itself. Even though some attempts have been made to include specific, culturally bound disorders in the most recent edition of the *Diagnostic and Statistical Manual of Mental Disorders, 4th Edition* (*DSM–IV*; American Psychiatric Association, 1994), it is highly prone to *category fallacy*, which is the use of a category developed for a particular population applied to members of another culture without establishing its validity (Good & Good, 1985). Dana (1993) noted that ethnic minority clients are vulnerable to misdiagnoses of dependent personality disorder or paranoid personality disorder related to differences in population values and experiences.

The many complexities involved in diagnosing Southeast Asian refugees are a good illustration of the cultural problems involved in assessment. Many Southeast Asian refugees consider headaches and nightmares to be a normal part of life and may not even mention them because they are so common among the refugee population (Tien, 1994). Response styles which from a Western perspective may seem like exaggeration or malingering may be related to cultural differences and difficulties in discussing things in a psychological manner (W. M. Lee & Nakagawa, 1996). Additionally, posttraumatic stress disorder may be erroneously diagnosed as schizophrenia among refugees (Gong-Guy, Cravens, & Patterson, 1991).

Such difficulties underscore the need to take more time and carry out an assessment interview in a more individualized fashion with a client who is from an ethnic or cultural minority background (W. M. Lee & Nakagawa, 1996). Repeating the same question in a variety of ways may be needed to obtain adequate information. Increased emphasis on exploring gender roles and expectations, childbearing or other reproductive events, and sexual behavior may prove helpful. Also important is the client's perception of the helping process (Dana, 1993). In addition to traditional areas of assessment, culture-specific information should be obtained. The counselor could begin addressing this topic with the question "What do you call yourself when asked about your ethnicity?" (Zuniga, 1988). Comas-Diaz and Jacobsen (1987) recommended inquiring about the client's mother's and father's cultures and countries of origin, circumstances of the client's immigration, the client's perceptions of his or her family's cultural identity, and the client's own cultural adjustment.

The use of an interpreter may be needed with clients who are not fluent in English. There are many problems with the use of interpreters (Gong-Guy et al., 1991; W. M. Lee & Nakagawa, 1996; D. Sue & Sue, 1987; Tien, 1994):

1. One language may lack the words to fully correspond to the meaning of a word in another language.

2. The interpreter may unintentionally change, embellish, or distort information.

3. The interpreter's own cultural norms and values may interfere.

4. The interpreter may lack an understanding of what is important from a psychological perspective.

5. Confidentiality issues may cause the client to provide more limited information when the interpreter is a friend or family member.

It is difficult to have access to an expert interpreter who is fluent in English and in the client's primary language and who is trained to accurately represent the content expressed. For example, an interpreter unfamiliar with the counseling process might leave out information that he or she might consider embarrassing or unimportant, such as reproductive or sexual history information (W. M. Lee & Nakagawa, 1996). To minimize some of the problems inherent in the use of interpreters, Marcos (1979) suggested meeting beforehand with the interpreter to discuss the goals of the interview, the areas to be assessed, and potentially sensitive topics as well as the interpreter's level of competence in both languages. Counselors can anticipate potential language difficulties and prepare themselves to use an interpreter effectively.

CHAPTER

Cultural Transition

All changes, even the most longed for, have their melancholy; for what we leave behind us is a part of ourselves; we must die to one life before we can enter into another!

—Anatole France (Ehrlich & DeBruhl, 1996, p. 79)

Many people have experienced the process of cultural transition as they have physically moved from one culture to another. Anyone who has visited another country, moved from one region of the United States to another, or moved from one country to another has experienced this process to some extent. There are many changes that occur in the life of someone who moves into a new culture, and change, even positively anticipated change, can be stressful. Studies of life stress using the Social Readjustment Rating Scale (Holmes & Rahe, 1967) have found that the cumulative change involved in moving from one culture to another is often so great that it puts a person at risk for serious illness or depression (see Table 4.1).

A score of 150 on the Social Readjustment Rating Scale in the previous 6 months can be indicative of stress, 200–300 in 1 year has been associated with a 50% risk of serious illness or depression, and 300 or more in 1 year has been associated with an 80% probability of illness or depression. These levels are easily reached during cultural transition, when the many changes in place of employment, school, living situation, family, friendships, recreation, and religious activities are added.

TABLE 4.1. Social Readjustment Rating Scale

Life event	Scale of impact
Death of spouse	100
Divorce	73
Marital separation	65
Jail term	63
Death of close family member	63
Personal injury or illness	53
Marriage	50
Loss of job	47
Marital reconciliation	45
Retirement	45
Health problems in family	44
Pregnancy	40
Sexual difficulties	39
Gain of new family member	39
Business readjustment	39
Change in finances	38
Death of close friend	37
Change in line of work	36
More/fewer arguments with spouse	35
Large mortgage taken out	32
Foreclosure of mortgage/loan	30
Change in work responsibilities	29
Son or daughter leaving home	29
Trouble with in-laws	29
Major personal achievement	28
Change in spouse's work	26
Starting or leaving school	26
Change in living conditions	25
Revision of personal habits	24
Trouble with boss	23
Change in work hours/conditions	20
Change in residence	20

Table 4.1 continues on page 38.

TABLE 4.1. *Continued*

Life event	Scale of impact
Change in schools	20
Change in recreation	19
Change in church activities	19
Change in social activities	18
Small loan taken out	17
Change in sleeping habits	16
More/fewer family reunions	15
Change in eating habits	15
Vacation	13
Christmas	12
Minor violations of the law	11

Note: Adapted from Holmes and Rahe (1967).

The changes are most dramatic when a person moves from one country to another. Immigrants, refugees, foreign students, military personnel, business assignees, and Peace Corps volunteers are all affected by this process. It is estimated that 2% to 10% of businesspeople on foreign assignments have adjustment difficulties, and 33% of their families return to the United States earlier than planned (Church, 1982). Similarly, 15% to 25% of foreign students have been reported to experience significant adjustment difficulties, and as many as 35% to 40% of Peace Corps volunteers in some years terminate prematurely (Church, 1982).

☐ Culture Shock

The term *culture shock* was first used by Oberg (1960) to describe the state of anxiety that arises from not knowing how to behave in a new culture. Pedersen (1995) elaborated on several characteristics of culture shock:

1. Familiar cues about how to behave are missing.

2. Personal values may not seem to be respected by host nationals.

3. Feelings of disorientation may lead to anxiety, depression, or hostility.

4. Dissatisfaction with the new culture may simultaneously be experienced while idealizing the way things used to be in the home culture.

5. Coping skills may no longer work.

6. There may be a sense that the situation is permanent and will not improve.

Several models have been proposed for the stages that a person may go through in the cultural adjustment process (P. Adler, 1975; Fontaine, 1983; Oberg, 1960; Pedersen, 1995). Most describe four or five stages, with the first being a "honeymoon" stage that lasts anywhere from a few days to 6 months. During this initial stage there are positive feelings of excitement and curiosity about the new culture. Short-term tourists may experience only this phase, which lasts an average of 3 months (Oberg, 1960). The second phase, characterized by dissatisfaction and feelings of inadequacy, may last approximately 2–3 months (Fontaine, 1983). The person in a new culture begins to confront cultural differences that are problematic: Language difficulties make it hard to make friends and keep up with current events; legal barriers to employment may become stressful; and dealing with the phone company, post office, or other basic services may be different in the new culture. The world as the person has known it seems to be disintegrating, and the person may blame him- or herself for not being able to cope with the differences in the new culture. The next phase may involve feelings of depression, and the person may want to return to his or her home culture, if that is an option. Feelings of grief and bereavement on losing familiar family, friends, and culture also may be present (Furnham & Bochner, 1986). With time, as a person's language facility and coping skills improve, the feelings of depression may begin to subside. Feelings of anger and active dislike of the new culture may surface. Eventually, however, the person reaches a stage where he or she cherishes the differences in the new culture. He or she begins to have a more balanced view of the positives and negatives of both his or her home culture and the new culture. A final stage, when the person is truly comfortable in both cultures, is controversial. It may not really be possible to be truly bicultural, as the person risks losing a stable sense of identity in continually adapting to two cultures (P. Adler, 1975). Other models posit the existence of continuing waves of negative and positive feelings that may continue for several years.

The overall pattern of cultural adjustment was described as a *U*-shaped curve initially by Lysgaard (1955), but empirical support for this is mixed at best (Church, 1982). Research has not verified that most people go through a period of excitement and later depression. The time it takes to go through the various stages also varies widely among models. It is important to note that not all people may experience changes or difficulties in cultural adjustment. However, the stress of acculturation can produce feelings of anxiety, depression, marginality and alienation, psychosomatic symptoms, and identity confusion (Berry, Kim, Minde, & Mok, 1987). If a client is experiencing culture shock, the stages of adjustment and *U* curve just described may be useful to consider as a way to increase clients' understanding of what they are experiencing.

A major point to remember is that there is a lot of individual variation in how well someone will adjust to a new culture. People's experiences may be different depending on the degree of difference between the home and new cultures. There is evidence suggesting that the cultural adjustment process is different, and often harder, for women (Bowler, 1980; Church, 1982; Sjogren, 1988; Useem, 1966), particularly if they are not employed in the new culture. An alternative explanation is that cultural adjustment is equally difficult for both men and women but that women are more likely to seek counseling for their difficulties, whereas men may cope by making job or other situational changes (Bowler, 1980). In general, sex differences in cultural adjustment are an important consideration (Rogler, Cortes, & Malgady, 1991). Hopkins (1982) identified some individual qualities that predicted effective adaptation to a new culture for adolescent exchange students: self-confidence, interpersonal interest, nonethnocentrism, and educational background match to the new school. Additional variables to consider for anyone going through cultural transition are attitudes toward acculturation, degree of prior knowledge of the new language and culture, previous intercultural encounters, voluntary versus involuntary reason for entering the new culture, and level of education and employment (Williams & Berry, 1991).

☐ Counseling Individuals and Families in Cultural Transition

Treatment for culture shock may be helpful for many individuals and families in transition from one culture to another. If possible, preventive education is advisable prior to or just after the move. Clients can be taught that the feelings they may experience are part of a normal, natural process and that adjustment may take time and be difficult (Boyer & Sedlacek, 1989). One recurrent finding in the research on cultural adjustment is that congruity between expectations and actualities when encountering a new culture affects mental health (Williams & Berry, 1991). Therefore, learning about the new culture should be encouraged. Observing behavior by viewing television and movies of the new culture is one potential source of cultural information. Cultural orientation workshops or counseling sessions also would be helpful for developing realistic expectations and anticipatory problem solving. Use of the new culture's language is an important component of acculturation and accounts for much of the variance in individual adjustment (Rogler, Cortes, & Malgady, 1991). Language training is highly recommended, and it is especially useful to include specific business communication practices, day-to-day conversational dialogue, and idiomatic expressions (Donnelly, 1994).

Once the person or family has moved to the new culture, it is helpful for them to have interpersonal support to help maintain a positive self-image. Having other people who will listen to them and developing networking skills to make new friends are desirable. A counselor may be useful in this process, and at this point a counselor who is native to the new culture is often preferable (Jones, 1975).

Specific issues may arise that are relevant to the particular circumstances of cultural transition; for example, temporary transition versus permanent transition. Two transitional groups counselors are likely to encounter will be discussed separately: international students and immigrants.

International Students

There were more than 400,000 international students studying at American universities in 1990–1991 and 82,000 high school exchange students to the United States in 1992–1993 (Sandhu, 1993). International students at the graduate level were awarded approximately 26% of the doctorates granted in 1989 (Pedersen, 1991). Most international students currently come from Asian countries (Pedersen, 1991).

International students are a high-risk population, because most of their home countries do not have a history of providing or encouraging counseling, and many international students seek help only as a last resort (Boyer & Sedlacek, 1989; Sandhu, 1993). Although as many as one fourth of international students may experience cultural adjustment difficulties (Church, 1982), one study revealed that only 13% of them made use of some sort of counseling services (Boyer & Sedlacek, 1989). When international students do seek help, they tend to view their difficulties as medical as opposed to psychological (Boyer & Sedlacek, 1989). International students tend to be more satisfied with their academic adjustment than with their social adjustment (Church, 1982). Although they may like American sports, foods, freedom of dress, and openness, they may have difficulty with English; living in a different climate; homesickness; discrimination; feelings of depression, irritability, and tiredness; and visa and employment issues. Isolation and negative attitudes toward international students and lack of cultural sensitivity by Americans also are barriers to their cultural adjustment (Pedersen, 1991).

The international students who have more understanding of and ability to deal with racism, a preference for long-term goals, and an openness to nontraditional ways of seeking knowledge are the ones more likely to seek counseling. It is interesting that these same three qualities also predict better outcomes in terms of grades and retention for international students (Boyer & Sedlacek, 1989). In other words, the students with the best coping skills are the ones more likely to seek counseling, and the students who may have the most difficulty may not seek treatment. Orientation workshops that address basic life and safety information for living in the United States, colloquial English, and the nature and availability of counseling at American schools and colleges have been suggested as a way to reach some of these high-risk students (Sandhu, 1993). Another possibility is group counseling of a cross-cultural discussion group nature. I and others have led such groups at an international-student dormitory, with good results. Each group session focused on a different educational topic or theme—for example, music or holiday celebration—while giving members an opportunity to socialize with and support one another. When international students seek help for difficulties with their academic progress, brief behavioral therapy as opposed to longer term personality-reorganization-focused treatment has been recommended (K. Thomas & Althen, 1989).

Immigrants and Refugees

Unlike international students, who plan on staying temporarily in the United States, immigrants and refugees become permanent members of their new culture. The immigrant population in the United States is growing: Nine percent of the U.S. population, or 22.6 million people, were foreign born in 1994 (Morrisey, 1995), up from 19.8 million in 1990 (Rogler, 1994).

One of the major changes immigrants experience is the economic, social, and psychological stress of job loss. It is very difficult for an individual to retain his or her former occupation on entering the new culture. Socioeconomic entry status in the new culture is often lower than status on departure from the home culture (Williams & Berry, 1991). The loss of a job is a multiple loss: The job itself may be mourned; economic stress may develop, especially if a new job is not found or is found at a lower income level; and there may be a loss of personal identity involved if the old job was lucrative, a professional career, or both. It may be helpful for the individual to develop or maintain some sort of personal or professional pastime to focus his or her sense of self-worth while transitioning to a new job in the new culture.

Undocumented status may be an additional source of stress for some immigrants (Lefley, 1989). A client who is undocumented may be initially reluctant to seek counseling and, once in counseling, he or she may be less self-disclosing and may appear more paranoid in behavior.

Another more subtle but growing issue of concern is cultural racism. Prior to 1970 most immigrants were Europeans, and from 1970 on they have been primarily Latinos and Asians (Kitano, 1989). From 1965 to 1993 the number of Americans who express the belief that immigration should be decreased rose from 33% to 61%. The lack of cultural sensitivity in the United States of Americans toward people from other cultures has been notable (Pedersen, 1991; Sandhu, 1993).

One study of immigrant and refugee college students at a large university suggested that their concerns are very similar to those of international students: unfamiliarity with American society and institutions; problems relating to students, teaching assistants, and professors; and difficulties making friends, feeling that they belong, and getting involved with campus organizations (J. McKay, personal communication, October 20, 1980). Most of the immigrant and refugee students majored in engineering or computer science, and their grades were comparable to those of other students. However, fewer of them had attended precollege orientation sessions. More information about student services, additional advising and orientation efforts, bilingual peer advisors, and student or faculty mentors are suggested remedies.

Refugees are particularly at risk for psychological problems because they come to their new culture not voluntarily but because they are forced to leave their homes, fleeing persecution for their beliefs, politics, or ethnicity. Most people who are displaced from their homes stay in their home country, yet in 1995 14.4 million refugees worldwide left their home countries ("In-country refugees," 1995). Fourteen percent of legal immigrants to the United States are refugees, primarily from the Soviet Union and Vietnam (Morrisey, 1995). Many refugees may have experienced traumas such as sexual abuse, physical torture, or internment in a refugee camp or the loss of one or more family members prior to coming to the

United States. In this respect, refugees are similar to disaster victims, and similar counseling strategies may be applicable (Lefley, 1989). The most frequent diagnoses for Southeast Asian refugees in psychological treatment are depression and posttraumatic stress disorder (Kroll et al., 1989; Mollica, Wyshak, & Lavelle, 1987). The frequent experience of trauma, coupled with the involuntary nature of their move, makes cultural transition especially difficult for refugees.

Morrisey (1995) proposed a multilevel model for counseling refugees. The multilevel model involves simultaneously working with the client on four levels:

1. Mental education—educating the client about the counseling process

2. Western individual, group, and family counseling—applying traditional Western counseling techniques as appropriate

3. Cultural empowerment—serving as the client's resource guide, culture broker, and advocate

4. Indigenous healing—working with traditional healers from the client's culture

This model may be useful in planning treatment that takes into consideration cultural differences not only for refugees but also for other cultural groups.

☐ Re-Entry Shock

Re-entry shock (Fontaine, 1983) is reverse culture shock that an individual may experience on returning to his or her home culture. Gullahorn and Gullahorn (1963) suggested modifying the *U* curve previously proposed to describe the cultural adjustment process to be more of a *W* curve instead, to include the re-entry process. Re-entry shock can be as strong or stronger than the initial culture shock and may be even more difficult (N. J. Adler, 1981), for several reasons. The individual may not expect to encounter difficulties on returning home. Also, the initial culture shock may be positively rationalized by the individual as "developmental," whereas re-entry shock may feel "regressive" (Harvey, 1970).

People who spend less time living in another culture seem to have an easier time readjusting (Mattox, Sanchez, Ulsh, & Valero, 1982), and some people do not experience re-entry shock at all, because psychologically they have never left their home culture (Sobie, 1986). In contrast, people who adjusted most successfully to the new culture may find going home the most difficult (Sobie, 1986). Once a few years have passed in a new culture, the individual may have developed friends and intimate relationships in his or her new culture and may have incorporated aspects of the new culture that he or she particularly likes—for example, American music, openness of expression—into his or her own life. The prospect of returning to the home culture at this point may be stressful, as the loss of new relationships, experiences, and freedoms becomes a reality. Foreign students, and people on temporary military, business, or humanitarian assignments may find the process of returning home to be more distressing than they had initially imagined. Family and friends in the home culture may not express more than superficial interest in their overseas experiences while simultaneously the people themselves may be missing their overseas friends. As a reaction to initial culture shock, they may have come to idealize their home country and may be surprised to find themselves feeling politically, economically, and socially estranged on their return (Koehler, 1980). The individuals' values and perspectives may have changed, they may think more globally (Scott, 1984), and they may find themselves drawn to others who have had similar expatriate experiences. Sometimes, there may be a loss of a sense of "specialness" in their identity or the realities of shrinking job responsibilities on returning home to contend with as well (Sobie, 1986). Two examples of problems that may bring someone in to see a counselor at this time are the East Indian or Arab woman who does not want to return to her home country and the prospect of an arranged marriage, or the military serviceperson who has a close intimate relationship with a local national in the new culture whom he or she must either leave or marry.

People experiencing re-entry shock may require 6 months to a year to readjust; some require more than 2 years (Sobie, 1986). Harvey (1970) reported that over 50% of business assignees needed over a year to readjust. Recommendations for minimizing re-entry shock have included prereturn training and education that re-entry shock is normal (N. J. Adler, 1981; Koehler, 1980), continued contact with the home culture while away (N. J. Adler, 1981), talking within the immediate family about re-entry experiences as they occur, and talking with others who are also returning (Sobie, 1986). In general, time and support seem to alleviate the accompanying stresses of this natural adjustment process (Koehler, 1980).

☐ Generational Effects of Acculturation

Acculturation continues to affect the descendants of immigrants in future generations. These generational effects can be so notable that, for example, Japanese Americans have specific terms to describe the first through fourth generations in the United States: *issei, nissei, sansei,* and *yonsei,* respectively.

Although there may be many cultural variations, often the first-generation immigrants in the United States are grappling with economic and other initial adjustment issues. If they have chosen to immigrate to achieve a better life for their family, they may strongly value their children's success in the new culture.

Second-generation immigrants grow up with American culture, education, and media all around them. They may want to be "American," although they may speak a language other than English at home. They learn to speak English in school and often have superior language proficiency compared to their parents. As a result, they may be placed in the position of translator for the family, upending traditional family structure. They may be embarrassed at their parents' lack of ability to communicate and negotiate American institutions and procedures and lose respect for their parents' authority. Lefley (1989) described intergenerational conflict and the ensuing erosion of family structure as the major problem facing refugees. One excellent example of this is the case study of a Vietnamese family in family therapy described by Lappin and Scott (1982). Having the mother teach her children about the Vietnamese language and culture was a successful technique used by the counselor as a way for the mother to retain her position of expertise in the family and restore family stability. Second-generation immigrants are often sandwiched between two cultures. One second-generation Chinese American college student described his social circumstances: "I don't mix with new immigrants, yet I know I am not part of the third- and fourth-generation families either. Sometimes I feel caught in the middle" (Scott-Blair, 1986, p. A10).

The third- and later generation immigrants grow up American in their culture and sense of identity. However, they may find that no matter how "American" they feel, they must continue to face discrimination based on their ethnicity. It is at this point that many descendants of immigrants rediscover their grandparents' culture, perhaps developing an interest in what is now a "foreign" language, taking ethnic studies classes, and in other ways learning about their history and cultural roots. This phenomenon of the third generation trying to recapture what the second generation has lost has been called the *Hansen effect* (Kitano, 1989).

Many aspects of the home culture remain even after many generations in the new culture. Sandy Dornbusch and colleagues (O'Toole, 1988) found that in six of the seven ethnic groups they studied, high school grades and the amount of homework done decreased for second-generation immigrants and even more for third-generation immigrants. However, the parents of the third-generation students still retained a more authoritarian parenting style compared to middle-class White American parents. F. A. Johnson and Marsella (1978) found that even third-generation Japanese American college students had less aggressive, less assertive, and less egalitarian speech tendencies than European Americans. Also, third- and fourth-generation Asian Americans continue to be reluctant to admit to psychological problems (Yamamoto & Acosta, 1982).

In summary, acculturation is a powerful process, with many potential effects on individuals and families. Counselors need to be aware of the ramifications of cultural transition on their clients even if unspoken by them. At the minimum, counselors would do well to inquire about the cultural transition experiences of their clients regardless of whether they seem directly related to the presenting problem.

5

CHAPTER

Cultural Identity Development

I went from being ashamed, to being accepting, to being proud. Really, honestly, I guess that would be the best way to present it. I didn't want to be Black. There was a time period when you can see in my writing: "Oh my goodness, this is the curse of my life." Then, "Well, I'm Black, so (sigh) deal." To the point now where, "I'm Black! Hey I'm glad." I wouldn't change it.

—18-year-old African American female (Tatum, 1993, p. 15)

Tajfel (1981) described *ethnic identity* as part of an individual's self-concept that comes from knowledge of membership in a social group and the value or emotional significance attached to that membership. Similarly, Phinney (1990) defined ethnic identity as consisting of self-identification as a group member, a sense of belonging, and one's attitudes toward one's group. These definitions can easily be broadened and extended to include other aspects of social status that constitute an individual's cultural identity, such as gender, sexual orientation, age, or disability status.

Of the many topics relevant to multicultural counseling, developmental models of cultural identity have perhaps received the most theoretical interest. Many stage models have been proposed to account for the incorporation of culture into an individual's sense of identity. As with other stage models of development, these models are based on the assumptions that (a) progression from one stage to another is desirable, and (b) the order, but not the rate of progression through the various stages is similar across individuals.

Caution should be taken in applying stage models of cultural identity development, in part because of their commonalities with other stage models. Although the people who developed a particular stage model may not have intended for it to be linear—such that a person may be in more than one stage simultaneously or return to a previous stage without it being perceived as negative (Helms, 1995; Zera, 1992)—in application, however, stage models typically are perceived as inherently implying linearity (Weinberg [1984], cited in Zera, 1992). Indeed, Hoffman (1991) offered two valid criticisms that apply to most cultural identity development models. From a feminist perspective, such models are hierarchical reflections of a masculine worldview, that progression through stages is likened to tasks to be completed rather than something that will increase the contextual range of responses available to an individual. Also, with few exceptions (Gutierrez, 1985), cultural identity development models have generally not been compared with other well-established developmental models.

Even given the assumptions and criticisms just mentioned, stage models of cultural identity development may be useful for counselors who want to understand the cultural context of their clients. This chapter explores some of the many stage models of identity development that have been described in the multicultural literature.

☐ Racial–Ethnic Identity Development

Many identity development models have been proposed and elaborated over the past two decades to describe the process an individual may experience in becoming aware, accepting, and positive in his or her attitudes about his or her own or others' racial–ethnic background. Some of these models are more specific to individuals of a particular ethnic minority group; for example, Blacks (Cross, 1995) and Chicanos/Latinos (A. S. Ruiz, 1990), and others are described as applicable to a broad range of ethnic minority groups (Atkinson, Morten, & Sue, 1989; Helms, 1995). Some models describe the experiences of people who belong to the dominant racial–ethnic group (Christensen, 1989; Helms, 1995), and some describe the experiences of those who are biracial (i.e., belonging to two different racial–ethnic groups; Poston, 1990). Three representative examples of racial–ethnic identity development models will be outlined and compared.

One of the oldest and most widely known developmental models relevant to people of an ethnic minority cultural background is the one developed by Atkinson, Morten, and Sue (1989), currently entitled the racial/cultural identity development (R/CID) model. This model was first proposed in 1979 and has since undergone some revision. It includes five stages: Conformity, Dissonance, Resistance and Immersion, Introspection, and Integrative Awareness. In the Conformity stage, an ethnic minority individual holds the same values as those of people in the dominant cultural group and tends to devalue him- or herself and others who are ethnic minorities. Such a client would probably prefer a counselor who is a member of the dominant cultural group and might be particularly amenable to a problem-solving approach to counseling. A client in the next stage, Dissonance, is in a state of psychological conflict. Clients in the Dissonance stage are beginning to question their cultural identity and their sense of self-esteem as they come to realize the impact of culture in their own lives. Here, a counselor who is knowledgeable about the cultural background of the client may be especially helpful. The third stage, Resistance and Immersion, involves a new sense of self, appreciation of one's own cultural group, and rejection of the dominant cultural group. A client in this stage may distrust people of the dominant cultural group and prefer an ethnic minority counselor. The client may put much of his or her energy into group action and efforts to combat oppression. Trust issues; racism; and feelings of guilt, shame, and anger may be important in counseling a client at this stage of cultural identity development. The fourth stage, Introspection, involves a growing concern over the basis of self-appreciation and a questioning of ethnocentrism as a premise for judging others. A client in this stage may benefit most from a counselor with a broad world view who can assist the client in a process of self-exploration to differentiate his or her individual views from those of others. The last stage, Integrative Awareness, involves a capacity to appreciate oneself as well as others. A client at this stage may have an ongoing desire and commitment to eliminate oppression, and a counselor with a broad world view would again be desired.

There is a growing body of research evidence relevant to the R/CID model. For example, Pang, Mizokawa, Moishima, and Olstad (1985) found that Asian American children felt less positive about their physical characteristics than did White children. These children may be in the Conformity stage, deprecating themselves and preferring the characteristics of the White cultural group. Similarly, Tatum (1993) found that half of the African American college students who had been raised in White communities did not consider attending a historically Black college because they were afraid that they would be labeled by other students as "too White." These students might be in the Dissonance stage, aware of but uncomfortable with their cultural identity. Kohatsu (1996) found that, among Asian Americans, racial mistrust of another ethnic minority group was positively related to levels of Resistance and Immersion attitudes and negatively related to Integrative Awareness attitudes. However, racial identity attitudes were less predictive for Latinos. Certainly, more specific research into the validity and utility of the R/CID model is needed. In the meantime, counselors may be able to apply the model on an individual basis as a way to understand some of the potentially contradictory and confusing feelings and actions that an ethnic minority client may experience over time with respect to his or her cultural identity.

Cross's (1995) Nigrescence model of Black identity development is very similar to the R/CID model. First described in 1971, it encompasses five stages: Pre-Encounter, Encounter, Immersion–Emersion, Internalization, and Internalization–Commitment. The nature of the issues and psychological stresses and attitudes at each stage are generally comparable to those of the R/CID model. Research on the Nigrescence model has yielded two themes: (a) at the Pre-Encounter stage, low salience is given to race, but most people in this stage are not confused, self-hating, or mentally ill and (b) at later stages an individual might express him- or herself by means of a range of ideological preferences, from Black nationalism to multiculturalism.

A. S. Ruiz (1990) proposed a Chicano/Latino ethnic identity model that also consists of five stages similar to those in the R/CID model: (a) Causal, (b) Cognitive, and (c) Consequence stages of identity conflict; the (d) Working-Through stage of intervention, when the client is ready to discuss ethnic identity concerns, increase ethnic consciousness, and reintegrate disowned parts of his or her ethnic identity; and the (e) Successful Resolution stage, characterized by greater self-esteem and cultural–ethnic appreciation. Because this model was developed from the point of view of a practitioner, little empirical validation is available for it. A. S. Ruiz's recommended counseling interventions include cultural assessment; cognitive restructuring of internalized negative injunctions and faulty beliefs related to ethnicity; and recognition of the client's cultural beliefs, values, and behaviors.

Several models have been proposed to account for the identity development of people who are members of the dominant racial group, which in the United States is White. The experience of being White is developmentally different from that of belonging to an ethnic minority group, because Whites in the United States learn that they are entitled to privileges associated with being White (McIntosh, 1988) and learn to deny or distort race-related reality in order to protect the status quo (Helms, 1995). According to Helms (1995, p. 184), "the general developmental issue for Whites is abandonment of entitlement, whereas the general developmental issue for people of color is surmounting internalized racism in its various manifestations."

Christensen (1989) described a cross-cultural awareness development model that included five stages for both majority and minority individuals. In the Unawareness stage a majority individual may deny being White, assert that racial differences are not important, and avoid any personal responsibility for a racist society. In the Transition stage there may be feelings of shame, guilt, anger, or depression as the individual begins to acknowledge what it means to be White. He or she may suffer impaired relationships with White relatives, friends, or colleagues if he or she makes his or her feelings known. The third stage, Conscious Awareness, may involve racial self-hatred as the person perhaps overidentifies with people of color. The person may attempt to join minority group activities and, to his or her surprise, be rejected and perceived as insincere. In the Consolidated Awareness stage, the individual recognizes his or her Whiteness, and negative feelings of guilt and anger begin to subside. In the final stage, Transcendent Awareness, the individual has an increased appreciation of cultural diversity and an increased commitment to societal change. Christensen noted that underlying this model are assumptions that racism is an integral part of life in the United States and that all Whites are racist whether they are aware of it or not.

Helms (1984, 1995) proposed a six-status (i.e., stage) White racial identity model that differs from Christensen's (1989) model primarily in that the third stage, Reintegration, involves an idealization of things perceived to be White as opposed to a fascination with non-White cultures, as in the Christensen model. In addition, stage models for racial consciousness development among White counselor trainees (Ponterotto, 1988) and White racial identity development in counselor training (Sabnani, Ponterotto, & Borodovsky, 1991) have been proposed.

Biracial Identity Development

A growing segment of the population is biracial. Estimates are that 1.9 million children in the United States live in homes with parents of different races, and other estimates suggest that there are 6 million mixed-heritage people of all ages in the country (Contin, 1996). Several identity development models that account for the unique needs of biracial or bicultural people have been developed (Gutierrez, 1985; Poston, 1990).

Poston (1990) proposed a five-stage biracial identity development model. In the first stage, the biracial person is independent of group identity as he or she develops within the context of the family. During the second stage, Choice of Group Categorization, the biracial person is compelled to choose a specific identification group (e.g., White, Black, etc.). Children of White–Asian or White–Hispanic background are more easily assimilated into predominantly White culture, whereas White-Black children are generally identified with the Black community (Keerdoja, 1984). In the Enmeshment/Denial stage that follows, feelings of guilt and self-hatred may be experienced as the biracial individual struggles with his or her own rejection of a part of him- or herself. The fourth stage, Appreciation, involves exploration of previously ignored heritage(s), and in the final stage, Integration, the biracial individual comes to value his or her multicultural identity. Another model, of bicultural personality development, proposed by Gutierrez (1985), reconciles Erikson's (1968) stages of development with cultural identity development stages. At each of Erikson's psychosocial developmental stages the individual's current cultural identity plays an important role in how developmental tasks are approached (Chavez, 1986). Kerwin and Ponterotto (1995) reviewed several other biracial identity development models.

There is scant research on bicultural people. Several scholars suggest that biracial status can be problematic: Biracial children must come to terms with a culture in which standards of beauty are White and other children may ask painful questions about why the child looks unlike his or her parents (Shackford, 1984). Many biracial adolescents indicate problems with racial identity (Gibbs, 1987). On the other hand, Burnette (1995) noted that interracial children are no less well adjusted than other children of color, and Brandell (1988) noted some advantages of biracial status: more tolerance of others and a greater hesitancy to develop biases toward any group of people. There is some consensus that parents may foster a healthy self-concept in interracial children by using labels such as "interracial," "mixed," or "tan" (Jacobs, 1992; Kerwin, 1993). Hall (1980) found that two thirds of her sample of biracial adults had resolved any earlier identity issues and identified themselves as multiracial, suggesting that they had reached the last stage of their biracial identity development.

In comparing these and other models of cultural identity development, one can note several similarities. Refer to Table 5.1 for a comparison of three of these models. Most of the models have five stages, with some outlining as many as seven. The initial stage is characterized by unawareness of culture as an important part of a person's sense of identity, and the final stage is a desirable state of self-acceptance and appreciation of culture as an important dimension of the self. The stages in between involve psychological discomfort and self-examination, often with a middle stage of overidentification with culture.

TABLE 5.1. Comparison of Racial/Ethnic Identity Development Models

Racial/cultural identity development model[a]	Cross-cultural awareness development model[b]	Biracial identity development model[c]
Conformity	Unawareness	Personal Identity
Dissonance	Transition	Choice of Group Categorization
Resistance and Immersion	Conscious Awareness	Enmeshment/Denial
Introspection	Consolidated Awareness	Appreciation
Integrative Awareness	Transcendent Awareness	Integration

[a]From Atkinson et al. (1989).
[b]From Christensen (1989).
[c]From Poston (1990).

☐ Other Dimensions of Minority Identity Development

Several other dimensions of minority status, such as gender, sexual orientation, and disability status, also may be strong influences on identity formation. For example, 74% of disabled Americans recognized a common identity with other people with disabilities, according to one Harris poll (Tainter, Compisi, & Richards, 1995).

Downing and Roush (1985) proposed a feminist identity development model that begins with a Passive Acceptance of Sexism stage; followed by a Crisis stage involving new revelations of the influence of sexism; an Embeddedness stage, marked by intense connections with other women; and an Active Commitment to Feminism stage, in which individual personal attributes are integrated with feminist principles.

Cass (1979, 1984) pioneered discussion about gay and lesbian identity development in her sexual identity formation model, which consists of Identity Confusion, Identity Comparison, Identity Tolerance, Identity Acceptance, Identity Pride, and Identity Synthesis stages. Her model became an inspiration and baseline of comparison for other models of gay and lesbian identity development (Zera, 1992) as well as for bisexual identity development (Zinick, 1985). A more recent model (Troiden, 1989) includes four stages. The first stage, Sensitization, takes place before puberty, when the gay or lesbian child experiences social feelings of marginality and difference and gender identification, not sexual behavior, is a primary concern. At this stage, being teased for cross-gender behavior may contribute to internalization of a negative self-concept. Identity Confusion, the second stage, is the most difficult and potentially dangerous. At approximately age 17 for males and 18 for females, homosexual feelings and behaviors develop, and the adolescent is at risk for suicide and other self-destructive behavior as he or she tries to come to terms with societally unacceptable aspects of the self. The third phase, Identity Assumption, incorporates Cass's Identity Tolerance and Identity Acceptance stages. At approximately ages 19–21 years for men and 21–23 for women, the young gay man or lesbian begins to reduce his or her isolation and increase his or her contact with other homosexual people as the stigma of his or her sexual orientation becomes more manageable. The last stage, Commitment, involves accepting homosexuality as a part of one's being and making a same-sex love commitment. Happiness and self-satisfaction increase as inner struggles diminish, and homosexuality may become a less important part of the individual's total identity. This may occur roughly at ages 21–24 in gay men and ages 22–23 in lesbians. These models of sexual orientation identity development are useful in helping counselors become aware of different issues that may be salient at different stages for clients. For example, having a counselor who is not gay may be less helpful when a client is in an identity confusion or identity pride stage (Chojnacki & Gelberg, 1995).

The convergence of more than one minority status on identity development may have complex implications for a client's life. Morales (1992) described a five-state process to integrate minority ethnicity and sexual orientation identity development. According to Morales (1992), a client may experience several states at the same time, unlike most models. Some elements of the process include denial of conflict and attraction to White lovers, conflicts in allegiance to ethnic and gay communities, and the integration of various communities into a multicultural support system. Furthermore, a client who is lesbian and blind, or another who is a physically disabled Latina, is dealing with a triple minority status, and what this may mean in terms of self-esteem, social acceptance, and other clinical issues must be explored carefully and thoroughly by her counselor for the issues' potential impact on the presenting problem.

☐ Counseling Implications

Each of the various stage models has specific implications relevant to counseling issues and the salience of the counselor's own cultural background at a particular stage of identity development. Counselors should review appropriate models of cultural identity development that may relate to the client they are counseling. More generally, the most important result of the growing literature on cultural identity development as it applies to counseling is to reinforce the concept that how a client feels culturally about him- or herself is evolutionary and not static. This notion helps break down stereotypes that all clients from a particular cultural background would have similar feelings about themselves. An adult client could be in any stage of cultural identity development and thus be very different from another client of the same cultural background who is in a different stage. Furthermore, a client could be in one stage of cultural identity development when he or she first enters counseling, and how the client feels about his or her cultural identity may change during the course of counseling, regardless of whether culture is an explicit focus of counseling (Chavez, 1986). This should be assessed on an ongoing basis. Comas-Diaz and Jacobsen (1987) suggested that a counselor might begin the exploration of the client's cultural identity by using reflection to acknowledge the role of ethnicity (Comas-Diaz & Jacobsen, 1987) or other aspects of cultural difference in the client's life. One potential treatment goal for a client might be to help the person make a transition into another stage of cultural identity development, which might result in increased feelings of self-esteem and an ability to act productively within his or her environment.

☐ Recommended Cultural Resources

Print Media

Mabry, M. (1995). *White bucks and black-eyed peas.* New York: Simon & Schuster.

6

Native Americans in Counseling

A sense of humor is an important characteristic of American Indian cultures. We believe there is a fine line between laughter and tears. They are both enabling means of survival.

—Joseph Iron Eye Dudley (1992, p. 139)

☐ Histories and Diversity

There are more than 2.3 million Native Americans in the United States (U.S. Bureau of the Census, 1991). States with more than 40,000 Native American inhabitants include California, Oklahoma, Arizona, New Mexico, North Carolina, Washington, and South Dakota (Axelson, 1993; Baruth & Manning, 1991; Lieberg, 1996). The total number of Native Americans living in the United States is most likely underreported because of difficulties in getting census information from lower income groups and because the federal government automatically classified American Indians whose origins are from Central or South America as *Hispanic* (Ponterotto & Casas, 1991). The federal Bureau of Indian Affairs restricts the definition of *Indian* to someone enrolled or registered as a member of a federally recognized Indian tribe or someone who can legally demonstrate that he or she has at least one fourth Indian heritage. There are an estimated 10–20 million people in the United States who have some Indian blood (Trimble & Fleming, 1989).

There is tremendous diversity among Native Americans, a term that includes American Indians, Eskimos, and Aleuts. Five hundred seventeen federally recognized Native American entities have been identified (Herring, 1991), with additional groups that as yet are unrecognized (Heinrich, Corbine, & Thomas, 1990). The Navajo tribe, with more than 110,000 members, is the largest, and the smallest tribe may have only 1 remaining survivor (Trimble & Fleming, 1989). There are an estimated 200–2,200 distinct languages spoken by Native Americans (Baruth & Manning, 1991; LaFromboise, Berman, & Sohi, 1994). Given the vast diversity among Native American cultures, much of what is written about Native Americans is based on generalizations, primarily from specific North American Indian tribes. There is research evidence that the degree of cultural variation within a tribal group can be greater than between Indians and non-Indians (Tefft, 1967).

When referring to the ethnicity of a Native American client, it is generally best to use the name of the person's tribe, because many Native Americans most strongly identify themselves as members of a tribe. If tribal affiliation is not known, *American Indian* is the term preferred by most Native American tribes and organizations. However, some individuals may dislike this term, because *Indian* originated with European explorers who mistakenly believed they had reached India when they came to the Americas. *First American, Amerindian,* or *Native People* are other common designations. Avoid using terms that refer to discriminatory stereotypes of Native Americans, such as *savage, noble warrior,* and *squaw* (Herring, 1991).

Roughly half the Native American population lives on federal reservations, which number 314 (U.S. Bureau of the Census, 1993b); the others live in urban or metropolitan areas (Baruth & Manning, 1991). Many urban Indians are of mixed blood, have limited contact with reservations, and may feel alienated or socially isolated (Attneave, 1982; Sage, 1991). Other urban Native Americans choose to return to the reservation of their people on a regular basis. On the reservation, a person's genealogy is common knowledge, and the sense of community and tribal identity is strong (Sage, 1991). Thus, a return to the reservation may bring a sense of balance, increased self-esteem, and tribal identity (Sage, 1991) and at the same time help counteract feelings of isolation, rejection, or anxiety experienced when living in Anglo society outside the reservation (Sanders, 1987). Migration between the reservation and the city also brings with it greater connection to others in terms of information sharing about travel plans and some pressure to remain connected with family (Sage, 1991). Miller (1974/1979, cited in Attneave, 1982) found that the most successful urban Indian families were both open to the learning and technology of the majority culture around them and interested in maintaining their tribal language, values, and customs.

Although there are many variations among tribal cultures, there are several experiences shared by Native American groups in the United States that bring a sense of common history and hardship. Loss of tribal lands to the U.S. government is common to all Native Americans (Axelson, 1993). The history of Native Americans in the United States can be described as fraught with ambivalence and filled with failed attempts at forced assimilation and a general lack of respect for their humanity. Refer to the text box below for a brief chronology of Native American history with the U.S. government.

Beginning in the late 1800s, the U.S. government guaranteed the provision of education and health care to many Native American groups as part of treaties signed in exchange for tribal lands (Dinges, Trimble, Manson, & Pasquale, 1981). This led to the establishment of government boarding schools. By 1902 there were 25 such schools in 15 states. Native

A Brief Chronology of Native American History With the U.S. Government

1787   Policy of reserving land for exclusive use of Native Americans began the formation of reservations.

1824   Bureau of Indian Affairs organized to supervise Native Americans.

1830   Indian Removal Act moved nearly all eastern tribes west of the Mississippi, and many died along the way, on the Trail of Tears.

1871   Congress ruled that tribes were no longer independent governments, thereby eliminating the need for treaties.

1887   Dawes Act gave land to individual tribe members in an effort to break up tribal groups and encourage farming.

1890   U.S. Army annihilated a band of Sioux, including women and children, at Wounded Knee, South Dakota.

1924   All U.S.-born Native Americans granted citizenship.

1980   Indian Child Welfare Act gave preference to Native Americans in foster care and adoption of Native American children.

American children as young as 5 years of age were separated from their parents and taken to these schools, which were often far from their homes. There Native American children were punished for speaking their tribal languages, because the schools were aimed at removing all traces of Indian and immersing the child in Western culture. In addition, the children often had to endure forced physical labor, food scarcity, overcrowding, and sickness, because these institutions were underfunded (Tafoya & Del Vecchio, 1996). In addition, government practices of placing Native American children in adoptive families who were non-Native also attacked Native American cultural continuity. It has been estimated that from 25% to 55% of all Native American children have been placed in non-Native foster homes, adoptive families, boarding homes, or other institutional settings at some time in their lives (Herring, 1991). Given the known negative effects of institutionalization, the governmental treatment of Native American children in this century has been described as cultural genocide.

Chronic unemployment and poverty are part of life for many Native Americans. The Bureau of Indian Affairs estimated that the unemployment rate for Native Americans living on or near reservations is 48% (Herring, 1991). Twenty-one percent of reservation Native Americans have no plumbing, and 16% have no electricity (U.S. Bureau of the Census, 1985). Native Americans have the highest school dropout rate of any U.S. ethnic group, 35.5% (Herring, 1991). Native Americans also have the highest rates of diabetes, kidney disease, and accidental death nationwide (J. Pease-Pretty On Top, personal communication, July 1997). The average life expectancy of Native Americans is 8 years less than that of Anglo Americans (American Association of Retired Persons [AARP], 1986), and the median age of Native Americans is 20.4 years—almost 10 years younger than the national median (LaFromboise, 1988). The high rates of unemployment, school dropout, and also teen pregnancy need to be viewed with the Native American history of 500 years of cultural trauma in mind (Sutton & Broken Nose, 1996). It is not surprising that many Native Americans share a sense of distrust of and frustration with the government, and these attitudes many greatly hinder the counseling relationship for a counselor working for any type of government agency.

☐ Cultural Values

For traditional Native Americans, everything in nature has a spirit: all animals, inanimate objects, the sky, and the earth. Respect and reverence for nature exists in both physical and spiritual ways. Respect may take the form of noninterference (Baruth & Manning, 1991), which can be mistaken for passivity or neglect by people who are unfamiliar with Native American cultures. In contrast, disrespect for and overuse of natural resources are believed by many Native Americans to lead to imbalance and disharmony in the world and dysfunction in human relationships (Axelson, 1993). Thus, harmony with nature is a very important value in many Native American cultures (Baruth & Manning, 1991). This harmony is based on belief in the constancy, timelessness, and predictability of nature (Herring, 1991). Harmony is desirable on a cosmic level, not only in one's nuclear and extended families, but also between the self and important others, trees, animals, land, ancestors, stars, and the Great Spirit (Herring, 1991; Matheson, 1986). Matheson (1986) gave as an example that an Indian would not waste natural resources by indiscriminately harvesting large quantities of herbs and would in addition give an "offering" back to the earth. Being ignorant of one's relationship to nature is not considered sinful but simply the direct cause of natural destructive consequences (Axelson, 1993). Mental illness may be believed to be a justifiable outcome of human weakness or a lack of discipline in maintaining harmony (Herring, 1991).

This holistic and inclusive view of nature gives the spirit world reality, making it not unnatural to "see" or "hear" spirits in everyday life (Matheson, 1986). There may be little distinction between mind and body, spirit world and reality. Many Native American cultures believe in reincarnation (LaFromboise et al., 1994). Dreams may be considered important and visions actively sought after (Matheson, 1986). This is a definite departure from typical Western psychological dualism, in which such experiences are often deemed pathological auditory or visual hallucinations. Spirituality in many Native American cultures may be described as mystical and integrated into everyday existence. Prayer may be a part of daily life (Axelson, 1993), and dance may be considered a form of religious expression (E. H. Richardson, 1981).

For many Native Americans the group, in terms of the tribe and extended family, comes before the individual (M. J. Anderson & Ellis, 1995; Baruth & Manning, 1991). Some of the ramifications of this group sense of self are that cooperation is valued, praise must come from others, and leaving the reservation may be difficult as it implies rejection of the tribe (M. J. Anderson & Ellis, 1995; Garrett & Garrett, 1994). Sharing and generosity are highly valued qualities in many Native American cultures (Attneave, 1982; Axelson, 1993; Baruth & Manning, 1991). In fact, acquisition and competition may be considered abhorrent (Matheson, 1986). Instead of material wealth, family and relatives are treasured, and many Native Americans may feel that to be poor is to be without family or relations (Sage, 1991). Some Native American cultures have ceremonies in which material goods are given away to recognize others' help, achievement, or kinship during important life transitions. Sharing with and gift giving to visitors and guests also is valued. This spirit of generosity can come into conflict with the modern American majority cultural emphasis on acquiring money and possessions, causing Native Americans in school and work situations to erroneously be viewed as unmotivated or unassertive if they freely share their possessions and do not try to compete for material or individual advancement. Sharing unemployment benefits or educational stipends with relatives whose needs are greater has been described as one of the major obstacles to career development among Native Americans (Attneave, 1982).

The "Indian way" means that families work together to solve problems (Sutton & Broken Nose, 1996). Decision making is preferably consensual (Attneave, 1982). Traditional family units often consist of an extended family that includes three or more generations (Attneave, 1982). In many Native American cultures children's primary relationship is with grandparents (who are largely responsible for rearing children) and not parents (who are responsible for economic support; Garrett & Garrett, 1994; Sutton & Broken Nose, 1996). Cousins may be called "brother" or "sister," and often no distinction is made between natural relatives and in-laws. It has been suggested that counselors take a family history early during the counseling process, because this is nonthreatening and recognizes the importance of the extended family (Sutton & Broken Nose, 1996).

Because of the oral historical tradition of most Native American cultures, words are viewed as powerful and valuable (Sage, 1991). Legends are used to convey cultural knowledge in many Native American cultures (Baruth & Manning, 1991). In this manner, taboos, which—unlike European laws—have flexible, mystical qualities, also are taught (Matheson, 1986). This suggests that counselors might consider making use of storytelling or the techniques of Milton Erickson (Erickson, Rossi, & Rossi, 1976) in their work with some Native American clients. Discipline often comes in the form of shaming, ridicule, or natural consequences, and Attneave (1982) suggested that feelings of guilt may be less prominent among Native Americans because there may be fewer assumptions regarding personal control over others or the environment.

Native American cultures often have a present orientation to time (Attneave, 1982; Baruth & Manning, 1991; Sutton & Broken Nose, 1996). Because change is not an inherent value, there is more emphasis on doing things well rather than quickly. The concept of "Indian time" referring to being late might more accurately be described as doing something when the time is right (LaFromboise et al., 1994).

Noninterference in the lives of others is a Native American value that may result in tolerance of others' behavior, even if it is extreme (LaFromboise et al., 1994). This can be misinterpreted as overindulgence, passivity, or a lack of concern. Direct confrontation may be limited to defining the consequences of an individual's behavior. On the other hand, a Native American client might be more open to a variety of counseling techniques because of an attitude of tolerance (Attneave, 1982).

Some other Native American values that may have relevance to counseling include patience and control of one's emotions, honesty, bravery, strength, endurance of natural pain and suffering, self-sufficiency, and working with one's hands (Axelson, 1993; Baruth & Manning, 1991; E. H. Richardson, 1981).

☐ Indigenous Treatment Methods

Medicine people, or shamans, are indigenous healers who are believed to possess psychic abilities to heal and to predict weather conditions and the migration of local animals (Axelson, 1993). *Medicine* refers to a way of life or doing things (Garrett & Garrett, 1994). The medicine wheel, or circle of life, represents the Four Directions of spirit, nature, body, and mind. After a person sits and talks with the medicine person and decides what the problem is, the medicine person will typically either suggest ways of dealing with the problem or ask the person to do some specific task. The healing process also incorporates a support system and some type of ceremony or ritual. Medicine people do not solely support themselves through healing (Attneave, 1982). These indigenous healers have great influence and play a significant role in Native American communities. DeAngelis (1992) wrote of a Fond du Lac reservation medicine man in Wisconsin who impresses on his people that alcohol and tobacco are both sacred substances that should not be used casually. Counselors can make their efforts with their clients more successful by consulting and working in conjunction with Native American healers whenever possible (Garrett & Garrett, 1994). Many Native Americans view both traditional and Western practices as helpful, and counselors can support their clients' attendance at prayer meetings, use of herbal medicines, and indigenous healing rituals (Sutton & Broken Nose, 1996). Also, any fees for counseling should be discussed explicitly and in a straightforward manner as fee-for-service may be handled differently when help is sought from a medicine person (Attneave, 1982).

Network therapy (Attneave, 1969, 1982) takes into account the Native American value of harmonious relationships from a family therapy, community psychology perspective. Counseling occurs during a network meeting in which an individual, his or her immediate family, extended family, and any significant others in the community (e.g., neighbors, police, teacher, priest, bartender) meet to help resolve problems. Network therapy mobilizes a tribal unit or clan to help its members (Attneave, 1969). The goal of tribal network therapy is to build the client's coping skills within the context of the group (Thomason, 1995). The network therapist or counselor's role has been compared to that of a participant who sometimes intervenes, or like the conductor of an orchestra (Attneave, 1969). Several kinds of skills are needed to conduct network therapy: family therapy and group process skills, individual assessment and crisis intervention skills, and the ability to provide links between the network and outside institutions whose services may be helpful. Although network therapy calls for much skill on the part of the counselor, it holds much promise for the successful treatment of Native Americans. Network therapy has similarities to indigenous ceremonies such as the Navajo "sing," a social and curative event in which all who play a part in the person's social life gather together. The curative properties attributed to such indigenous treatments—the reaffirmation of social bonds, social support received, hope inspired, and a general expectation of positive change (Dinges et al., 1981)—may also be activated by network therapy. There is research evidence of the effectiveness of network therapy for prevention and treatment (Schoenfeld, Halevy-Martini, Hemley-Van der Velden, & Ruhf, 1985). Even if network therapy is not attempted, community and tribal leaders can be helpful resources for counselors (Herring, 1991).

The sweat lodge and vision quest are indigenous treatment rituals common to many Native American cultures. A sweat lodge is a small hut constructed from animal hides and supported by saplings. Over a period of many hours, herbal water is sprinkled over hot stones, creating steam, for the purpose of physical and spiritual self-purification. Many aspects of the sweat lodge ceremony are symbolic. For example, the steam represents prayers ascending to the Great Spirit above (Heinrich et al., 1990).

A vision quest is a male rite of passage or renewal preceded by a sweat lodge ceremony. During the vision quest, the person has no contact with other humans and sits for days without food and water, spending the time in reflection, prayer, and a search for a vision. "Whether it be in a dream state or in full consciousness, something, some one thing or series of events, will reveal to this young Native American man a strikingly real element of the future he must follow" (Heinrich et al., 1990, p. 131).

A modified version of the vision quest may be incorporated into the counseling process through the use of guided imagery. The client carries out the vision quest in imagery and is instructed to seek an animal who will befriend the client and help answer his or her questions. This combination of guided imagery and inner dialogue work has parallels to the vision quest and might perhaps yield similar benefits.

Another Native American technique that has been adapted by some counselors is the "talking circle" (Heinrich et al., 1990). The talking circle is a forum for expressing one's thoughts and feelings without a time limit and in an atmosphere of acceptance. In a Native American talking circle, sacred objects (e.g., a feather or stone), a pipe, and prayer are part of the process. Thomason (1995) described the use of talking circles in group counseling with Native American students: An object is passed around the circle of participants and only the person holding the object speaks, only for him- or herself, and for as long as he or she needs. The talking circle also was reported to be a highly successful activity in a treatment program for sexually abused Native American adolescents (Ashby, Gilchrist, & Miramontez, 1987).

The Navajo create sand paintings during special ceremonies as a means of curing afflictions (Axelson, 1993). Parallels between sand painting and the uses of a sand tray as a counseling technique have yet to be explored. Here again, consultation with Native American healers would be beneficial.

☐ Treatment Implications

Educational Concerns

Native Americans have the highest school dropout rate of any ethnic group in the United States—35.5% (Herring, 1991)—and their representation among dropouts is more than triple their proportion of all elementary and secondary students (National Center for Educational Statistics, 1989). Only 57% of Native Americans have obtained a high school degree or its equivalent (Sanders, 1987). On or near the reservation, even fewer Native Americans have much formal education, with only 43% having completed high school and 16% having less than 5 years of schooling according to a 1987 Bureau of Indian Affairs estimate (cited in Herring, 1991). The education of Native Americans is a particularly acute concern given that Native American children function at an average-to-superior range until the third grade (Sanders, 1987) but by the 12th grade test at three grade levels below the national average (Dillard, 1983).

Many factors have been suggested as being responsible for Native American achievement difficulties in school. Baruth and Manning (1991) summarized several, including English as a second language, low self-esteem, and health problems such as fetal alcohol syndrome and ear disease. M. J. Anderson and Ellis (1995) suggested that cultural value differences may contribute to the situation. They asserted that Native Americans emphasize living in the present and not long-term projects that require delayed gratification and sacrifice, such as formal education. Herring (1991) attributed the problem to chronic poverty and unemployment, which result in few positive career role models and low career aspirations.

The educational issues of Native Americans are compounded at the college level. Only 16% of Native Americans complete an undergraduate degree (Astin, 1982). Native American tribal groups have begun to develop their own solution to this problem. The first American Indian tribal college was founded in 1968 on a Navajo reservation (D. Johnson, 1994). In time, many more tribal colleges were started; most are community colleges, but three offer bachelor's and master's degrees. When counseling a Native American student who is preparing to attend college, it may be helpful to consider a predominantly Native American college. For a list of some American Indian colleges (compiled by R. McNeil, personal communication, December 12, 1995), refer to the box on page 67.

Alcoholism

Alcohol use is a significant concern for Native Americans, whose alcoholism rate is estimated to be double the national average (Heinrich et al., 1990). Alcohol or drug abuse has been described as problematic for 52% of urban and 80% of reservation Native Americans (U.S. Senate Select Committee on Indian Affairs, 1985). However, alcoholism rates vary extensively among tribes (LaFromboise et al., 1994).

There is no physiological or psychological support for the myth that Native Americans have a lower tolerance for alcohol (M. J. Anderson & Ellis, 1995). Tafoya and Del Vecchio (1996) considered alcoholism, as well as other addictive behaviors, such as gambling, to be consequences of the historical trauma endured by Native Americans. Addictive behavior serves as a coping skill that is used as a means of denial to avoid dealing with the impact of years of traumatic conditions. Alternatively, M. J. Anderson and Ellis (1995) suggested that drinking alcohol is a social behavior and a social facilitator for Native Americans. Binge drinking in a group setting is done to have a good time with others, and effective counseling must address the social context in which abuse was developed and maintained. Native Americans have begun to develop their own culturally relevant treatment programs for alcohol abuse. According to Hall (1986, cited in Heinrich et al., 1990), approximately 50% of Indian Health Service alcohol programs incorporate sweat lodge ceremonies in treatment.

Some American Indian Colleges
(Members of the American Indian College Fund)

Bay Mills Community College, Brimly, MI

Blackfeet Community College, Browning, MT

Cheyenne River Community College, Eagle Butte, SD

College of the Menominee Nation, Keshena, WI

Crownpoint Institute of Technology, Crownpoint, NM

D-Q University, Davis, CA

Dull Knife Memorial College, Lame Deer, MT

Fond du Lac Tribal and Community College, Cloquet, MN

Fort Belknap Community College, Harlem, MT

Fort Berhold Community College, New Town, ND

Fort Peck Community College, Poplar, MT

Haskell Indian Nations University, Lawrence, KS

Institute for American Indian Arts, Santa Fe, NM

Lac Courte Oreilles Ojibwa Community College, Hayward, WI

Leech Lake Tribal College, Cass Lake, MN

Little Big Horn College, Crow Agency, MT

Little Hoop Community College, Fort Totten, ND

Navajo Community College, Tsaile, AZ

Nebraska Indian Community College, Winnebago, NE

Northwest Indian College, Bellingham, WA

Oglala Lakota College, Kyle, SD

Salish Kootenai College, Pablo, MT

Sinte Gleska University, Rosebud, SD

Sisseton Wahpeton Community College, Sisseton, SD

Southwest Indian Polytechnic Institute, Albuquerque, NM

Standing Rock College, Fort Yates, ND

Stone Child Community College, Box Elder, MT

Turtle Mountain Community College, Belcourt, ND

United Tribes Technical College, Bismarck, ND

☐ General Counseling Issues

Native Americans tend to underuse mental health services and, when they do seek services, have a high dropout rate. Among their dissatisfactions with counseling are distance to the service location, limited operating hours, impersonal interactions, ambiguous agency procedures, long waits before they can be seen, high fees, transportation problems, and lack of child care (Baruth & Manning, 1991). It is evident that many of these barriers could be minimized by changing agency policies and procedures to be more accommodating of the needs of Native American clients. Lack of understanding of cultural differences and language also are barriers (W. E. Martin et al., 1988). Other contributors to low mental health service use may be the enduring influence of negative historical interactions with non-Native people (Herring, 1991), who make up the vast majority of counselors, as well as perceived conflict in acculturation goals and power differentials within the counseling relationship (LaFromboise, Trimble, & Mohatt, 1990). On the reservation, a Native American of mixed blood may be reluctant to seek the services of an Indian Health Service counselor because of concern that he or she would be perceived as not really being an Indian if he or she sought government assistance (Sage, 1991). In urban areas, the lack of an identified central agency with which to communicate complicates matters (W. E. Martin et al., 1988).

Native Americans are most commonly diagnosed with alcohol abuse and dependence, depression, anxiety, and adjustment disorders (Foster, 1995a). Diagnosing depression among Native Americans is particularly difficult, because there are several culturally appropriate behaviors that may be misdiagnosed as signs of depression. Trimble and Fleming (1989) described the "cultural time out," or *wacinko*, among Siouan-speaking people, which includes withdrawal. Similarly, a Native American client who is simply waiting with hope for the natural consequences to evolve that will resolve the problems he or she is facing may appear hopeless or passive. However, the suicide rate for Native Americans is the highest in the country and is twice the national average (Baruth & Manning, 1991; J. Pease-Pretty On Top, personal communication, July 1977). Suicidal behavior may be another reflection of historical trauma (Tafoya & Del Vecchio, 1996) or even a family characteristic within some tribes, and the counselor should be aware that suicide rates vary tremendously among tribes (Shore, 1975).

Nonverbal Behavior

Nonverbal behavior is extremely important in counseling Native Americans. Attention to how the counselor enters the room, the furnishings in the room, and the presence of coffee or food can make the counselor's office seem more comfortable (Sutton & Broken Nose, 1996). Casual dress on the part of the counselor may be perceived negatively (Trimble & Fleming, 1989) because the degree of care the Native American client takes in preparing his or her appearance for counseling sessions may be an indication of respect for the counselor (M. J. Anderson & Ellis, 1995). Also, the counselor needs to respect and appreciate any gifts given (Attneave, 1982). Several authors have noted the importance of feeling comfortable with and using silence (Foster, 1995a; Garrett & Garrett, 1994; Heinrich et al., 1990; E. H. Richardson, 1981; Sage, 1991; Sutton & Broken Nose, 1996; Thomason, 1995). Thomason (1995) suggested mirroring the client's nonverbal and verbal styles. For example, Native American children tend to speak more slowly and softly than White children do (Baruth & Manning, 1991). Nonverbal signs of attention, such as head nodding or *uh huh*s, are uncharacteristic for many Native Americans (Sanders, 1987). Prolonged eye contact may be considered disrespectful to Native Americans from some tribes (Garrett & Garrett, 1994; Matheson, 1986; E. H. Richardson, 1981).

The Initial Session

The first session is critical in counseling Native Americans even though the client may disclose little information while he or she assesses the therapist and the initial problem he or she presents may not be the major issue (Attneave, 1982; Herring, 1991). Counselors might consider several recommendations that have been made regarding the content of the first session.

1. Disclose who you are and where you come from before asking the client to self-disclose (Sutton & Broken Nose, 1996). Anecdotes and short stories are good ways to model self-disclosure (Garrett & Garrett, 1994).

2. Ask questions. Questions that make the client the expert are a way to address client passivity (M. J. Anderson & Ellis, 1995). The first session is useful for asking open-ended questions about family history as this is nonthreatening and shows concern for the extended family (Attneave,

1982; Sutton & Broken Nose, 1996). However, avoid direct questions about religion, tribal ceremonies and politics, and traditional healing and medicine practices (W. E. Martin et al., 1988; Thomason, 1995). Broach these and other cultural topics slowly, perhaps letting the client initiate the topic.

3. Acknowledge any awareness you may have of the client's tribal identity and family configuration (Herring, 1991).

4. It may be important to open the issue of Native American–White relationships if the counselor is White (P. Katz, 1981).

5. Be flexible in ending the session, and be prepared to extend the first session (Foster, 1995).

In general, these suggestions are more applicable the more traditional the client is in terms of acculturation. The first session may be treated as time to get acquainted in an unhurried, interested fashion (Lum, 1986), and the counselor is well advised to listen carefully and make no assumptions (Sutton & Broken Nose, 1996). The counselor demonstrates patience by not interrupting the client and withholding advice or interpretation until invited (Garrett & Garrett, 1994).

Therapeutic Modalities

No one mode of counseling has been proven to be better than others in counseling Native Americans (Heinrich et al., 1990; Thomason, 1995). Attneave (1982) suggested that many therapeutic approaches would be acceptable to Native American clients as long as the counselor is sincere. Although there is little process research on what works in counseling Native Americans, many writers who are knowledgeable in the field have made a variety of recommendations. Reviews of the literature suggest that counselors use a more directive style (Trimble & Fleming, 1989), concentrate on problem solving (E. H. Richardson, 1981; Thomason, 1995), and make the counseling more informal by welcoming drop-in meetings (Heinrich et al., 1990) and conversations in social settings (Thomason, 1995). Nonverbal play and creative arts for children, spirituality, humor, storytelling, metaphors, imagery, paradoxical interventions, modeling, and role play have been recommended (Foster, 1995a; Garrett & Garrett, 1994; Lazarus, 1982; Sutton & Broken Nose, 1996). Restatement and summarizing a client's comments at the end of the session are recommended, and confrontation is best avoided because it is perceived as rude and disruptive of essential harmony in many Native American cultures (Baruth & Manning, 1991; Garrett & Garrett, 1994).

Family therapy has been frequently recommended for Native Americans (Baruth & Manning, 1991; Sutton & Broken Nose, 1996; Thomason, 1995). Particular attention should be paid to encouraging family stability and taking into consideration the many demands made by relatives (Thomason, 1995). At the very least, counselors need to be open to the participation of family members and tribal elders in the counseling process (Foster, 1995a).

Group counseling may be helpful with Native American clients, but not if the group is heterogeneous (Baruth & Manning, 1991). Sage (1991) described an example of a Native American women's group during which the women participated in beading and other crafts. The counseling approach was indirect, with the group focusing on problems by way of members relating stories of how similar situations had been handled. Thomason (1995) recommended small-group counseling for Native American students, using values clarification and resolution of cultural conflict as themes. A group program might begin with introductions that include family background and extent of identification with Indian heritage and in future sessions cover such topics as ways Native Americans differ from non-Indians; stereotypes about Indians; strengths of traditional Native American culture; conflict over societal pressure to conform to non-Indian ways; assertiveness; and sharing of Indian artwork, music, and literature.

Cultural Knowledge

It is essential that counselors work toward becoming knowledgeable about Native American cultures (Trimble & Fleming, 1989) and begin to read literature about specific individual tribes (Sutton & Broken Nose, 1996). Establishing credibility as a helper is a long-term, community-based process (Lowrey, 1983). It has been recommended that counselors acknowledge the depth of cultural loss that Native American clients experience, even for assimilated clients who may need to grieve for what they never had (Sutton & Broken Nose, 1996). Also, given the depth of historical trauma Native Americans have experienced in the United States, there is a need for counselors to become systemic-change agents (Herring, 1991).

☐ **Recommended Cultural Resources**

Print Media

Dudley, J.I.E. (1992). *Choteau Creek: A Sioux reminiscence*. Lincoln: University of Nebraska Press.
Holm, T. (1996). *Strong hearts, wounded souls*. Austin: University of Texas Press.
Innu Nation & Mushuan Innu Band Council. (1995). *Gathering voices: Finding strength to help our children*. Vancouver, British Columbia, Canada: Douglas & McIntyre.
Journal of American Indian Education
Miles, M. (1971). *Annie and the old one*. Boston: Little, Brown.

Multimedia

Barnes, M. (Writer/Producer). (1979). *The long walk of Fred Young* [Videotape]. Washington, DC: PBS Video.
Costner, K., & Wilson, J. (Producers). (1990). *Dances with wolves* [Film]. Chatsworth, CA: Orion Pictures.
Millar, S. (Producer). (1988). *Little big man* [Videorecording]. Livonia, MI: CBS/Fox Video.

Organizations

American Indian College Fund, 21 West 68th Street, Suite 1F, New York, New York 10023. Phone: (212) 787-6312.

African Americans in Counseling

If you're black, you still carry the problems that your people have been going through. You're never gonna forget that and once you know that, you wake up with that every single day. And so for me, I have to wake up every day and realize where I come from all over again, realize the struggle we went through, and understand that I am different.

—Reggie Simmons, African American college student
("Voices of diversity," 1993)

☐ Histories and Diversity

African Americans constitute the largest ethnic minority group within the United States. Thirty million Americans, approximately 12.1% of the population, have an identifiable African heritage (Ponterotto & Casas, 1991). Because of the longstanding prejudice and discrimination against African Americans throughout United States history, many descendants of African Americans do not identify with or claim that part of their ethnic heritage (G. West, personal communication, February 21, 1997). People who are identifiable as African Americans are a relatively young ethnic group, with children and young people constituting close to half the population. The median age of these African Americans is 26.9 years, compared to a median age of 32.7 years for the European American population (U.S. Bureau of the Census, 1986). Unemployment is on the increase for African American youths (Hoyt, 1989), and young African American men are at risk to experience violence. Homicide is the leading cause of death among African American men aged 15–24 (Freiberg, 1991a), and a young Black man is six times more likely than a young White man is to be killed (Pania, 1992). Nearly one in four African American men aged 20–29 are in prison, on parole, or on probation; they outnumber those in college (Pania, 1992). Only 11.5% of African Americans have completed four years of college, compared to 22.2% of Whites. The high school graduation rate is 66.7% for African Americans and 79.9% for Whites (McDavis, Parker, & Parker, 1995). The rate of teenage pregnancy among African Americans is more than twice that of Whites ("Black and White," 1988). In 1990 the divorce rate for African Americans was twice that of all Americans in general (U.S. Bureau of the Census, 1990b).

Unlike any other ethnic group who migrated to the United States, most African Americans had ancestors who were brought to the country against their will, as slaves, beginning in the early 1600s. The effects of slavery on the majority of African Americans cannot be overstated as slavery not only created conditions of economic exploitation, but it also left a legacy of disconnected family histories and, for some, a sense of hopelessness. African Americans were called "African" or "Black" during the slavery era, and "Negro" or "Colored" during postemancipation times, and "Black" or "African American" became preferred terms during the civil rights era. However, some African Americans may still be reluctant to use the most recent terms and prefer "Negro" because of a perception that an African identity is not positive (Dobbins & Skillings, 1991).

Although slavery has been illegal for more than 100 years, the economic recovery from its effects on many African Americans has been largely unnoticed. However, a substantial proportion of African Americans in the United States were never slaves. These free people trace their roots to ancestors who were indentured servants and worked off their financial obligations over several years. These African Americans often moved to urban areas, among them New Orleans; Charleston; Washington, DC; and northern cities, and have been prominent in the Black middle class (Axelson, 1993). Also, between 1940 and 1970 1.5 million African Americans migrated from the South to urban areas in the North and the West coast for better employment prospects (Hines & Boyd-Franklin, 1982). In 1987, 36% of Black families had middle-class annual incomes of $25,000 or above. From 1970 to 1989, the percentage of Blacks with annual incomes greater than $50,000 grew by 182% (Edwards & Polite, 1992). These statistics suggest that there is a large African American middle class that has developed despite societal racial barriers and that the number of affluent African Americans is growing substantially. On the other side of the economic spectrum, 29% of Black households had zero net worth in 1987 (Edwards & Polite, 1992), and the chances of a Black person finding employment are half that of someone who is White (Pania, 1992). There is a great diversity of economic conditions among African Americans, but images of unemployment and poverty continue to predominate in both print and televised media.

The 1896 Supreme Court case Plessy v. Ferguson legalized "separate but equal" use of railroad facilities for African Americans. The ruling contributed to segregation in education and housing as well. One of the outcomes was the further development of predominantly Black colleges and universities, a trend that had first begun in 1869. Legally segregated schools ended with the 1954 Brown v. Board of Education Supreme Court ruling that racial segregation in public schools was unconstitutional. The Civil Rights Act of 1964 ended legalized discrimination in public restaurants and hotels, employment and union membership, and programs receiving federal assistance (Axelson, 1993; McDavis et al., 1995).

Racism and discrimination, however, continue to be strong influences in the lives of most African Americans. According to one review (Fendel et al., 1996), Blacks and Latinos were denied jobs which were then offered to equally qualified Whites 15%–20% of the time, and 46% of Blacks compared to 11% of Whites say they have been discriminated against in the workplace during the past 5 years. The overall unemployment rate remains higher for Black high school graduates than for White high school dropouts (Hoyt, 1989). Many African American parents have attempted to teach their children how to respond to discouragements such as name-calling or stereotyping (McDavis et al., 1995). They also know that they must prepare their children for dealing with police and the criminal justice system, which arrest, convict, and incarcerate higher proportions of African Americans than Anglo Americans (Jaynes & Williams, 1989). One Black mother (cited in Pania, 1992) instructed her son as follows:

> If you're ever stopped, . . . answer when spoken to. Say yes sir, no sir, and provide only what is asked. Keep your hands visible at all times and be polite. Don't question authority. And make your exit as soon as it's permitted. (p. 17A)

Some vestiges of racism that have been internalized by segments of the African American community continue to be manifested in a color "caste" system, with lighter skinned Blacks being preferred over others (McDavis et al., 1995). These skin color preferences are even an issue within some families (Block, 1981).

It is important to note that the term *African Americans,* as used in the United States, is very broad; it includes Spanish-speaking Blacks, American Indian Blacks (Ponterotto & Casas, 1991), West Indian Blacks, and Haitian Americans, as well as recent immigrants from Africa. Counselors are cautioned against making assumptions about people from some of these subgroups, because the vast majority of research on African Americans in the United States is based on people whose ancestors experienced the American version of slavery and racism and their effects for generations. For example, whereas many West Indian Blacks also have a history that includes slavery, in the West Indies slaves were emancipated earlier and were able to become landowners and enter the middle or upper classes. Many skilled, educated, middle-class West Indian Blacks immigrated to the United States between 1940 and 1978. These African Americans often identify ethnically more as immigrants with island, regional, or colonial (e.g., British) roots (Brice, 1982). Haitian Americans, some of whom speak Creole—a blend of French and African languages—constitute another distinct subgroup that has immigrated to the United States in large numbers since 1970 (Axelson, 1993).

☐ Cultural Values

Spirituality

For many African Americans, religion has been an integral part of their ancestral cosmology and an important resource during hard times (Hines & Boyd-Franklin, 1982). A national survey of Black Americans conducted in 1979–1980 (cited in Billingsley, 1992) indicated that 84% of African Americans consider themselves religious, and 77% said that the church was very important in their lives. In addition to providing a sense of hope, communal religious practices provide a network in which to socialize, exchange support, develop leadership, and take social action. Consequently, African Americans with a strong sense of spirituality may initially seek help from spiritual resources before approaching a counselor.

The African American church is a generic term for religious institutions within African American communities, which include a multitude of Christian denominations, such as African Methodist Episcopal Zion; African Methodist Episcopal; Apostolic; National Baptist Convention of America; National Baptist Convention, USA; National Primitive Baptist Convention; Progressive National Baptist Convention; Church of God in Christ; Church of God; Congregational; Episcopal; Lutheran; Roman Catholic; Seventh

Day Adventist; and others (Axelson, 1993; B. L. Richardson, 1991). The Nation of Islam practices an American version of Islam (Axelson, 1993). In general, 80% of African Americans are Protestant (Billingsley, 1992). B. L. Richardson (1991) wrote that

> Slavery and then segregation denied African Americans access to the rights and privileges accorded other Americans. The church was the only institution that African Americans had to meet their emotional, spiritual, and material needs. . . . Today, the church remains at the center of community life, attending to the social, spiritual, and psychological needs of scores of African Americans. No other institution claims the loyalty and attention of African Americans as does the church. (p. 65)

The church continues to serve many functions in addition to spiritual guidance: (a) It is a source of support and enhancement of self-esteem gained through service to the church, (b) it is a source of role models, and (c) it is a community base around which to organize collective efforts to confront oppressive systems and practices. For example, some African American parents who live in White neighborhoods and whose children attend predominantly White schools may seek African American churches as a means of balancing their children's identity development (B. L. Richardson, 1991). This may counteract the possibility of feeling alienated from both Blacks and Whites and experiencing interpersonal rejection as personal rather than cultural, which may occur when growing up in a White community.

In 1984 a Gallup survey revealed that 74% of Black adults belonged to a church, compared to 68% of White adults (cited in Hill, 1993). More recently, however, Jackson (cited in Foster, 1995b) suggested that although the African American church was a primary focus and had a calming effect on the family, its influence has diminished because many African American men no longer attend as regularly. He recommended that counselors encourage their African American male clients, in particular, to become more involved in church, among other treatment options.

Family

The myth regarding the deterioration of the Black family as a major cause of African American problems suggests a lack of understanding of the Black family. Strong kinship and tribal ties common among African cultures were damaged by slavery, which often physically separated family members (Hines & Boyd-Franklin, 1982). However, the resilience of African American family values may be currently evidenced in a variety of ways, including acceptance of children born out of wedlock, frequent extended family contact, and multigenerational households. A child raised by persons other than his or her parents is not rejected in the community, as alternative living arrangements are a practical solution to economic and other problems (Hines & Boyd-Franklin, 1982). The mother is often considered the family's strength and emotional center, acting as a stabilizing influence if the father does not have the level of education or employment needed to protect or provide for the family (Pinderhughes, 1982). However, the father may be considered the head of the household even when he is physically absent from the family. Long separations may be more tolerable than the idea of divorce when marital conflicts occur, and marital issues may be addressed indirectly. At the same time, there may be pressure on family members to remain close to home and to assist family members in need (Hines & Boyd-Franklin, 1982). In some families, economic necessity results in a de-emphasis on sex role related division of labor within the household and encouragement of educational accomplishment for women. Grandparents may take on the responsibility of raising their grandchildren (McDavis et al, 1995) and, indeed, 85% of African American teenage mothers live in three-generational households with their grandparents at the head (Billingsley, 1992). Black families also have been characterized as having a strong work and achievement ethic and a strong religious orientation (Baruth & Manning, 1991; D. W. Sue & Sue, 1990). The family is often used as a solution to individual problems. According to Hines and Boyd-Franklin (1982), a high tolerance for problems in the family may be related to religious convictions or to having dealt with a long history of oppression. African Americans may be disinclined to view the family as a source of problems, and the counselor would do well to draw on the family as a strength and consider including or consulting extended family members. For example, a "parent effectiveness group" may not appeal to African American families with extended or non-nuclear structures, whereas a more inclusive description, such as a group on "raising children," may be better received (M. B. Thomas & Dansby, 1985).

The Afrocentric Worldview

In an Afrocentric view of the world, the individual is validated in terms of others (Asante, 1987; Cheatham, 1990). This is a definitive concept, and this basic value is complemented by emphases on family and collective survival. The family is a reference point for interconnecting the person to all other family members—past, present, and future—and includes relationships based on blood, marriage, and both formal and informal adoption (Rogers-Dulan & Blacher, 1995). The traditional vocational choices of African Americans, teaching and the social sciences, tend to actualize Afrocentric values. Other elements of an Afrocentric worldview include a holistic rather than dualistic mind-versus-body focus, self-knowledge revealed through symbolic image and rhythm, interpersonal relationships that are cooperative and interdependent, harmonious blending with others and the universe, emphasis on the present more than the future, animated emotional expression, obedience to authority, and respect for the elderly because they have accumulated life's wisdom (Pinderhughes, 1982; Robinson & Howard-Hamilton, 1994; White & Parham, 1990).

Oral tradition is another important aspect of African American cultures (White & Parham, 1990). Parables, folk verses, folk tales, biblical verses, songs, and proverbs contribute to this oral tradition. A sample of Black proverbs collected by White (1984) are listed in the box below. Much Black humor has evolved from this strong oral tradition.

African American vernacular, or *Ebonics*, is a variation of American English that evolved in the United States over several hundred years. In fact, many African Americans are bilingual, speaking Ebonics as well as the more widely accepted American English. Recently, controversy has

---

Some African American Proverbs

The truth will out.

Don't sign no checks with your mouth that your ass can't cash.

Hard head make a soft behind.

You better be yourself or you gonna be by yourself.

One monkey don't stop no show.

Only a fool plays the golden rule in a crowd that don't play fair.

If you lay down with dogs you gonna come up with fleas.

What goes around, comes around.

You better learn how to work before work works you.

You don't git to be old being no fool.

arisen over programs that use Ebonics as a means of teaching African American schoolchildren American English (Darling, 1997). An African American client's decision to speak the mainstream American version of English could be indicative of responsiveness to the social context in which he or she is speaking. Wilson and Stith (1991) noted that poor Blacks may have difficulty communicating their feelings, behaviors, and thoughts in American English. They recommend that counselors become familiar with Ebonics and accept its use by their clients. Counselors unfamiliar with Ebonics might do well to consider getting training and or increased exposure to Ebonics as a means of more fully understanding their clients. African American clients do not expect their counselors to imitate either Ebonics or Black humor in an attempt to create rapport, however, because African American clients frequently are more adept at switching back and forth between Ebonics and American English than most counselors.

☐ Indigenous Treatment Methods

The African American church may be a source of great assistance to some African American clients. B. L. Richardson (1991) noted that some African Americans may associate the counseling process with institutional or individual racism they have experienced, and such perceptions promote defensiveness and hinder the counseling process. This tendency is exacerbated when counselors have limited knowledge of and sensitivity to racism. African American clergy are a form of traditional healer, and the counselor may benefit from consulting them (Hines & Boyd-Franklin, 1982; B. L. Richardson, 1991). B. L. Richardson (1991) offered some guidelines for consulting with traditional healers. When a client's spiritual beliefs are counterproductive to positive mental health, consultation is recommended. The church can also provide resources and support for families in crisis or who have experienced loss and assist isolated families in forming a new social network. Counselors might also consider the benefits of "pastoral initiative," the expectation that clergy will go to people and intervene on their own initiative and without specific invitation. Counselors can establish contact with African American clergy, for example, by giving a workshop at a ministerial alliance, a weekly meeting where clergy discuss clerical and community concerns, and later, presenting a workshop to the congregation (B. L. Richardson, 1991).

There also has been interest in studying indigenous healing as currently practiced in Africa (Anwar, 1995; Levers & Maki, 1995). This process may have potential benefits with respect to understanding African

American concepts of healing. Medicine and religion are connected in several African cultures, and the healing process is characterized by spiritual transformation (Levers & Maki, 1995). Generally, healers had been ill for some years themselves and perceive their abilities as inherited or received as a gift from God or ancestral spirits. Healing is spiritual in that it involves a sense of community, of being reunited with ancestors.

> Transformation occurs from the state of being afflicted to being healed; transcendence occurs in the act of being healed and in the process of becoming healer. Becoming healer and the process of healing allow for reconnection— the reconnection of the healer as well as of those the healer heals—to self, to community, to ancestors, and to universe. (Levers & Maki, 1995, p. 139)

Identification with a mythical figure and adopting the role of the spirit is another way traditional healing occurs (Anwar, 1995).

Kwanzaa is "a movement that seeks to establish, express, and celebrate aspects of African-American cultural identity" (Axelson, 1993, p. 103). Dr. Maulana Karenga developed it in 1966 on the basis of the African harvest celebration. The 7-day festival celebrates the life principles of unity, self-determination, collective work and responsibility, collective sharing, purpose, creativity, and faith (Axelson, 1993). Kwanzaa can be viewed as an indigenous healing ritual for African Americans.

Robinson and Howard-Hamilton (1994) proposed that the African value system called *nguzo saba* can be integrated into the counseling process in a more Afrocentric approach. The seven major principles of *nguzo saba* are *umoja* (unity), *kujichagalia* (self-determination), *ujima* (collaborative work and responsibility), *ujaama* (cooperative economics), *nia* (purpose), *kuumba* (creativity), and *imani* (faith).

Yet another form of indigenous treatment was described in an article by Charles (cited in Lefley, 1989), who used cultural values and strengths in treating African Americans from the Caribbean. For example, the Haitian value placed on not lying or stealing was used to generate motivation to attend vocational training. Similarly, achievement orientation and group commitment values were used as incentives to treat depression.

☐ Treatment Implications

Black Rage and Trust

One of the most important issues for the counselor to initially consider when counseling an African American client is that of trust. Because of the legacy of slavery and realities of present-day racism and discrimination, trust in counselors and the counseling process may be difficult to develop. The history of slavery in the United States continuously makes African Americans angry and, whether consciously or unconsciously, every African American deals with it internally, according to Clemmont Vontress (Foster, 1995b). In some segments of the African American community, a client might ask him- or herself, "Is counseling something Black people do? Will counseling help me?" This is especially salient when the counselor is White. It may be easier for some African American clients to develop a counseling relationship with a counselor of color, but a degree of wariness might still exist. Block (1981) compared a Black getting help from a non-Black therapist as "like asking a Jew to be treated by a German, an Irish Catholic by an Irish Protestant, an Arab by a Jew, a white South African by a black" (p. 191). The real reason for counseling may be disguised, and a pseudoneed may be presented instead to first test the safety of the counselor and the counseling process (Block, 1981).

Because counseling or therapy may be perceived as something for "crazy" people, other sources of help, such as ministers, doctors, aunts, or grandmothers, may have been tried first (Hines & Boyd-Franklin, 1982). By the time many African American clients encounter a professional counselor they may feel desperate and at the end of their rope. According to Morris Jackson (Foster, 1995b), the counselor must ask him- or herself, "Can I deal with the rage that African Americans may be having?" knowing that that rage may be directed at people very similar to the counselor, and "Do I have enough confidence and competence as a counselor to work through that, or am I too timid?"

The counselor is cautioned not to interpret African American anger as simple transference; the client's feelings are a realistic response to the counselor as a part of a social system that has historically proven inhospitable and deserving of mistrust. Client issues concerning trust may constructively be viewed as healthy suspiciousness (Hines & Boyd-Franklin, 1982). Sometimes clients' expression of affect or other responses may be subdued because the clients expect a negative response from the counselor. The counselor may help the client feel more comfortable expressing emotions by responding to a client's description of a situation with "Some people might feel . . . (discouraged, outraged, etc.) with that experience."

The client being "cool," acting unconcerned and worldly, has been mistakenly interpreted at times as limiting the personal risk of counseling and promoting a sense of power and control, especially for African American men (Freiberg, 1991a). On the other hand, counselors need to keep in mind that verbal directness does not necessarily imply hostility (Baruth & Manning, 1991). A somewhat different, but also stigmatizing issue is that of internalized oppression (see Chapter 2). Some African American clients may have internalized societal messages about racial inferiority with the results being self-hatred and self-limiting of potential, with concomitant hostility and mistrust (McDavis et al., 1995). This self-hatred hypothesis has been destructive to understanding Black adjustment and may result in a counselor erroneously blaming the client, when the client may actually have been victimized.

Historically Black Colleges

Low expectations, lack of role models, disregard for cultural diversity, and grouping or tracking practices have been identified as barriers to African American educational success in schools (Locke, 1995). Counselors with African American clients who are considering college can be of great assistance by helping them consider the potential benefits of attending a historically Black college, which may minimize many of these barriers. Some traditionally Black educational institutions are Clark Atlanta, Howard, Florida A&M, Fisk, Hampton Institute, Morehouse, Morgan State, North Carolina Central, John C. Smith, Southern, Tennessee State, Tuskegee Institute, and Virginia State (Backover, 1992; DeAngelis, 1997; Pruitt & Isaac, 1985; "Voices of diversity," 1993). Many historically Black colleges and universities (HBCUs) are private institutions. HBCUs provide a distinctive, positive educational experience for their students. According to Locke (1995), getting good grades in high school can lead to an African American student being accused of "acting White" and can result in him or her questioning the value of academic achievement because it puts him or her at odds with peers. This dilemma loses significance at HBCUs. African American students at Black colleges and universities are often more diverse with respect to socioeconomic and educational background. Historically, Black colleges and universities have produced a large majority of African American PhDs, Army officers, physicians, and federal judges (Kemp, 1990). Graduation rates for African American students are higher at HBCUs compared to graduation rates at predominantly White institutions. According to a 1992 report, 44% of all bachelor's degrees earned by African Americans were awarded by HBCUs, even though only 17% of all enrolled African American college students attend them (Backover, 1992). Some of the advantages of attending a Black institution of higher education are a higher level of psychosocial adjustment and a better self-image gained from being part of a majority experience (Kemp, 1990). Communication and identification with faculty also happen more spontaneously (Backover, 1992). The disadvantages include fewer campus resources and more limited choice of majors and advanced-study programs (Kemp, 1990). Faculty may be less nationally recognized than at predominantly White institutions, but they frequently place more of their emphasis on teaching.

In 1990, 73% of African American students attended predominantly White universities (Kemp, 1990). It may be that many counselors have little knowledge about Black institutions as an educational alternative. The choice of colleges for African Americans is complex and also interacts with issues of ethnic identity. Tatum (1993) found that many African American students did not consider attending a historically Black college for the reason that they were afraid to be labeled "too White" by their college peers. Indeed, Edwards and Polite (1992), in their book, *Children of the Dream*, found that a common trait among successful African Americans was a positive sense of ethnic identity. Other similarities included a strong sense of family, self-confidence, a willingness to get along with Whites, and an ability to keep anger or resentment from detracting from their goals (Siegel, 1992).

Diagnostic Issues

Psychological disorders may express themselves differently depending on the client's ethnic and economic background. For example, Blacks with depressive disorders are more likely to report hallucinations and delusions, whereas manic symptoms or feelings of guilt are more common in Whites with depressive disorders. W. B. Lawson asserted that "the increased likelihood of hallucinations in Black and Hispanic patients with bipolar affective disorder (manic depression) may contribute to the misdiagnosis of schizophrenia" (Ziegler, 1986, p. E2). The rate of depression among Blacks is actually no different than among Whites when socioeconomic status is taken into account (Ziegler, 1986). African Americans with depressive disorders may also display more agitation and aggression, weight gain, difficulty crying, and self-destructive symptoms such as not going to work or victim-precipitated homicide (Block, 1981). As with depressive disorders, no differences have been found between Blacks and Whites in rates of sociopathy or antisocial personality (Cloninger, Reich, & Guze, 1975; Robins et al., 1984).

Historically, African Americans have had more access to health services than to mental health services, and somatic complaints sometimes have helped bring about positive change in terms of relief from situational stresses. However, African Americans continue to have differentially higher rates of infant mortality, hypertension, heart disease, obesity, anemia, AIDS, and other physical conditions than European Americans (Axelson, 1993; Baruth & Manning, 1991; DeAngelis, 1992; Mayo, 1974; Pinderhughes, 1982). On average, Blacks die 7 years earlier than Whites (DeAngelis, 1992).

Counselors must be sensitive to issues of bias in diagnosing African Americans. Jordan (1993) reviewed studies that indicated that African Americans tend to be rated by clinicians and therapists as less verbal, more impaired, and having poorer family relations, more so when the therapist is White.

Other Counseling Issues

There are several ways in which the counselor may want to modify his or her behavior when working with African American clients. For some African Americans, eye contact may not be a sign of attentiveness (Baruth & Manning, 1991), and the counselor needs to look more closely at other nonverbal behavior instead. Although many African Americans may value openness and action, being out of control is not valued (Block, 1981). Self-disclosure may be low, and the counselor may want to share more personal information and opinions of his or her own (Block, 1981; McDavis et al., 1995) and provide an orientation to the counseling process to first-time clients (Hines & Boyd-Franklin, 1982; McDavis et al., 1995). The orientation might include:

1. Discussing the importance of being present at the time of the appointment,

2. Emphasizing the need to notify the counselor about cancellations,

3. Telling the client that he or she needs to bring up important issues,

4. Explaining to the client that trust will develop over time,

5. Explaining to the client that counseling occurs outside the session as well, in terms of how he or she thinks and acts between sessions (Block, 1981; Hines & Boyd-Franklin, 1982).

Giving specific, explicit answers to client questions also has been recommended (Locke, 1995). In addition, it may be helpful to specifically address cultural differences (Wilson & Stith, 1991). This may be appropriate during the initial session. The counselor may want to give the client a summary of what the counselor understood from the session, particularly at the end of the first session.

African American clients may prefer a more active, problem-focused, time-limited therapeutic style (Hines & Boyd-Franklin, 1982) from an authoritative counselor who will be vigorous and committed in his or her interactions (Pinderhughes, 1982). A cognitive behavioral approach has been recommended for African American women and people of color in general because of its active, present orientation (McNair, 1992; Ponterotto & Casas, 1991). However, role playing with some adult clients may be resisted as childish (McRoy & Oglesby, 1984). More passive approaches, such as psychodynamic or client-centered approaches, may increase clients' anxiety about counseling and may be more appropriate with African American clients who have more education. Others have recommended an eclectic approach with an existential philosophical base (McDavis et al., 1995). An additional recommendation has been that counselors be ready to assume the role of client advocate in working with African American clients (Locke, 1995; Paster, 1985).

Specific questions a counselor might ask to get a more accurate picture of the family of an African American client are "Who is in the family?" or "Whom can you depend on for help when needed?" instead of "Who lives in the home?" (Hines & Boyd-Franklin, 1982). Pinderhughes (1982) recommended that, because powerlessness is a major issue in the lives of many African Americans, the counselor should focus on client strengths rather than weaknesses. It may be helpful to connect discussions of actions with other people in the community: "What would your parents, other kinfolk, church members, etc. think about this behavior?" (Locke, 1995). Among the goals a counselor might consider with an African American client could be helping the client understand more about his or her cultural history and learning to express anger effectively, and to convert negative feelings into creative productivity (Foster, 1995).

Group counseling may be beneficial, because it is consistent with the communal focus of many African American cultures (Locke, 1995). Counseling in an all-Black group would provide opportunities for clients to deal with issues of cultural identity, feelings of racial hostility, identification of new goals, and getting feedback on their presentation to others.

Family therapy with African Americans, as commonly practiced, is somewhat controversial. Gwyn and Kilpatrick (1981) reported an 81% dropout rate for family therapy with low-income Blacks. Counselors may make many errors that may contribute to premature termination. For example, a counselor who uses first names before asking permission may be perceived as treating African American clients disrespectfully (Hines &

Boyd-Franklin, 1982). Bowen family systems therapy, on the other hand, has been specifically recommended for West Indian Black families because it is compatible with the education and upward mobility values of this African American subgroup (Brice, 1982). In general, Pinderhughes (1982) recommended focusing on African American family strengths to counteract societal experiences of powerlessness.

☐ Recommended Cultural Resources

Print Media

Haley, A. (Ed.). (1965). *The autobiography of Malcolm X*. New York: Ballantine.
Journal of Black Psychology
Journal of Black Studies
Lincoln, C. E., & Mamiya, L. H. (1990). *The Black church in the African American experience*. Durham, NC: Duke University Press.
Mabry, M. (1995). *White bucks and black-eyed peas*. New York: Simon & Schuster.
Murray, P. (1956). *Proud shoes*. New York: Harper.
Walker, M. (1966). *Jubilee*. Boston: Houghton Mifflin.

Multimedia

Margulies, S. (Producer). (1992). *Roots* [Videorecording]. Burbank, CA: Warner Home Video.
Riggs, M. (Producer). (1995). *Black is, black ain't* [Videorecording]. San Francisco: California Newsreel.
Shange, N. (1976). *For colored girls who have considered suicide when the rainbow is enuf* [Sound recording]. New York: Buddah Records.
Worth, M., & Lee, S. (Producers). (1992). *Malcolm X* [Videorecording]. Princeton, NJ: Films for the Humanities.

CHAPTER

Latinos and Latinas in Counseling

We Would Like You To Know

We would like you to know
we are not all docile
nor revolutionaries
but we are all survivors.
We do not all carry
zip guns, hot pistols,
steal cars.
We do know how
to defend ourselves.

We do not all have
slicked-back hair
distasteful apparel
unpolished shoes
although the economy
doesn't allow everyone
a Macy's chargecard.

We do not all pick
lettuce, run
assembly lines, clean
restaurant tables, even
if someone has to do it.

We do not all sneak
under barbed wire or
wade the Rio Grande.

These are the facts.

We would like you to know
we are not all brown.
Genetic history has made
some of us blue eyed as any
German immigrant
and as black as a descendant
of an African slave.
We never claimed to be
a homogeneous race.

—Ana Castillo, Latina poet and novelist[1]
(1995, pp. 81–82)

☐ Histories and Diversity

Latinos and Latinas are people of Hispanic ancestry living in the United States, they constitute the second largest minority group in the country, numbering 22 million in 1990 (U.S. Bureau of the Census, 1992). The Latino population is even larger when the number of undocumented workers is included. Latinos and Latinas are the fastest growing ethnic minority group in the country (Santiago-Rivera, 1995) and will be the largest ethnic minority group by the year 2020 (Vasquez, 1994). The majority of Latinos and Latinas live in California, Texas, New York, or Florida (Zapata, 1995). Most live in urban areas (Arredondo, 1991; D. W. Sue & Sue, 1990; Zapata, 1995) and work in blue collar jobs as laborers or machine operators if they are male and as service personnel if they are female (Arredondo, 1991; Zapata, 1995). Latinos and Latinas are undereducated (Zapata, 1995), even in comparison to African Americans, with an average educational level of 6th grade and a high school dropout rate of nearly one in two (D. W. Sue & Sue, 1990). By their senior year, only 31% of Latinos and Latinas are taking college preparatory courses (Baruth & Manning, 1991). Only 51% of Latino and Latina adults have completed 4 years of high school,

---

and only 10% have completed 4 years of college (U.S. Bureau of the Census, 1988). Latinos and Latinas are a young population compared to other ethnic groups, their birth rate is higher, and their households tend to be larger (D. W. Sue & Sue, 1990; Zapata, 1995). Nearly one in four Latinos and Latinas lives in poverty (Zapata, 1995). More Latino families live in poverty than European American families, and separation and divorce rates are higher among Latinas than among other women (Arredondo, 1991). A contributing factor to higher rates of family discord may be the necessity of the father to leave the family in order to seek or follow employment (D. W. Sue & Sue, 1990). Although Latinos and Latinas make up only 7.8% of the population, they make up 15% of the total number of people with AIDS (Freiberg, 1991b). Latinas are 11 times more likely to contract AIDS than other women, perhaps because of a combination of heterosexual male intravenous drug use and a reluctance among Latinos to use condoms ("Waking up," 1988).

The term *Hispanic* is a designation of the federal government that includes people whose cultural origins are in Mexico (60%); Puerto Rico (14%); Cuba (6%); and other countries, including El Salvador, Guatemala, Honduras, the Dominican Republic, and Spain (20%; U.S. Bureau of the Census, 1990c). It was originally used in Mexico to refer to people of Spanish heritage. The use of the term *Hispanic* is controversial, because it implies the influence of colonialism and ignores the contribution of indigenous American influences to Latino life (D. W. Sue & Sue, 1990). *Chicano* is a term used by many poor or militant Mexican Americans as an indication of cultural pride and history, but among many elderly Mexican Americans the same word may be derogatory, representing a poor, uneducated, and exploited farm worker (Avila & Avila, 1995; Burciaga, 1989). It tends to be used as a positive symbol of ethnic identification most often by young, educated, urban, bilingual English- and Spanish-speaking Latinos and Latinas. Cesar Chavez began the Chicano movement by mobilizing the United Farm Workers to organize themselves to struggle to get better working conditions. *Chicano* may also refer to a Latino from Mexico or even to an ex-convict, when used by some elderly Latinos or Latinas. *Mexican* is a term favored by older, often poor, rural, monolingual Spanish-speaking Latinos and Latinas of Mexican heritage. People who call themselves *Mexican Americans* are likely to be somewhere in between Chicanos and Mexicans politically and educationally. *La Raza* ("the race"), *Mexicano*, and *Spanish American* are other terms for Latinos and Latinas (D. W. Sue & Sue, 1990). *Puerto Riqueno*, *Newyorican*, and *Tejano* are additional terms Latinos may use to describe themselves, which refer to their birthplace (Puerto Rico, New Yorker of Puerto Rican heritage, and Texan of Mexican heritage, respectively). Clearly, the specific words a client uses to describe his or her ethnic background may provide important clues to his or her cultural identity, and further exploration with the client may be worthwhile. The counselor's cultural sensitivity to the client's choice of terms is also important when talking about immigration status. The term *undocumented workers* rather than *illegal aliens* should be used because it is much more positive, taking into account the working status of people in these circumstances and acknowledging one of their major presenting problems, the lack of official papers.

Latinos and Latinas are a very diverse group socioeconomically and demographically (Rogler et al., 1991), with differences in subgroup membership, immigration status, skin color, and bilingual ability (Arredondo, 1991). One major dimension of diversity is along the lines of country of cultural origin. For example, Central American immigrants experience more symptoms of depression than immigrants from Mexico (Salgado de Snyder, Cervantes, & Padilla, 1990). Leal and Menjivar (1992) noted that Latinas whose ethnic roots were in different countries were not necessarily supportive of each other. Similarly, there has been said to be a rivalry between Mexican Americans and Cubans, with Mexican Americans getting along better with Puerto Ricans (Burciaga, 1989).

The largest Latino ethnic group, Mexican Americans, are frequently of *mestizo* ancestry, a combination of Aztec Indian and Spanish European influences (Avila & Avila, 1995; Burciaga, 1989). Because the United States and Mexico share a border, travel back and forth is natural, and original culture is thereby renewed. However, motivation to learn English is diminished (Smart & Smart, 1995). Mexican Americans have the highest illiteracy rate of any ethnic group in the United States. Forty percent have not completed high school, and only 1% have gone to college. One out of three Mexican Americans lives in poverty.

Puerto Ricans, the second largest Latino ethnic group, are the least educated, having the highest dropout rate (D. W. Sue & Sue, 1990; Zapata, 1995). They are also most likely to be unemployed and poor (Zapata, 1995), with 40% living below the poverty level (D. W. Sue & Sue, 1990). Given their level of environmental stress, it is not surprising that Puerto Ricans have the highest rate of depression among Latino ethnic groups (Moscicki, Rae, Regier, & Locke, 1987).

Cubans have the most economic power of any Latino ethnic group (Zapata, 1995). This might be related to several influences: Many Cubans appear to be of White European descent (Smart & Smart, 1995); the average Cuban is older, and has had longer potential time in the workforce; and more Cuban immigrants may have initially come from middle and upper classes.

There is a long history of discrimination against Latinos and Latinas in the United States. In the 1848 treaty with Mexico, the United States acquired Texas and most of the Southwest. According to the treaty, Mexican landowners were offered citizenship, but their lands were often taken away from them later.

The realization that racism and discrimination are part of life in the United States can take Latino and Latina immigrants by surprise. In many of their countries of origin, a wide variation in skin color among people is the norm (Smart & Smart, 1995). Also, 98% of "Hispanics" identified their racial background as White according to U.S. Bureau of the Census data (A. Leal-Idrogo, personal communication, March 28, 1995). A Latino or Latina client may not expect discrimination on the basis of skin color.

Linguistic discrimination is one of the major modes in which Latinos and Latinas are discriminated against today. In 1974 the Supreme Court ruled (in Lau v. Nichols) that public schools must provide programs that do not prevent non-English–speaking students from receiving meaningful education (D. W. Sue & Sue, 1990). Bilingual education programs developed as a result of this ruling but remain controversial even two decades later. Part of the controversy is due to a belief held by many English-speaking majority people that the English language is preferable to Spanish because it is the language of the majority and in part due to suggestions that bilingual education provides Spanish speakers with a segregated, lesser quality educational experience.

☐ Cultural Values

Family

Loyalty to the family is highly valued among most Latinos and Latinas. *Compadrazgo* describes a formalized system of kinship relationships that tends to be both hierarchical and patriarchal (Arredondo, 1991). A large extended family may be part of the client's interpersonal world. Strong kinship bonds may exist between friends as well as family (C. C. Lee & Richardson, 1991). Godparents, often the parents' closest friends, can play an integral role in the client's life and may be an integral part of the family system. Sabogal, Marin, Otero-Sabogal, Marin, and Perez-Stable (1987) described *familism,* or the importance of the family, among Latinos and Latinas as having three components: (a) family obligations, (b) perceived support, and (c) family as referents or role models. Sabogal et al. found Latinos and Latinas to be familistic even when they were acculturated. Indeed, family support is a cultural resource for Latinos and Latinas. Family support has been shown to be associated with success in college for

Chicanas (Vasquez, 1982). It would be helpful for many Latino and Latina clients for the counselor to explore ways in which they can draw on their family as a source of strength.

Children in the family are taught respect—*respeto*—and obedience to parents, and adults in general, is valued (S. A. Gonzales, 1979). *Respeto* may come into play in the counseling setting as deference to the counselor and an unwillingness to disagree, ask questions, or speak up in order not to show a lack of respect (M. K. Ho, 1987).

Machismo

Within Latino cultures, *machismo* has a meaning that is far different from the male chauvinistic stereotype typically associated with the word in the United States. In Spanish, the term originally referred to honor, loyalty, and the following of a gallant code of ethics, comparable to that often associated with knighthood and chivalry in European history. Misinterpretation of the term in U.S. culture has led to misconceptions and erroneous negative stereotypes. The situation is complex. For example, research has shown that marriages between Latinos and Latinas are no more traditional in terms of sex roles than other marriages, yet anecdotal clinical evidence suggests that sex role expectations may be problematic for many Latinas (Zuniga, 1988). The rate of separation and divorce is higher for Latinas (14.1%) than for other women (9.8%; U.S. Bureau of the Census, 1981). The authority of the Latino husband may vary by region and social class, yet *aguantando*, or enduring, a quality involving passivity and deference to male authority, is valued in women among many Latino cultures. Although the role of homemaker is often valued among Latinas and many Latinas respond to stress by crying, praying, and enduring, the role of women remains complex. In the United States, Latinas have sometimes been mistakenly described as hysterical because of a comparatively demonstrative style of dress and communication. Also, stereotypes of Latinas as powerless, submissive, and self-sacrificing are contradictory to the valued quality of *marianismo*, which is a concept connected to the admiration of the Virgin Mary and implies a female spiritual superiority (C. C. Lee & Richardson, 1991).

The value placed on *machismo* among Latinos might play a role in the higher incidence of AIDS among Latinos and Latinas compared to the U.S. population in general (Freiberg, 1991b). Two thirds of Latinos who were diagnosed with AIDS or were HIV positive reported having had unprotected sex with a woman in the preceding year (Freiberg, 1991b). *Machismo* may contribute to a cultural homophobia that masks sexual contact between Latinos who do not identify themselves as gay. It is important to note, however, that other factors, such as a lack of educational information about AIDS prevention in Spanish, may have an even greater role in the higher impact of AIDS on Latinos and Latinas.

Spirituality

Religion and spirituality have a great influence on the lives of many Latinos and Latinas. Most are Christian, usually Roman Catholic (Arredondo, 1991). Religion and family life may be intertwined, and the church may be regarded as a social gathering place and community center as well as a place of worship. The strong influence of Catholicism on Latinos and Latinas may have several implications for counseling. The teachings of the Roman Catholic Church may suggest that health and illness are influenced by God, and as a result some Latinos and Latinas may be less likely to seek preventive medical exams or procedures. Mental illness may similarly be viewed as an act of God. The influence of Catholicism on the client may sometimes be perceived by the counselor as an attitude of fatalism. In counseling, the client might appear to be unmotivated to change. The client may appear to behave unassertively if he or she acts consistently with beliefs in sacrifice leading to salvation, charity to others, and the value of enduring wrongs (D. W. Sue & Sue, 1990). A tendency toward larger families and an avoidance of divorce may also be related to religious teachings regarding artificial contraception and divorce. Continuing with an unhappy marriage or maintaining a permanent separation may be preferable to divorce for some traditional Latinas who may believe they will be treated as outcasts or prostitutes within their own community if they ever begin a new relationship.

In addition to the influences of Catholicism, some Latino cultures include elements of spirituality such as witchcraft, sorcery, belief in anthropomorphic or animistic supernatural beings, sacred objects, rites, and ceremonies that are complementary or coexistent with Catholicism (Fabrega & Nutini, 1994; Sandoval, 1979). For example, in a rural Mexican community, grief reactions over several cases of SIDS were tempered by indigenous spiritual beliefs that catastrophes and unhappy events happen for a reason (Fabrega & Nutini, 1994).

Personalismo

Personalismo refers to a preference for personal contact and individual interactions over more formal or bureaucratic dealings (R. A. Ruiz & Padilla,

1977). For the client, this could mean a preference for more personal small talk, and for the counselor this might suggest engaging in more self-disclosure and using one's first name instead of a title.

In summary, some of the cultural values that are important to understand when counseling Latino and Latina clients include

- the importance of family
- *respeto*
- *machismo* and *marianismo* and their effect on sex roles
- the influence of the Roman Catholic Church and other forms of spirituality
- *personalismo*

☐ Indigenous Treatment Methods

Curanderos are folk healers who use herbs and spirituality to treat the mystical or supernatural roots of psychological disturbance in some Latino cultures, especially Mexican Indian. *Curanderos* might make use of candles, a rosary, an altar, incense, praying in Spanish, massage, or ointments made from natural sources in their treatment (Davidson, 1993). True *curanderos* are believed to be "chosen" and receive further training through an apprenticeship process. *Boticas* and *pharmacias* dispense nonprescription remedies for psychological and physical ailments.

Another approach to indigenous counseling with Latino clients has been to make use of cultural folk tales and proverbs. *Cuento therapy* (Costantino, Malgady, & Rogler, 1986; Malgady, Rogler, & Costantino, 1990) was developed as a treatment for young children; it makes use of Puerto Rican folk tales, or *cuentos*. The *cuentos* have themes—for example, delay of gratification or control of aggression—and are read, discussed, enacted and videotaped, and summarized for full effect. *Cuentos* adapted to U.S. settings have been found to be more effective compared to either their original Puerto Rican versions or art therapy. Similarly, Zuniga (1991) described the use of *dichos*, or Spanish-language proverbs, for use with Latino clients. Some examples of *dichos* collected by R. Gonzales and Ruiz (1995) are included in the box on page 96.

Some Mexican *Dichos*, Translated Into English

Getting up at dawn will not make the morning come sooner.

Experience is the mama of science.

Pig out while you have the chance.

If you don't ride, you can't fall.

A good listener needs few words.

If you hang out with wolves you will learn how to howl.

A good rooster can crow anywhere.

After the rain comes the sun.

If you get wet early, you'll have time to dry off.

Small, but very hot.

When you use force, not even your shoes fit.

One bee doesn't make a hive.

Many littles make a lot.

You only visit the cactus when it is bearing fruit.

Sing every day and chase the mean blues away.

If you know how to swim you won't drown.

A lesson well learned is never forgotten.

Each head is a world of its own.

A painting is a poem without words.

Note: From R. Gonzales and Ruiz (1995).

☐ Counseling Issues

Language and Acculturation

Language is a very important consideration when counseling Latinos and Latinas. English language use is an important component of acculturation and accounts for much of the variance attributed to acculturation (Rogler et al., 1991). One study found that Mexican Americans who were either bilingual or primarily English-speaking perceived mental health issues no differently than Anglo Americans, whereas those who were primarily Spanish-speaking tended to believe mental illness was inherited and used more somatic attributes to describe mental problems (Edgerton & Karno, 1971). Mexican Americans who prefer to speak Spanish are more likely to be monolingual, born in Mexico, and have lower levels of education and stronger ties to religion than other Mexican Americans. The language (or languages) spoken is a key indicator of cultural traditionalism in Latinos, with clients who speak only Spanish tending to be more traditional. However, whatever languages they speak, it is important to note that Latino parents strongly encourage their children to speak both Spanish and English (Edgerton & Karno, 1971; Fernandez, 1989). Many second-generation Latinos and Latinas, although they spoke Spanish at home and are considered bilingual, may prefer to function in English, which they learned in school and through television (D. W. Sue & Sue, 1990).

Lijtmaer (1993) suggested that it is important to explore when and where a client learned English. If at all possible, give the client the choice of which language he or she wishes to use in counseling. In addition, the counselor may be able to make use of the client's bilingualism in therapeutic ways. For example, using a non-native language may allow the client to temporarily separate him- or herself from intense emotions. The counselor may use "language switching" to moderate the client's level of emotional involvement rather than freely allowing the client to choose the language used during sessions (Santiago-Rivera, 1995).

In addition to languages spoken, other important areas to assess are socioeconomic status, religious training and current spiritual identification, politics, birthplace and immigration status, generational level of immigration, geographic location of ancestors (including any effects of continuing immigration, proximity of the mother country, etc.), level of acculturation, and experiences with prejudice or discrimination.

Adolescents

Baruth and Manning (1991) listed several potential counseling problems for Latino adolescents: identity issues, effects of negative stereotypes, cultural value conflicts, struggle between individual advancement versus family commitments, failure to comply with traditional family roles, academic problems, language problems, developmental differences in height and weight when compared to others, and the effects of racism and discrimination. Gang involvement among Latino youths may give some members a sense of identity (Curry & Spergel, 1992); however, Latinos and Latinas, in general, have a lower delinquency rate compared to other Americans (Lyon, Henggeler, & Hall, 1992).

Career Concerns

Given the lack of educational and economic success for many Latinos and Latinas, career counseling needs are great. Information about the world of work would be helpful in combating the tendency toward low educational goals, unrealistically high career goals, and less specific educational and career goals. When expectations are high, career disappointment can be great, and many Latinos and Latinas leave the corporate world to start their own businesses, which further limits the role models available to new workers. As mentioned earlier, one review suggested that when Blacks and Latinos were denied jobs, 15%–20% of the time these same jobs were later offered to equally qualified Whites (Fendel et al., 1996).

Some suggestions for increasing the workforce participation of Latinos and Latinas include recruiting at minority job fairs, offering employer-paid training programs, sponsoring career events that feature popular musicians or athletes in order to draw a larger audience, and distributing information to a wider audience through ethnic clubs and ethnic studies departments on college campuses. Figueroa (1996) also added advertising jobs where they will be seen by a wider range of applicants, expanding internship and outreach programs, developing mentoring partnerships with inner city schools, and providing educational scholarships as ways to increase the pool of qualified minority applicants.

There may be some conflict between workforce values and the personal values of the Latino or Latina. For example, traditional Latino values of community, cooperation, modesty, and hierarchical relationships do not mesh well with modern values of individualism, competition, achievement, and egalitarianism in many work environments. Also, effective communication in individual interpersonal relationships may differ from what is effective in management. These career conflicts may be productively explored in counseling. Prejudice and discrimination may make advancement and promotion in the workplace even more difficult.

Undocumented Workers

There are many undocumented workers in the United States, many of whom have a Latino background. Undocumented persons have limited access to the job market as well as education and economic benefits. They live in fear of deportation, and their lives are filled with caution and mistrust because anyone could report them. They are vulnerable to exploitation, blackmail, and pressure to work for substandard wages. Although the Immigration Reform and Control Act of 1986 declared an amnesty and allowed access to citizenship for many of these people, fear and distrust may have kept many from seeking amnesty. One suggestion for counseling this population is to provide training in problem-solving and social skills to combat stress and to increase social support. In addition, counselors need an understanding of immigration law to be maximally helpful with this population. Although undocumented immigrants are ineligible for food stamps, they are eligible for emergency medical care and some programs for children. American-born children of undocumented people are eligible for full educational and public assistance (Smart & Smart, 1995).

Other Counseling Issues

In terms of nonverbal communication, when counseling Latinos and Latinas, the counselor may want to decrease interpersonal distance by placing chairs a little closer together. Lapses in eye contact may signify respect rather than pathology and should be evaluated with the client's level of traditionalism in mind.

There are many barriers, both economic and psychological, to Latino and Latina clients getting counseling. Arranging child care, forfeiting hourly wages, and making use of public transportation all contribute to low utilization rates. Latinas, in particular, may approach counseling with mixed feelings of relief and embarrassment or apprehension, because self-disclosure by women outside the home may be discouraged in some Latino cultures (Arredondo, 1991). Similarly, Mexican Americans with a traditional cultural orientation may have some difficulty with being open and self-disclosing in the role of the client (Sanchez & Atkinson, 1983), *personalismo* notwithstanding.

Although clients rarely enter counseling stating that culture is a concern, cultural differences may have an impact on many presenting problems. It may be helpful for the counselor to help the client distinguish between individual difficulties in functioning and the effect of broader social problems on the client. A. Ruiz (1981) recommended examining external causes first, among them exposure to environmental toxins, fears of deportation or creditors, poverty, poor housing, lack of English facility, and difficulties in dealing with governmental agencies. Some suggestions that have been made regarding counseling Latinas that would apply to Latinos as well include identifying sources of personal and environmental stress, exploring the positive aspects of the client, locating community resources, and identifying specific cultural assets (Rodriguez-Nelson, 1993).

The counselor is advised to take a present time orientation during counseling and to focus on getting the client current relief. The counselor's role might include listener, problem solver, advocate, and interpreter. Waiting a little longer in using confrontation with the client and in general proceeding slowly to allow trust to develop may be helpful when counseling Latinos and Latinas. In their review of the literature, D. W. Sue and Sue (1990) noted recommendations for active, concrete, problem-solving, behavioral or cognitive behavioral approaches lasting four to five sessions.

Although the client may prefer an active orientation and direct advice, there is no evidence that Latinos and Latinas are not good candidates for gaining insight. Wampold, Casas, and Atkinson (1981) found that a majority of the practicing psychotherapists studied had subtle stereotypic attitudes in which Latinos were perceived as lazy, unintelligent, unclean, and overemotional. Negative stereotypes easily influence the counseling process, and counselors should be especially wary of such countertransference.

Family therapy also has been recommended, particularly structural family therapy, which complements the often-hierarchical structure of many Latino families (D. W. Sue & Sue, 1990). Although the mother may be the spokesperson for the family, it is usually the father who holds the power. The family counselor is encouraged to be active, polite, willing to offer advice (Padilla, 1981), and nonconfrontational (M. K. Ho, 1987). However, family therapy may not work if the parents do not bring out issues for fear of being embarrassed in front of their children. In such cases it might be better to meet with parents and children separately.

In summary, when counseling Latinos and Latinas, the counselor needs to be cognizant of the potential impact of cultural differences and external stresses on the client. Either an active, yet not confrontational, individual approach or family therapy may be especially useful. It may be helpful to consider an eclectic therapeutic approach to counseling Latinos and Latinas.

☐ Recommended Cultural Resources

Print Media

Esquivel, L. (1992). *Like water for chocolate*. New York: Doubleday.
Gonzales, R., & Ruiz, A. (1995). *My first book of proverbs* (*Mi primer libro de dichos*). San Francisco: Children's Book Press.
Hispanic Journal of Behavioral Sciences

Multimedia

Coppola, F. (Producer). (1995). *My family mi familia* [Videorecording]. Atlanta, GA: Turner Home Entertainment.
Musca, T. (Producer). (1988). *Stand and deliver* [Videorecording]. Burbank, CA: Warner Home Video.
Redford, R., & Esparza, M. (Producers). (1993). *Milagro beanfield war* [Videorecording]. Universal City, CA: MCA Home Video.
Thomas, A. (Producer). (1984). *El Norte* [Videorecording]. Farmington Hills, MI: CBS/Fox Video.
Valdez, L. (Writer/director). (1991). *Zoot suit* [Videorecording]. Universal City, CA: Universal Pictures.

CHAPTER

Asian and Pacific Islander Americans in Counseling

Asians are silent people
Never speaking of distress
Bearing much in their heart
The burden of the silent one.

Standing up to their rights
Trying to prove loyal by working hard.
America, a place of hopes...
For White people only!

—Leah Appel, elementary school student
(D. W. Sue, 1973, p. 398)

☐ Histories and Diversity

Asian Americans are people of Asian ethnicity who are making their home in the United States. They are a very diverse group. Chinese, Japanese, Koreans, Filipinos, Malays, Vietnamese, Cambodians, Laotians, Hmong, and Mien living in the United States are the among the ethnic groups categorized as Asian American. Hawaiians, Samoans, and Tongans (all Pacific Islanders), and Asian Indians also are sometimes grouped and counted with Asian Americans, depending on whose classification system is used. The history of Pacific Islanders in the United States and their cultural traditions are in many ways more similar to those of Native Americans than to those of Asian Americans, and classifying these peoples with Asian Americans is often a matter of convention rather than utility. Although there are a few references to Pacific Islander Americans in this chapter, the reader is referred to Chapter 6, Native Americans in Counseling, for further material that may be even more relevant when counseling Pacific Islander Americans.

According to the U.S. Bureau of the Census (1993a), 7.3 million Asian Americans lived in the United States in 1990, making up 2.9% of the population. Estimates range from 30 to 50 different cultural subgroups of Asian Americans (in part depending on whether Pacific Islanders are included), with the most populous being the Chinese, Filipino, Japanese, Asian Indian, Korean, and Vietnamese (D. Sue & Sue, 1995a; S. Sue, 1994). The Chinese, Japanese, and Filipinos were the earliest Asian ethnic groups to begin immigrating to the United States in the 19th century. Many other groups followed, with a large number of Southeast Asians arriving after 1975. The Asian American population continues to change dramatically even today (Kitano, 1989; S. Sue, 1994). Because of recent immigration, Asian Americans in general are currently one of the fastest growing ethnic groups in the country, and the majority of any Asian American subgroup is foreign born, except for Japanese Americans (D. Sue & Sue, 1995).

To make any generalizations about Asian Americans is extremely difficult, given the variety of ethnic groups included under the designation and the changes in migration patterns that the population continues to undergo. The history of each ethnic group, including dates and circumstances of immigration/refugee resettlement and ensuing treatment within the United States, is entirely different. For example, the forced internment of 110,000 Japanese Americans for up to 5 years without due process of law during World War II is an integral part of the history of Japanese Americans as a group (Tomine, 1991). This traumatic experience still affects not only the elderly adult survivors of the camps but also the families they have reared. Another example is the devastating level of war atrocities and refugee camp experiences of many Southeast Asian Americans, particularly, according to Rumbaut (1985), the Hmong and Cambodians, for whom posttraumatic stress symptoms may go unnoticed by individuals themselves because they are so common within a community. In addition, any two Asian Americans may differ in degree of acculturation, English fluency, socioeconomic status, and education. Unfortunately, more of the available literature in counseling and psychology related to Asian and Pacific Islander Americans has been written about Chinese and Japanese Americans than any of the other groups. Keeping this in mind, some generalizations will be presented in order to illustrate some cultural differences as they relate to counseling and to give counselors an idea of specific issues that may be involved.

☐ Cultural Values

Many Asian cultures are influenced by the philosophies of Confucianism, Buddhism, and Taoism. Among the values that appear common to many Asian cultures are those of harmony; humility; and respect for family, authority, and tradition.

Harmony is a widely held value in many Asian cultures. To promote interpersonal harmony, emotional restraint and indirect communication as opposed to confrontation are often preferred (Homma-True, 1990; Huang, 1994; Mattson, 1993). The Buddhist concept of moderation is valued by some Asian Americans, and humility is valued over competitive pride. For example, at times it might be preferable to take second place in a contest rather than first, because this facilitates interpersonal harmony, does not provoke as much envy from others, and does not embarrass others that their performance was inferior. Similarly, moderation of affect may be valued as a means of expressing intrapersonal harmony, and in a counseling setting this can result in a client's problems being understated or ignored.

The Confucian notion of filial piety teaches respect and obedience to authority figures beginning with the males in the family (Cerhan, 1990). The family in general, including extended family, is often highly valued in Asian cultures (Homma-True, 1990; Kitano, 1989). Hierarchical relationships within and without the family are prevalent (Kitano, 1989). The significance of roles in interpersonal relationships is very important, and birth order and sex roles are strongly emphasized (Huang, 1994). The group often takes precedence over the needs of the individual. For example, when emphasis is placed on education, as in many Asian cultures, its purpose may be more to directly increase the status and wealth of the family as a whole, not to advance one's individual career, as is more common in northern European American families. The societal group focus also tends to emphasize dependency and respect for authority as compared to independence and egalitarian relationships. As part of a respect for authority, some Asian Americans may expect advice or specific direction from their counselor. Internal means of control, such as guilt, shame, obligation, and duty, rather than individual freedom of choice and expression, also are more valued in many Asian cultures. In a related fashion, the concept of dating and choosing one's spouse does not exist in some Asian cultures where arranged marriages are traditional, so when a first- or second-generation Asian American dates, the relationship may be taken very seriously by the individual and/or his or her family.

The extended family as well as the nuclear family are important. In many Asian cultures a sense of the time continuum includes past and future generations, not just present family. Sometimes comparisons are made by parents, aunts, uncles, or grandparents between a client and someone else in his or her extended family as an indirect form of motivation. The family counselor should consider including extended family members, especially if they are living in the same household.

A more passive (listening, observing) versus active (doing, experimenting) approach to learning is typical in some Asian cultures, and this has implications for counseling. Counseling techniques that demand more activity from the client during the session—for example, role playing or hitting a pillow—may be less comfortable for some Asian Americans.

An especially important point to note is that each Asian culture is different in its values, and greater familiarity with a particular culture is important to understanding the values a client may bring to the counseling setting. In Japanese culture, for example, the concept of "self" may have multiple facets: an interactional self, an inner self, and a boundless self (Yamaguchi, 1995). Behavior may change on the basis of the social context without threatening an individual's coherent sense of self. Thus, a client's behavior may appear as more inconsistent, unpredictable, or inscrutable to a counselor who is unaware of Japanese cultural viewpoints.

One Japanese value has been termed *enryo*, or not dominating others in a social situation. Hesitancy to speak up in class or to contradict someone in authority and devaluing or disparaging oneself, one's children, or one's possessions to others so others will not feel inadequate are examples of *enryo* (Uba, 1994). *Enryo* can easily be mistaken by a counselor who is unaware of Japanese culture as passivity or low self-esteem. Another Japanese value is that of *gaman*, meaning the endurance of hardships (Kristof, 1996). This value has been offered as a possible explanation of the low rate of divorce in Japan. The somewhat fatalistic orientation of some Japanese to problems, called *shikata ga-nai*—literally, "it cannot be helped" (Kitano, 1981)—may originate in a Buddhist attitude toward living life without struggle. In the worst case, *shikata ga-nai*, when combined with *gaman*, may render a victim of spousal abuse dangerously resistant to leaving a violent relationship.

One sample of Asian American practitioners identified the cultural values they felt were most important to understand when counseling Asian American clients. These were, in descending order of importance (as summarized by Uba, 1994):

- the importance of family
- shame and guilt
- respect for others based on their role and status
- interpersonal styles of behavior
- stigma of mental illness
- restraint of self-expression
- group orientation
- achievement
- sense of duty and obligation
- role expectations

☐ Indigenous Treatment Methods

Traditionally, many Asian Americans may believe that hard work, effort, and character development are the best cure for mental disorders (Kitano, 1989). Handling problems through internalization has been described as common for Japanese Americans (Kitano, 1981), and it may be frequent for other Asian Americans as well. Keeping active also is often viewed as helpful (Homma-True, 1990), and behavioral counseling techniques are culturally consistent with this view.

One view of mental illness in many Asian cultures is that it is related to organic factors, and physical remedies may be expected (Kitano, 1989). Because many Asian cultures do not promote a mind–body dichotomy, a concept that is more common from a Western view, somatic symptoms are often reported and may be indicative of concurrent psychological disorders (Homma-True, 1990; Mattson, 1993; Tung, 1978, cited in Nishio & Bilmes, 1987).

Many first-generation and more traditional Asian Americans may turn to indigenous cultural healers and remedies when distressed. Much diversity exists within Asian cultures as to whom they will go to seek assistance outside the family. The Hmong may seek out herbalists or shamans, who may use herbal remedies, animal sacrifices, or other religious rituals (Cerhan, 1990; Kitano, 1989). Lao (Bliatout et al., cited in Kitano, 1989) and Vietnamese (State of California Department of Mental Health, 1981b) may consult Buddhist monks, whereas other Vietnamese may consult Catholic priests (State of California Department of Mental Health, 1981b) or Taoist scholars (Bliatout et al., cited in Kitano, 1989). Acupuncture, massage, fortune telling, and physiognomy (reading palms and facial features) also are among the folk remedies used by Southeast Asian Americans (Chung & Okazaki, 1991). See Das (1987) for a review of the folk, mystical, and medical traditions of Buddhist, Hindu, and Islamic societies. Thai traditional healers have been discussed by Hiegel (1983). In general, C. C. Lee and Armstrong (1995) recommended working in conjunction with traditional healers in a concerted effort to assist clients.

There has been limited discussion of Asian cultural concepts in Western psychological literature. Okonogi (1978) described the *Ajase complex*, which is based on Buddhist writings and focuses on the consequences of a strong mother–child relationship and forgiveness after conflict. In an interestingly related manner, Doi (cited in Homma-True, 1990) described the Japanese concept of *amae* as the intense dependence of a child on his or her mother.

Morita therapy also incorporates the mother–child relationship through the acknowledgment of client indebtedness to significant people in his or her life. This therapy is based on the work of Shoma Morita of Japan and emphasizes the recognition and acceptance of feelings. Clients are assumed not to be able to control their feelings and are not responsible for them (Willms, 1990). Morita therapy has been adapted for use in the United States and called *constructive living*. It has been compared to rational–emotive therapy and other cognitive therapies (Ishiyama, 1990; Le Vine, 1993) and, although the focus is on altering thoughts, the emphasis is more on constructive actions rather than regulating feelings as the goal. Morita therapy, like client-centered counseling (Rogers, 1951), promotes the acceptance of subjective experiences and, like existential therapy (Frankl, 1978), the concept of facing anxiety and taking responsibility for life choices is central. Morita therapy incorporates some Zen Buddhist philosophy in guarding against too much effort as being possibly immobilizing rather than successful. One example given (Ishiyama, 1990) is that of a donkey tied to a post. The donkey can get tangled in its own attempts to walk around the post in order to get free, or it could graze freely around the post without becoming trapped. Moritist interventions are confrontational with the goal of "anxious action taking" as preferable to inaction.

There are many other indigenous treatment approaches. *Naikan therapy* has been described as group centered, ritualistic, behavioristic, and focused on the here and now (Kitano, 1989). A group-oriented indigenous approach is the Samoan *fa'a aiga* family unity process (State of California Department of Mental Health, 1981a). In this process, a leader entreats all family and community members affected by the client's problems to meet. At the meeting, prayers are said; the problem is identified; each person discusses the problem; and errors by the client are admitted, repented, and forgiven. Restitution may be made as well. Chung and Okazaki (1991) suggested using folk tales with Eastern concepts and philosophies (see the text box on page 109 for examples) as a culturally consistent technique in counseling Southeast Asian Americans. These folk tales could be integral within the counseling process a lá Milton Erickson (Haley, 1973).

☐ Counseling Issues

Spirituality

Buddhist, Confucian, Taoist, Shinto, and Catholic spiritual views underlie many of the beliefs of Asian Americans toward mental health, as mentioned previously, and this should be considered in forming treatment plans. For example, Taoist spirituality emphasizes the harmony between yin and yang, the female and male, dark and light, passive and active aspects of life. Avoiding direct confrontation and respecting the natural course of events also are part of the philosophy. This suggests that client-centered counseling (Rogers, 1951) might be a complementary approach for counseling someone with Taoist beliefs, because the process of self-actualization may assist in releasing the natural tao in the client. This approach also tends to minimize confrontation and, through unconditional positive regard, accepts the natural course of the client's life.

Many Cambodians put great importance on the attainment of personal spiritual enlightenment in accord with Thervada Buddhism, whereas many Laotians believe in animism, in which gods and spirits pervade much of daily life (Chung & Okazaki, 1991). Relaxation or visualization techniques may be helpful in counseling some of these clients. Engaging in spiritual activities is often the self-help remedy chosen by Cambodians in America (D'Avanzo, Frye, & Froman, 1994). Given the diversity within the Asian American population, spending some time early in the counseling process to explore the spiritual beliefs of the individual client is paramount in order to avoid stereotyping that could negatively affect treatment planning.

Myth of the Model Minority

The academic and economic success of Asian Americans as a group has led to their sometimes being described as the "model minority." College enrollment and graduation rates for Asian Americans, in general, are higher

Two Chinese Folk Tales

The Story of the Bamboo

During a fierce storm, the bamboo bends every which way the wind blows, while the other trees (e.g., oak) stand straight and resist the wind. But after the storm the bamboo tree stands proudly, looking into the heaven and reaching for life, dreams, and hopes. The other trees lie on the ground lifeless and without hope because they resisted the wind; they were not flexible and did not move with the wind.

The Frog

A frog sitting at the bottom of a well looks up toward the opening of the well and asks, "Oh! That's the size of the sky?" In reality the frog will not know how big the sky is until it steps out of the well. The frog in a well is limited in its knowledge by a narrow vision.

Note: Adapted by Chung and Okazaki (1991).

than for any other ethnic group (Government Accounting Office, 1990). This positive stereotype can have damaging repercussions. On a societal level, this stereotype suggests an erroneous notion that any minority group can (and should) succeed if the members work hard enough. Also, the model-minority myth separates Asian Americans from other ethnic minority groups by pointing them out as an example to others (D. W. Sue & Sue, 1990). Finally, in many instances Asian Americans are not categorized as a minority group and are not eligible for affirmative action programs (D. Sue & Sue, 1995), even though specific subgroups of Asian Americans may be underrepresented in terms of graduation, employment, or promotion rates.

On an individual level, teachers may not only have higher expectations of Asian Americans, but they also may judge them more negatively when they do misbehave or fail to achieve, and other students may be hostile toward them because of their reputation as good students (Baruth & Manning, 1991). Individuals with problems or concerns counter to the positive stereotype may be ignored (Fendel et al., 1996). Counselors may neglect to assess Asian Americans for substance abuse, teen pregnancy, domestic violence, and so on.

In order to allow their children to receive what they feel are superior educational experiences, affluent parents from some Asian countries, Taiwan in particular (Le, 1996), may split up their family in order to send their children to school in the United States. Children may be living with a grandparent, with only their mother while their father remains in Asia, or even with a paid guardian, all situations that could potentially be emotionally stressful in themselves for a student and that also may put additional pressure on them to do well in school. In addition, schoolwork also may be a source of stress for some Asian American students who face family expectations to support their parents and other family members as soon as they graduate. This may not only put excessive pressure on them for academic success, but it may also affect their choice of field of study and subsequent career satisfaction (Scott-Blair, 1986).

Mordkowitz and Ginsburg (1986) attributed the academic success of Asian Americans to what they termed *academic socialization*, meaning a combination of authoritative families, high expectations, emphasis on effort, supervision of children's time, allocation of resources for educational purposes, and reinforcement of beliefs and behaviors conducive to learning. In this interview study of Asian American college students at a prestigious university, families placed studying as the students' principal obligation and limited other chores expected of them. The other side of academic success, however, could be social discomfort, as these same families seemed to engage in little family conversation, discourage inviting guests into the home, and compare their children's performance to exemplary others. Another explanation of the higher average grades of Asian Americans may be attributed to increased time spent studying at the expense of leisure time or social relationships.

Career Concerns

Effort and family pride may be more important to many Asian American families than individual interests. One review of the literature on the career development of Asian Americans concluded that as a group they are more field dependent and segregated in their occupational choices, less tolerant of ambiguity, and more socially anxious than European Americans. Being *field dependent* means that external factors such as security, money, and status play a large role in vocational choice (Leong, 1991). Asian Americans tend to cluster in computer science, engineering, pre-med, and business majors. Underrepresentation of Asian Americans in certain majors and subsequent occupations may be due to several influences: Demonstrative self-expression is not encouraged in many Asian cultures, counselors may unintentionally steer students toward sciences because of stereotypical notions of their aptitudes, and some Asian Americans may choose technical career fields in which more objective evaluation occurs and discrimination may be more easily avoided (D. Sue & Sue, 1995). A frequent issue in career counseling with Asian Americans may be a mismatch between a vocation chosen for external factors and contradictory individual interests or aptitudes. A counselor assisting an Asian American client with such an issue is cautioned not to mistake what may be a collectivist decision making style that takes family concerns into account as being an overly dependent style (Leong, 1991). One third of students of Asian descent taking the SAT intend to seek vocational counseling—more than any other ethnic group (Leong, 1991). This may indicate a perception of vocational counseling as relevant to educational goals and an acknowledgment of the increased complexity of career decision making for Asian Americans. There is great potential for a counselor to make a significant difference in the lives of Asian American clients through skillful handling of career issues.

For Asian Americans already participating in the workforce, still other counseling issues may arise, such as discrimination in hiring or advancement or role strain for Asian American women. On the average, Asian–Pacific Islanders with college degrees earn 26% less than Whites with similar degrees (Fendel et al., 1996). Although a larger percentage of Asian American women work compared to other ethnic groups in the United States, the stereotype of Asian American women as "hardworking, uncomplaining handmaidens" (Homma-True, 1990) may result in their being exploited at work or denied promotion. Asian American women who believe strongly in their duty to be homemakers may more keenly experience the discomfort of role strain between their career and family obligations that is common among working women (Homma-True, 1990).

Other Counseling Implications

During the initial assessment phase of counseling some Asian Americans may appear to be doing more "complaining" than seeking help, which could be indicative of a more fatalistic, accepting approach to life. For some Asian Americans personal problems may come up only indirectly while physical, school, or vocational difficulties are readily discussed. W. M. Lee and Mixson (1995) noted the need for counselors to address presenting academic or career problems and simultaneously reduce client reluctance to deal with personal concerns. Because so many Asian Americans are born outside the United States and are experiencing cultural transition, intergenerational conflicts are especially common, including difficulties in communication, struggles over moving out of the family home, and interracial relationships.

Berg and Miller (1992) recommended emphasizing the client's goal during the first meeting, because many Asian Americans, like members of many other ethnic minority groups, are focused on problem solving and are not likely to stay in extended treatment otherwise. Relationship questions are suggested as a way to elicit information about the client's worldview and his or her view of other's perceptions of them. An example of a relationship question would be "What do you think _____ would say he or she likes about you?"

Because interpersonal relationships are often defined by roles, clients may be more comfortable once roles have been clearly established. The counselor, for example, is in a role of authority and expertise. Silence and avoidance of eye contact could be signs of respect from an Asian American client. A client may express agreement in order to be polite when he or she really does not agree with or does not understand the counselor and instead may not return for another session. Once counseling has begun, client transference regarding age or sex may be more likely because of the importance of such distinctions and roles in many Asian cultures.

Several authors have written about culturally consistent counseling approaches for Asian Americans. Homma-True (1990) summarized the recommendations to include the following:

1. Use bilingual–bicultural counselors whenever possible.

2. Respect the client's reluctance to express him- or herself verbally or emotionally.

3. Be attuned to somatic complaints as potential indicators of psychological distress.

4. Focus on issues within the context of the family.

5. Consider taking a more active role in the sessions.

6. Take an educational or informational approach.

Other counseling recommendations have included use of behavioral counseling, structured family therapy, assertion training, communication skills training, cognitive therapy (especially Morita therapy), supportive therapy, client-centered therapy, and role exploration (e.g., life script). When counseling families, M. K. Ho (1987) recommended addressing the parents first, which heightens the role differentiation in the family and is consistent with the hierarchical family structure of many Asian cultures. Berg and Miller (1992) recommended discussing exceptions to the problem when counseling Asian Americans as this helps the client "save face" and provides information about the client's strengths for further development.

Some caveats also have been raised regarding what not to do in counseling with most Asian Americans:

1. Avoid putting the client at odds with his or her family.

2. Traditional group therapy is not recommended (Kitano, 1989; Nakao & Lum, 1977); however, when appropriate, use a support group (Mattson, 1993).

3. Be generally cautious with psychodynamic, Gestalt, and confrontational approaches (Nakao & Lum, 1977) or approaches that seem to demand expression of feelings.

☐ Recommended Cultural Resources

Print Media

Kingston, M. H. (1976). *The woman warrior*. New York: Knopf.
Tan, A. (1989). *The joy luck club*. New York: Ballantine.

Multimedia

Colesberry, R. F. (Producer). (1991). *Come see the paradise* [Videorecording]. New York: CBS/ Fox Video.
Sternberg, T., Wang, W., & Yung, D. (Producers). (1987). *Dim sum: A little bit of heart* [Videorecording]. Beverly Hills, CA: Pacific Arts Video.
Wang, W., Tan, A., Bass, R., & Markey, P. (Producers). (1994). *The joy luck club* [Videorecording]. Hollywood, CA: Hollywood Pictures Home Video.
Yamamoto, K., & Kelly, N. (Producers). (1992). *Thousand pieces of gold* [Videorecording]. Los Angeles: Hemdale Home Video.

10
CHAPTER

European Americans in Counseling

It's a complex fate, being an American, and one of the responsibilities it entails is fighting against a superstitious valuation of Europe.

—Henry James (Bartlett, 1992, p. 548)

Although the term *European American* is meant here to include Americans whose ancestors immigrated to the United States from a country in Europe, most European Americans would not immediately identify themselves with this label for their cultural background. A European American client is more likely to use the expressions *American, Caucasian,* or possibly *Anglo American, WASP* (White Anglo-Saxon Protestant), *Southerner,* or *White.* Many European Americans are either unaware of or do not identify with the European aspects of their culture. However, because Americans from Europe are the dominant cultural force in the United States today, it is hoped that examining their cultural background will not only promote greater understanding of their counseling issues but that it also will illuminate the extent to which counseling itself, as it has developed to date, is a Eurocentric process (Das, 1995).

According to the 1990 census, German (58 million), Irish (38.7 million), and English (32.7 million) ethnic groups from northern Europe are currently the most populous in the United States ("German heritage," 1992).

Another 12.4 million Americans listed their ancestry as "American" or the "United States," or named a particular state. The latter responses came from people in mostly Appalachian and Southern states and, on further inquiry, most were found to be Scottish Americans whose families had been in the United States for many generations.

Some scholars have noted the lack of emphasis on encouraging Whites to explore what it means to be White or have called for Whites to explore their own cultural identities (Carter, 1990; J. H. Katz, 1989; Pope-Davis & Ottavi, 1994), and the dearth of information about counseling European Americans published in the last decade is remarkable. During the same period, the number of articles about counseling people of non-European ethnic backgrounds has grown tremendously. This discrepancy may be an indication of a lack of cultural awareness among majority (European American) researchers about the importance and uniqueness of their own ethnic backgrounds even though research results have found White racial identity attitudes to be related to racism toward others (Pope-Davis & Ottavi, 1994). The best resource about counseling European Americans continues to be *Ethnicity and Family Therapy*, 2nd ed., by McGoldrick, Giordano, and Pearce (1996), which includes specific chapters devoted to family therapy with many distinct European cultural groups in America.

☐ Within–Group Characteristics and Variability

Northern European Americans

Northern European Americans may include people whose families immigrated from England, Wales, Scotland, Ireland, France, Germany, Sweden, Norway, Denmark, Finland, Belgium, and so on. Although there are many differences between, among, and within ethnic groups that emigrated from northern Europe, some important similarities are worth noting, especially as they have in turn shaped current American culture. Four of these characteristics seem frequent among northern European immigrants: the importance of work, an emphasis on individuality, suppression of feelings, and distancing as a mode of coping with interpersonal conflict.

Work as a predominant value seems to have its roots in British culture. Sixty-five percent of the top executives of the largest American corporations in 1950, and 78% of Supreme Court justices through 1957 were of British heritage (Axelson, 1993). It is worth considering that these accomplishments may be indicative of political as well as economic power. A strong work value is also consistent with German, French, and other northern European cultures (Langelier, 1982; McGill & Pearce, 1982; Winawer-Steiner & Wetzel, 1982). In general, the work ethic has evolved in the United States to an emphasis on individual achievement, such that "all persons can, and therefore should, be individually successful" (McGill & Pearce, 1982, p. 458). This core value is evidenced in negative attitudes toward anyone who is not obviously successful—for example, people of color, disabled persons, and people on welfare. In counseling, this value may be reflected in high self-expectations and corresponding feelings of failure as well as in positive motivation to "work" on relationships and other problems.

The northern European American, especially British, emphasis on individuality may bring with it feelings of alienation, emotional isolation, and withdrawal (McGill & Pearce, 1982). Das (1995) noted that many successful middle-class Americans feel alienated and lack a sense of community after putting their emphasis on individual achievement and the self.

Another commonality in northern European countries that appears to have become characteristic of mainstream American culture is a reluctance to directly express feelings, which has been noted in British, French, German, and Irish cultures (Langelier, 1982; McGill & Pearce, 1982; McGoldrick, 1982; Winawer-Steiner & Wetzel, 1982). The expression of feelings often becomes a goal of counseling with European Americans, and several counseling techniques seem to have developed to address this need—for example, psychodrama, Rogerian reflection of feeling, Gestalt "empty chair."

Northern European Americans may cope with interpersonal conflicts by distancing or cutting off the relationship, as is common in British, German, and Irish cultures (McGill & Pearce, 1982; McGoldrick, 1982; Winawer-Steiner & Wetzel, 1982). Current European American concerns with divorce and teenage runaways may be indicators of this problem-solving style. Counseling techniques that focus on communication training and family therapy may have developed as remedies for these problematic interpersonal coping strategies.

Some other "typically American" characteristics appear to have their roots in northern European culture, for example, the British tendency to use the legal system, and especially money and property, to regulate human relationships, as currently evidenced in American divorce and custody battles. Similarly, the German propensity for structuring time and relationships may have contributed to the sense of hurriedness and need for time management so common to current American life. The political and social pressure on German Americans not to claim their German heritage, which grew out of the world wars, has no doubt further blurred the influence of German culture on American life.

Southern European Americans

After 1900, and prior to the 1965 Immigration Act, most immigrants to the United States came from southern and eastern European countries, such as Italy, Greece, Poland, and Russia (Stave & Sutherland, 1994). In 1882, 87% of immigrants were from northern and western European countries, but by 1907 the focus of immigration had shifted, and 81% were from southern and eastern European countries instead. Immigrants from southern and eastern European countries are sometimes called *White ethnic Americans* (Axelson, 1993). This term, however, seems to ignore the ethnic roots of northern and western European Americans. As cultural groups, southern European immigrants have some general cultural differences from northern Europeans that bear discussion: the importance of the family over the individual, expression of feelings, and physical punishment and prescribed roles as a mode of coping with interpersonal conflict.

The family is of great importance to many southern European Americans (Herz & Rosen, 1982; C. L. Johnson, 1985; Rotunno & McGoldrick, 1982; Welts, 1982), so much so that the needs of the individual may be considered secondary. This can make individuation from the family a difficult issue, especially in contrast to popular emphases on American independence. Moving out of the house, going away to college, or marrying outside the culture could each be viewed by the family as an act of betrayal and might become a presenting problem in counseling (Herz & Rosen, 1982; C. L. Johnson, 1985; Sleek, 1995; Welts, 1982).

Variability exists within southern European cultures with respect to individual achievement, ranging from idealistic family demands in Jewish culture that seem to render individual accomplishments as more like failures (Herz & Rosen, 1982); to Italian American culture, which may seem to support achievement only when compatible to family solidarity (Rotunno & McGoldrick, 1982); to Polish Americans, who may disapprove of higher education and upward mobility (Mondykowski, 1982). In the case of Italian Americans, for example, an Ivy League college might be judged too distant or expensive if the student cannot continue to live at home (C. L. Johnson, 1985).

Emotional expression is another common theme among southern European cultures (Herz & Rosen, 1982; Rotunno & McGoldrick, 1982). For example, among many families with Jewish cultural backgrounds, expression of feelings may not only be accepted but may also be a highly valued part of family interaction (Herz & Rosen, 1982). In other southern and eastern European cultures—Polish and Greek American, for example—some emotions related to joy or sexuality may be easily expressed, whereas other emotions that might indicate anxiety or weakness may be censored (Mondykowski, 1982; Welts, 1982).

Physical punishment and other forms of external control are more acceptable in many southern and eastern European cultures, such as Italian (C. L. Johnson, 1985), Greek (Welts, 1982), and Polish (Mondykowski, 1982). Such actions are possibly related to cultural emphases on respect or honor (Mondykowski, 1982; Rotunno & McGoldrick, 1982; Welts, 1982). Proscribed roles for men and women also may contribute to a more formalized behavioral conformity in carrying out relationships, with men often viewed as the authority and provider and women viewed as the nurturer within the family sphere (Herz & Rosen, 1982; C. L. Johnson, 1985; Rotunno & McGoldrick, 1982; Welts, 1982). The implication for counseling is that models for negotiation and role flexibility may be lacking in some southern European American homes (Herz & Rosen, 1982; Rotunno & McGoldrick, 1982).

☐ Indigenous Treatment Methods

Many indigenous treatments for European Americans are already part of traditional counseling practice. Because most counseling techniques taught today were developed by European Americans (Ivey, Ivey, & Simek-Morgan, 1993), it seems logical that they would be effective when applied to European Americans. The rational and complex explanations of psychodynamic approaches to counseling may be especially suited to British Americans (McGill & Pearce, 1982) and Jewish Americans (Herz & Rosen, 1982). Sigmund Freud, originator of psychoanalysis, was Jewish. Carl Rogers and Virginia Satir, both European Americans living in the Midwest, developed counseling approaches that may be especially compatible to midwestern British Americans, whereas structural and strategic family therapy approaches may be less helpful with these European Americans (McGill & Pearce, 1982). In contrast, structured, paradoxical techniques or positive reframing have been noted as possibly being more helpful to Irish Americans than nonverbal or body techniques (McGoldrick, 1982). Behavioral or action-oriented approaches have been described as culturally consistent for Franco-Americans (Langelier, 1982) and Polish Americans (Mondykowski, 1982). The use of videotape has been recommended for Greek Americans, and nondirective or family approaches may be counterindicated (Welts, 1982). Meanwhile, Milan-style family therapy was developed by Italians and is well suited for issues of family enmeshment when it becomes problematic (Rotunno & McGoldrick, 1982).

☐ Counseling Issues

Spirituality

The Association for Spiritual, Ethical and Religious Value Issues in Counseling recently defined *spirituality* as "the animating force in life, represented by such images as breath, wind, vigor and courage. Spirituality is the infusion and drawing out of spirit in one's life" ("Summit results," 1995, p. 30). Spirituality is further described as both an active and passive process, innate and unique to all people, which moves the individual toward knowledge, love, meaning, hope, transcendence, connectedness, and compassion, encompassing the religious, spiritual, and transpersonal.

Spiritual differences, only one facet of culture, are often confused with ethnic differences. For example, one study of Italian Americans frequently compared them to Protestants rather than to another specific ethnic group (C. L. Johnson, 1985). The differences between the groups might be more related to differences between Catholics and Protestants than between Italians and other ethnic groups. When counseling European Americans, the spiritual differences within these ethnic groups are particularly diverse and relevant to counseling. A client from one ethnic group, German American for example, might be Catholic, Protestant, Jewish, or have other spiritual beliefs.

It is important for the counselor to assess the client's individual views of spirituality and to not assume that membership in a particular ethnic group implies religious convictions common to that group. It has been suggested that the counselor explore the dynamics and religious practices of each client's family of origin, asking about the importance of these customs for the individual and, when counseling a couple, that each person be aided in learning about the history and practices of each other's religion so they can avoid misunderstandings and create new options for overcoming differences (Sleek, 1995).

Catholics have been described as tradition-oriented, guilt-ridden, and concerned about outward appearances, whereas Protestants have been described as stressing individual responsibility and emotional isolation (McGill & Pearce, 1982).

The Protestant faith has contributed to the work ethic in America. In Protestantism, work and productive activity are considered an expression of the spiritual being and eventually as indicative of one's self-worth. The external controls and behavioral conformity attributed to Catholicism in American culture have been contrasted with the Protestant emphasis on self-direction (C. L. Johnson, 1985). The implications for counseling are many, including those related to the work ethic mentioned earlier. There might possibly be more difficulties with guilt for Catholics and with dependency for Protestants. One suggestion has been for the counselor to make use of *clerical transference,* a tendency to see a counselor as a powerful clergyperson who can help with advice and problem solving (Langelier, 1982). However, McGoldrick (1982) warned that it may be counterproductive for a Catholic client to view counseling as if it were confession, a place to tell one's sins and seek forgiveness.

Most of the 6 million Jews in the United States, as of 1982, emigrated from eastern European countries, Russia, and Poland in response to religious persecution. Suffering is culturally important for many Jews because it connects them to their heritage and may provide some feeling of specialness because of the oppression they have endured (Herz & Rosen, 1982). Srole, Langner, Michael, Opler, and Rennies (1962) found that Jews were more likely to seek outpatient treatment than were Protestants or Catholics. Talking, insight, and complex explanations are culturally consistent with Jewish culture, making psychodynamic approaches to counseling a treatment of choice (Herz & Rosen, 1982). One cultural issue for Jews in counseling may be interfaith marriage. Jewish–Christian interfaith marriages have a higher rate of divorce than same-faith unions do, and this has become an issue of cultural survival because the frequency of outmarriage has risen to 52% in recent years (Sleek, 1995).

Church activities also can be used in counseling as a source of social support for Greek Orthodox clients (Welts, 1982), Protestant clients, and clients from other organized religions.

Intercultural Marriage

As the population of the United States has become increasingly ethnically diverse, intercultural marriages have become more frequent. Less than 30 years ago, 17 states still had laws prohibiting interracial marriages. The last miscegenation laws were repealed by the Loving v. Virginia Supreme Court decision of 1967 (Bachman, 1996; Burnette, 1995; Marino, 1995; Tucker & Mitchell-Kernan, 1990). In 1994 there were 1.3 million mixed-race— defined as White with non-White—couples in the United States according to government data cited by Bachman (1996). In addition, there were 1.3 million marriages between Hispanics and non-Hispanics in 1990.

Intercultural marriage may occur between members of any ethnic groups. Indeed, many of the concerns of intercultural couples may occur between people from different ethnic subgroups within the same broad ethnic grouping; for example, a Chinese American–Japanese American couple. However, the most noticeable intercultural couples are those between European Americans and people of color, especially African Americans. Although the topic of intercultural marriage may be applied appropriately with respect to many Americans, it is discussed here particularly in the context of European Americans.

Intercultural marriages most frequently occur between middle-class individuals who have been married before and live and work in integrated areas (Marino, 1995).

On top of the usual difficulties in maintaining a marriage, intercultural marriages may face societal discrimination and other complications due to cultural differences in gender roles, child rearing, language and communication style, food preferences, and spirituality (Burnette, 1995). Americans in general seem ambivalent about interracial marriage, verbally expressing their approval as long as the marriage does not occur within their own family (Marino, 1995). Perhaps as a consequence of these additional stresses, the divorce rate for interracial marriages is higher than for other marriages. Also, children raised in interfaith households may possibly be more at risk for depression and unruly behavior, particularly if they are not raised in one of their parents' faiths (Sleek, 1995).

Intercultural marriages need to come to a common definition of marriage, family, fidelity, and privacy. Agreements about sex roles, the role of extended family, and the language to be spoken in the family are necessary. If the couple lives in an area that is not integrated and is foreign to one of the partners, there needs to be a recognition that the person who is living in a foreign culture will always have some needs that will go unfulfilled (Bishop, 1989).

The degree of prejudice and discrimination the couple may experience may depend on many factors, including their place of residence, level of education, and socioeconomic status (Marino, 1995). The European American partner in an intercultural marriage may be shocked by the experience of racism from other European Americans (Burnette, 1995; Marino, 1995).

☐ Recommended Cultural Resources

Print Media

McGoldrick, M., Giordano, J., & Pearce, J. K. (1996). *Ethnicity and family therapy* (2nd ed.). New York: Guilford Press.
Wehrly, B. (1996). *Counseling interracial individuals and families*. Alexandria, VA: American Counseling Association.

Multimedia

Feldman, E. S. (Producer). (1985). *Witness* [Film]. Hollywood, CA: Paramount Pictures.

Schwary, R. L. (Producer). (1981). *Ordinary people* [Videorecording]. Hollywood, CA: Paramount Home Video.

CHAPTER

Counseling Women

Wives, submit yourselves unto your own husbands, as is fit in the Lord.

—Colossians 3:18 (Starr, 1991, p. 122)

It is the law of nature that woman should be held under the dominance of man.

—Confucius (Starr, 1991, p. 118)

☐ Histories and Diversity

Women in the United States do not have status that is comparable to that of men. Women make up only 5% of top executives, 8% of the Senate, 10% of full professors, and 11% of the House of Representatives (Heitner, 1995; Hoyt, 1989). Women are reportedly also more frequently sexually harassed, interrupted in conversations, and addressed with inappropriate forms of familiarity than are men (Enns, 1992).

Attempts have been made to combat discrimination against women (H. B. Wolfe, 1995). Congress passed the Equal Pay Act of 1963, and some government commissions were appointed to examine changes in the roles of women. The Women's Educational Equity Act of 1974 allocated funding for counseling women. The 1975 passage of Title IX of the Educational Amendments Act was aimed at eliminating sexual discrimination in college admissions, financial aid, physical facilities, curricula, sports, counseling, and employment in educational institutions receiving federal funds. However, relatively minimal real gains have been made because of lax enforcement and subsequent court decisions that restricted the impact of legislation. In the late 1970s, the Comprehensive Education Training Act began programs to retrain displaced homemakers, but these limited programs were ended by the Reagan administration in the early 1980s. During the same time, failure to ratify the Equal Rights Amendment contributed to further stagnation and erosion of women's rights.

Women of color have specific issues that in part reflect their dual minority status as both ethnic minorities and women. For example, Black and Hispanic women represent 72% of women with AIDS, yet they constitute only 19% of all women in the United States (Freiberg, 1991b). *Women of Color*, by Comas-Diaz and Greene (1994), is an excellent resource on ethnic minority women. Ethnic minority women have been described as having little trust in the health care system, believing that they will encounter racism (Burnette, 1996), and this reluctance may apply to seeking counseling as well.

Seventy-six percent of Native American women using the Indian Health Service are diagnosed with some form of depression. This has been attributed to a variety of causes, including historical trauma, feelings of discrimination, acculturation stress, or greater personal losses (LaFromboise et al., 1994). Native American women have a higher rate of alcoholism than American women in general. According to the Indian Health Service, the death rate for alcohol/substance abusers among Native American women aged 15–24 is 40% higher than their male counterparts (LaFromboise et al., 1994). However, it is again worth noting that alcoholism rates vary from tribe to tribe. For example, among the Navajo and Plains tribes, fewer women drink any alcohol at all compared to national surveys of women in general.

African American women are more likely than White women to endorse the goals of the women's movement, according to a 1979 Harris poll (Reid, 1993). Because of slavery, African American women have historically been in the position of working outside the home and raising children (Davenport & Yurich, 1991). Many never-married Black female college graduates are single heads of households raising children. Counselors need to be prepared to work with their non-nuclear families. Alcoholism and suicide are on the increase among African American women. Depression has been diagnosed more frequently among Black women than among White women (E. McGrath, Keita, Strickland, & Russo, 1990). Many Black women feel that they are ugly when they compare themselves to European American majority standards of beauty, and if they are intelligent, strong, persistent, or express anger they may be told they are "too masculine" (J. F. Brown, 1993). According to J. F. Brown, Black women may isolate themselves from other women to protect themselves from rejection and hurt for being considered "not Black enough," and counselors need to encourage these women to develop a friendship with a Black "sister" for support.

Among Chicanas, Latinas of Mexican heritage, many have been taught not to express affection openly, with marriage containing the only acceptable role (wife) for a woman. They have not been encouraged to strive for higher education or a career. S. A. Gonzales (1979) cited a source that suggested that men of Mexican heritage may be even more reluctant than White men to hire a Chicana for an administrative position. Instead, unselfish self-sacrifice is often extolled for Chicanas: *abnegada y sufrida*. In Spanish, *la vida de la mujer es dura y asi ha sido siempre*, meaning that a woman's life is hard and that is the way it has always been. Access to 24-hour child care and contraceptives are particularly salient issues for Chicanas. Because of factors such as discrimination or lack of education, many Chicanas have limited employment prospects. Jobs with odd work hours are out of the question unless evening and late-night child care are possible. The strong influence of the Catholic Church makes any decision about how many children to have a particularly difficult one for Chicanas. Latinas in general are at greater risk for contracting AIDS than other women ("Waking up," 1988). A majority of Hispanic males who are either diagnosed with AIDS or intravenous drug users at risk for contracting HIV report unprotected sex with a woman in the past year (Freiberg, 1991b). AIDS education, especially for Spanish-speaking Latinas, is needed.

A larger percentage of Asian American women work outside the home when compared to other groups of American women (Homma-True, 1990). Asian American women may often be exploited at work and denied promotions in accord with stereotypes of their hardworking and uncomplaining nature. Counseling regarding specific skills needed for advancement and successful role models may be particularly useful. Meanwhile, many Asian American women value the role of homemaker and subsequently experience much role strain between career and family obligations. Emphasis on traditional sex roles may make language learning and cultural adjustment in general more difficult for Asian American female immigrants. Somatization and social isolation are frequent among Southeast Asian refugee women (Mattson, 1993). Additionally, many of these women have experienced sexual abuse, putting them at risk for depression or post-traumatic stress disorder (E. McGrath et al., 1990).

☐ Cultural Values

It has been said that women tend to define themselves in relation to others (Miller, 1976). Chodorow (1978) and Gilligan (1982) similarly assert that female development emphasizes attachment and connection, whereas male development emphasizes separation and independence. A woman's sense of ethics may be based on caring, whereas male ethics seem based on logical principles of justice. However, both female and male "voices" can be equally valid. A more relational focus can lead women to place the needs of others before their own or have difficulty being aware of their own needs (B. C. Murphy, 1992).

Society gives women the message that they should not be too smart in order to protect men's feelings. Knowledge and power are often devalued for women (Saakvitne & Pearlman, 1993). In adolescence, when traditional societal views of women as less competent become salient, girls are much more at risk for loss of self-esteem than boys are (American Association of University Women, 1991). This is a crucial time for girls, as self-confidence drops and they begin to restrict their views of their future potential and place in society. *Fear of success* is a term used to describe women's anxiety or avoidance of success that is due to a belief that career success would jeopardize their relationships with men (Horner, 1972).

Women value intimacy. This is reflected in their communication patterns (Tannen, 1990). It seems that women talk as a means of becoming more intimate, whereas men talk more to share information. Men also tend to talk more in public or with lesser known people as a way to negotiate their status, and they may talk less at home because there their status is not in question. The resulting mismatch in communication styles can leave women feeling unheard and invalidated and men feeling helpless to assist their partners in solving problems.

☐ Indigenous Treatment Methods

Feminist Therapy

Feminist therapy is a theoretical orientation toward counseling that was developed by and for women. A comprehensive review of feminist therapy by Enns (1993) concluded that feminist therapy is difficult to define. A wide variety of theories and techniques have been used by counselors who practice feminist therapy. Also, feminist therapy evolved out of political, sociological, and philosophical perspectives of feminism as opposed to traditional psychological theories (Enns, 1993). Feminist theories have been characterized as more relational, more egalitarian, and emanating from women's experiences compared to the major theories of counseling, which tend to stress individualism, autonomous decision making, and a linear cause-and-effect worldview (Nwachuku & Ivey, 1991). Two other differences are that feminism calls for a commitment to activism and value-laden activity, in contrast to mainstream therapies, which encourage the counselor to be value free and that feminist counselors intentionally blur boundaries between clients and counselors (Enns, 1993). Ballou and Gabalac (1984) described six characteristics of feminist therapy:

1. The counselor promotes an egalitarian counselor–client relationship.

2. Use of community resources is emphasized.

3. The counselor takes an active, participatory role.

4. Giving information is appropriate.

5. Personal validation of the client is encouraged.

6. Traditional theories are used with an awareness of their cultural implications.

Feminist therapy developed out of women's consciousness-raising groups. Early premises were that the "personal is political," which symbolized women's solidarity, and that counselor–client relationships should be egalitarian and collective rather than hierarchical. Social conditioning was attributed to be the cause of women's distress. Personal change and support were the primary beneficial outcomes of consciousness-raising groups. Over time feminist therapy groups became more focused on specific issues. By the early 1980s individual feminist therapy had become the most frequent form of feminist practice. Social and gender role analysis, working on expressing anger, and self-disclosure are among the techniques that are most often associated with feminist therapy (Enns, 1992, 1993).

Gender role analysis may involve examining gender role constrictions, how behavior is currently maintained, costs and benefits of change, and commitment to take action (Enns, 1992). Helping clients name their problems may involve renaming and reconceptualizing their issues in a feminist framework, placing problems within a social context, confronting myths that contribute to self-blame, and identifying ways that symptoms serve as survival mechanisms within American culture. Gender role analysis can be facilitated by a variety of techniques, including guided inquiry, transactional analysis of cultural scripts, Gestalt two-chair exercises, and guided imagery (Enns, 1992). For example, the counselor might ask the client questions such as "What did it mean to be female or male in your environment? What direct and indirect lessons did you learn about gender? What happened when you deviated from gender role norms?" (Enns, 1992, p. 10). Another example is to have the client first visualize herself in an imaginary box that represents gender role definitions, then explore the interior of the box that constrains her and, finally, imagine breaking out of the box.

Women have been socialized to inhibit expressions of anger (B. C. Murphy, 1992). Assertiveness training has often been incorporated into feminist therapy as a means of developing new skills for women. Assertiveness training is consistent with a feminist perspective in that it can involve becoming aware of interpersonal rights, altering negative beliefs, transcending stereotypical gender roles, and influencing the environment. Women who completed assertiveness training programs did tend to increase their range of behaviors and self-esteem; however, they also had to face negative perceptions by others that they had become aggressive or pushy. Enns (1992) summarized earlier criticisms of assertiveness training techniques as defining assertive responses too narrowly, assuming that assertiveness leads to positive social consequences, reinforcing traditional emphases on power, and defining human "rights" without consideration of gender role complexities.

Other techniques used by feminist therapists have included use of fantasy and imagery, role playing, behavior modification, coping and decision-making training, cognitive restructuring, self-confirmation and nurturing, body therapy, poetry and storytelling, creating new support systems, and client advocacy. The overall goals of feminist therapy have been described as personal effectiveness, independence, autonomy, and a feminist social perspective (Enns, 1993).

Goddess Psychology

Another indigenous approach to counseling women is goddess psychology. Goddess psychology applies the Jungian concept of female archetypes to counseling women. By exploring the myths of female archetypes, women are able to gain an awareness of the coping behaviors they use to deal with their lower status in contemporary society and release self-blame. Goddess psychology tends to draw heavily on Greek mythology. Major goddess archetypes often include Athena (intellectual life, wisdom, achievement), Aphrodite (love and intimacy), Persephone (spiritual and mystical experiences), Artemis (adventure and the physical world), Demeter (nurturing and motherhood), and Hera (leadership and power). This kind of archetypal psychology encourages clients to look for the heroine within and place less emphasis on material and external satisfactions. It is consistent with feminist values in that Jung, like feminists, de-emphasized pathology and the authority of the analyst (Enns, 1994).

When counseling from a goddess psychology approach, clients may be invited to identify favorite fairy tale or mythical characters or role models from their real lives, visual media, or biographies. The counselor may use questions to guide the client in identifying strengths and limitations in these characters, what attracted them to these people, and how the characters deal with adversity. In this manner, the client can be helped to reflect on how stereotypes can be transcended in establishing individuality. Similarly, clients can create their own myths by drawing or describing themselves as they would like to be, noting important qualities of their images, and identifying characters from books, television, and fairy tales with similar qualities. In this manner, clients come to create their own stories in counseling. One caution in using archetypal approaches is that some archetypes may magnify gender differences or limit behavioral or emotional responses of clients, making it important to identify archetypal models who defy stereotypes (Enns, 1994).

☐ Counseling Issues

Gender and Diagnosis

Men and women are equally likely to be diagnosed with a mental health disorder; however, women are more likely to be diagnosed with an affective, anxiety, or somatization disorder (Morrissey, 1995). More specifically, major depressive episodes, agoraphobia, simple phobia, dysthymia, obsessive–compulsive disorder, schizophrenia, somatization disorder, and panic disorder are all more prevalent in women than in men (Robins et al., 1984). Women are also disproportionally diagnosed as having dependent personality disorder compared to men (Landrine, 1989).

Women are especially at risk of experiencing clinical depression. Worldwide, women tend to be more likely to be depressed than men, and this relationship holds true for White, Black, and Hispanic women (Ritter, 1993), and is likely for other women as well. Poverty, marital dissatisfaction, being the mother of several young children, and having experienced physical or sexual abuse are all related to the presence of depression in women (McGrath, Keita, & Strickland, 1990). Roughly 70% of antidepressant medications prescribed are given to women, with sometimes-questionable diagnosis and monitoring.

Premenstrual syndrome (PMS) has been a recent issue for women. Between 20% and 90% of American women experience one or more premenstrual symptoms, among them irritability, tension, anxiety, depression, fatigue, mood lability, fluid retention, headaches or backaches, breast tenderness, acne, and food cravings (T. Adler, 1990; M. Hamilton, 1984; Snyder, 1990). Treatments for these symptoms include progesterone therapy, dietary changes, vitamin supplements, stress reduction techniques, and exercise (M. Hamilton, 1984; Snyder, 1990). Counseling, diuretics, and oral contraceptives also have been selectively recommended ("PMS," 1989). Before seeking a medical intervention, a trial of nondrug self-care lasting at least 3 months may be advisable (M. Hamilton, 1984). Reducing caffeine, alcohol, sugar, and salt, along with relaxation and regular exercise, may have a substantial impact on symptoms. Increasing a woman's awareness of her body and its cyclical changes may also help in giving validity to her feelings and experiences, thereby reducing the effects of PMS. Self-statements such as "I'll feel better in a few days," "My feelings are more intense than usual right now," and "I need to take good care of myself now" may be useful.

PMS is controversial for many reasons. Little is known about the biological mechanisms involved. Research in this area is extremely complicated because it is difficult to validate self-reports of PMS with objective measures; PMS differs for women who have borne children or are taking contraceptives; and a majority of women seeking treatment for PMS have another ongoing condition, often depression, that tends to worsen premenstrually (Payer, 1989). In fact, 84% of women with PMS were diagnosed as having a major affective disorder, according to one psychiatrist (T. Adler, 1990). Sociopolitically, PMS conforms to Western cultural apprehensions about the female reproductive cycle. Only 2%–5% of women actually require treatment for their PMS, suggesting that the lives of many women are not significantly affected (Payer, 1989). However, PMS as a bona fide psychiatric diagnosis would carry with it a social stigma, fueling the myth that women have "raging hormones" and poor emotional stability, which might provide an easy excuse for not hiring, promoting, or electing a woman. PMS could then be used as a legal defense, as it has been in Great Britain. In *DSM–III–R* (American Psychiatric Association, 1987), PMS was given the term *late luteal phase dysphoric disorder* and, after political controversy, was relegated to the appendix. *Premenstrual dysphoric disorder* was included in *DSM–IV* (American Psychiatric Association, 1994).

Self-defeating personality disorder (SDPD), presented in *DSM–III–R* (American Psychiatric Association, 1987), is another controversial diagnostic classification because it seems to negatively label codependency or affiliation. Landrine (1989) found that respondents assumed that a description of someone with SDPD was female.

Violence Against Women

Many women are victims of violence at some time in their lives. From 22% to 37% of women have been sexually abused as children, 25%–50% have been battered by a partner, and 12%–46% have been raped (Nolen-Hoeksema, 1990; Russell, 1986). Women are most at risk for violence from people they know. Nearly half of child sexual assaults, and more than two thirds of sexual assaults on adult women, are perpetrated by acquaintances, including family members (N. F. Russo, 1990).

Walker (1984) delineated three phases of a cycle of violence affecting battered women. In the first, the tension-building phase, stress and frustration build in the relationship, along with communication difficulties. During this phase the woman may try to pacify the batterer's anger. When the tension can no longer be controlled, the second phase, violence, occurs. The third phase is the aftermath, a honeymoon period during which the batterer apologizes and tries to convince the woman that it will never happen again. Tension eventually mounts again, and the cycle repeats itself.

The first goal in counseling an abused woman is getting her to a safe physical environment. Then, examining the client's experience as part of a larger political, social, familial, and spiritual context can help transform the trauma into something meaningful beyond the self (Saakvitne & Pearlman, 1993).

The costs of violence against women are unknown. Many women with eating disorders have a history of sexual abuse, incest, or both. Counseling goals with a client who has an eating disorder might include increasing self-esteem, eliminating maladaptive behaviors, and focusing on factors other than external appearance for one's identity (Mintz & Wright, 1993). Effective treatment for eating disorders may combine behavioral, cognitive, and insight-oriented affective strategies as well as nutritional information.

Career Concerns

Pay Discrimination and the Glass Ceiling

Although the disparity between what women earn and what men earn has been getting smaller, one review of the literature indicated that in 1993 women still earned only 71.5% of the amount men earned. Although women constitute almost half of the United States workforce, 62% of working women in 1991 were employed in service, sales, and clerical fields, areas long traditional for women, according to a National Committee on Pay Equity study (McGowan, 1993). In law, for example, a less traditional field, a 1990 survey conducted by the U.S. Department of Labor found that female lawyers earned 25.7% less than male lawyers (Backover, 1991). Women in upper management at the level of vice president or above earned 58% of what men at similar levels earned. Women with 5 of more years of college earned 62% of what men with equivalent education earned (Weiss, 1991). In some specific fields—for example, financial service representatives and health care managers—the gender gap has widened to the point that women earn only 55% and 67%, respectively, of what men were paid. In other fields the pay is equitable, but access is still problematic ("Women narrow," 1996). These statistics suggest that there remains a substantial inequity in both pay and employment opportunities for women. The shortage of women in upper management and leadership positions is often attributed to a "glass ceiling," an invisible barrier that keeps women from further career advancement (H. B. Wolfe, 1995). Morrison and Von Glinow (1990) suggested that discrimination and systemic barriers are responsible for the lack of representation of women in management positions. Women themselves often perceive sex discrimination and childrearing as career barriers (Swanson & Tokar, 1991). Lack of information and self-esteem issues may also play a role, because most women do not know how to engage in salary bargaining and tend to underestimate their worth in pay negotiations (McGowan, 1993).

Research suggests that female clients are especially drawn to feminist therapy approaches when career and employment issues are the presenting concerns (Enns, 1993). H. B. Wolfe (1995) recommended that counselors help women examine alternatives so that they can surmount workplace barriers. She also recommended training in communication skills such as self-promotion and projecting confidence and in deciding on a long-term career plan. Bartholomew and Schnorr (1994) described several practical exercises for broadening career options for school-age girls; they also recommended exposure to female role models by way of biographies, videotapes, and guest speakers in math- and science-related fields.

Sexual Harassment

Sexual harassment on the job is a reality for many women. In a 1995 survey, 59% of women reported that they had experienced sexual harassment on the job (Fendel et al., 1996). Sexual harassment can include sexual innuendo, suggestive stories or jokes, remarks about personal appearance, sexual advances, sexual assault, or sexual coercion. The effects of harassment can include depression, insomnia, and feelings of frustration and anxiety. Fouad and Carter (1992) suggested that the counselor first help the client become aware of what sexual harassment is and help the client realize that she has a right not to be subjected to it. Next, the counselor should help the client to not blame herself for the actions of others and, finally, to develop ways to confront and effectively respond to the undesirable behavior. As mentioned previously in the discussion of how to counsel someone who has experienced discrimination, other recommendations are that the counselor validate the victim's feelings, provide information, encourage the safe expression of anger, assess maladaptive coping patterns by the victim or any impact on her family, provide a place to mourn losses, and offer hope (Koss, 1990).

Multiple Role Strain

Most women with families work because of economic necessity, but many of them would continue to work if given a choice, perhaps because of job satisfaction and commitment, adult companionship and support, and contact with the larger world (Scarr, Phillips, & McCartney, 1989). However, women are especially susceptible to role strain between their family and work roles. More than half of two-parent families have two wage earners. Yet even when a woman is employed full time outside the home, the majority of household and childrearing tasks is still accomplished by her (Levant, 1990). When employed, the average adult woman spends more time on housework, childrearing, and caregiving to sick or elderly family members than the average adult man, yielding a 74-hour total week for women, compared to 56 hours for men, according to studies conducted by Nolen-Hoeksema (as cited in Azar, 1996a). The effects of employment on a woman's mental health is moderated by her husband's approval and support and by her own level of satisfaction with child care (Elman & Gilbert, 1984; Van Meter & Agronow, 1982). Employed mothers with unsupportive partners and child-care problems tend to be the most depressed (N. F. Russo, 1990). Dual-career concerns, child care, and maternal employment issues may all compound routine work stress. The sum total of role demands can result in fatigue, guilt, and irritability, as well as depressed mood. Betz and Fitzgerald (1987) enumerated nine coping mechanisms for adapting to role conflict that were suggested by Epstein:

1. Eliminate unsupportive social relationships.

2. Reduce the number of contacts with others.

3. Reduce the number of obligations.

4. Redefine the occupational role as adjunctive to the family.

5. Plan schedules to emphasize the most salient role at the time.

6. Carefully separate work and family.

7. Delegate tasks to family or outside help.

8. Increase the observability of demands so that others will be aware of time demands.

9. Rely on rules, deadlines, or other devices to legitimize nonparticipation in family or social events.

Reducing standards for oneself within roles is yet another way of reducing role strain (Stoltz-Loike, 1992). On a family level, discussion of time management, role overload, childbearing plans, role conflict, identity issues, and career orientation may be useful (H. B. Wolfe, 1995). Improved child care, flextime, and maternity leave benefits on the part of employers also are needed.

Other Counseling Implications

Women are more likely to seek help for mental health problems from their general medical practitioner than from a counselor. Women also are more likely than men to be seen in outpatient treatment (N. F. Russo, 1990). Ironically, more money is spent on mental health treatment for men even though women are more likely than men to seek mental health services. Women are more likely to receive a prescription for psychotropic medication than are men (Morrissey, 1995).

Counselors need to become knowledgeable about resources and information relevant to women, including child-care and eldercare services (H. B. Wolfe, 1995), laws regarding sexual harassment and spousal abuse, and information about nontraditional careers.

☐ Recommended Cultural Resources

Print Media

Comas-Diaz, L., & Greene, B. (1994). *Women of color: Integrating ethnic and gender identities in psychotherapy*. New York: Guilford Press.

Hochschild, A. (1989). *The second shift*. New York: Viking.

Kim, E. (1983). *With silk wings: Asian American women at work*. San Francisco: Asian Women United of California.

Wasserstein, W. (1990). *The Heidi chronicles and other plays*. San Diego, CA: Harcourt Brace Jovanovich.

Multimedia

Young, V. L. (Producer and Director). (1980). *The pinks and the blues* [Videorecording]. Paramus, NJ: Time Life Video.

Spielberg, S. (Producer). (1987). *The color purple* [Videorecording]. Burbank, CA: Warner Home Video.

Organizations

9to5 Working Women Education Fund, 238 West Wisconsin Avenue, #700, Milwaukee, WI 53202. National Job Survival Hotline: (800) 522-0925.

12

Counseling Men

At a time when women want men to love, raise babies and remember our birthdays, it is also required that they be the ones who rescue people in burning buildings. (Emerson, 1985, p. 14)

☐ Histories and Diversity

Men in the United States seem to be the recipients of many privileges. All of the U.S. Presidents have been men, along with the vast majority of corporate executives, members of the Senate and House of Representatives, and university professors. However, the wealth and power are primarily available to European American men.

Current societal sex roles have negatively affected men as well as women. Men also experience *gender role conflict*, which is defined as internal conflict or violation of others' rights that results from socialization messages that are either unrealistic or contradictory (Enns, 1993). Gender role conflict has been reported to be linked to depression, lower psychological well-being, physical illness, and poor self-care in men (Enns, 1993). Similarly, male college students rated concern about sex role conflicts as a potential barrier in their careers, whereas women were more concerned about sex discrimination and childrearing issues as barriers (Swanson & Tokar, 1991).

The normative sex role for men in this country can be hazardous to their health. Men have been reported to have higher rates of several physical illnesses compared to women: heart disease, lung cancer, cirrhosis of the liver, and AIDS. Men are also more likely to experience homicide, suicide, and accidents than women. Men, in general, have a lower life expectancy than women by 8 years, and the gap has widened during this century (Leafgren, 1990a; May, 1990).

White men constitute only 33% of the U.S. population, but they are overrepresented in positions of power and influence, making up 80% of the House of Representatives, 85% of tenured professors, and 90% of senators (Fendel et al., 1996). In contrast, men of color experience much less success in the United States.

Many of the traditionally respected gender roles for Native American men—for example, hunter or warrior—are no longer viable. Some Native American women have associated the anger and physical abuse Native American men direct toward them as related to the loss of these roles (LaFromboise et al., 1994).

African American men are at risk for increased death by violence, inadequate health care, lower life expectancy rates, imprisonment, decreased educational opportunities, unemployment, and underemployment (Parham & McDavis, 1987). Most avenues of power in American society, with the exception of achievement in sports, are relatively inaccessible to African American men (Davenport & Yurich, 1991). The suicide rate for Black men is increasing, and "Black men are rapidly becoming an endangered species" (Parham & McDavis, 1987, p. 24). Counselors may represent a social system that has rendered Black men powerless, and the counseling process may be perceived as unmanly. C. Lee (1990) recommended an active outreach approach for Black men that uses Black churches, fraternal organizations, and other African American community organizations. He proposed an intensive, developmental, group consciousness-raising experience that incorporates Black songs, books, and plays into the group process.

Asian American men seem to acculturate to life in the United States more slowly than Asian American women do. They experience great pressure for academic success and greater career restriction than Asian American women. Asian American men are heavily represented in the physical sciences. The reasons this occurs may be related to greater perceived financial returns, lower perceived potential for discrimination, or even counselors' stereotypical beliefs about their abilities in these fields (D. Sue, 1990).

☐ Cultural Values

It is particularly hard to delineate male cultural values because they are so intertwined with the dominant, majority values of U.S. society. It is difficult to differentiate the values of men, in particular, from Americans in general. Because men lead, own, or manage most of the major institutions in this country, it may be assumed that most of what is currently the status quo is what is valued by men. Wealth, power, sexuality, and competitiveness have been emphasized in U.S. culture, and people who are successful in these areas seem to have a higher status and may feel more worthy (Moore, Parker, Thompson, & Dougherty, 1990). Achievement, power, and strength have been particularly associated with masculinity in our society (Forrester, 1986).

There is considerable overlap between the cultural values placed on individual achievement and strength in many northern European cultures and the values associated with being male in the United States.

Achievement

Men have been socialized to validate their sense of maleness through achievement-oriented behaviors such as winning in sports, physical fights, intellectual debates, or financial endeavors and other forms of attaining power over others. They are trained to be goal oriented and productive and, consequently, to base their sense of self on external standards, particularly their achievements (Leafgren, 1990b). Some men, who for whatever reason are not able to be successful according to these external, societal definitions, may instead involve themselves in compensatory masculine role behaviors such as risk-taking, aggression, and violence (Leafgren, 1990a).

Power and Strength

Cultural expectations encourage men to remain strong and do not encourage expressions of intimacy, gentleness, caring, weakness, or needing help. Weakness is associated with a loss of masculinity and an ensuing loss of self-worth. Feelings other than aggression or anger are usually kept hidden.

Boys were told that "big boys don't cry," or, in sports, that they should learn to "play with pain," exhortations that served to train them to be out of touch with their own feelings, particularly those feelings on the vulnerable end of the spectrum. (Levant, 1990, p. 84)

Research suggests that although men and women self-disclose equally (Wilcox & Forrest, 1992), men tend to mention their strengths and conceal their weaknesses. This may contribute to the difficulty many men have in communicating personal concerns and the fact that men participate less frequently in counseling than do women (Leafgren, 1990b). Many men are not comfortable with the intimate sharing and one-down position of being a client if they have adopted power-oriented values, and they may expect or prefer more self-disclosure from counselors (Wilcox & Forrest, 1992).

O'Neil and Egan (1993) contended that men are more comfortable with overt social, political, and economic power, relative to women, because they have more practice and support using it. Boys are often trained to resolve conflict through the exercise of power, in terms of physical strength, verbal facility, or superior strategy (Levant, 1990). In contrast, girls are socialized to use power indirectly through emotionally expressive and nurturant roles.

Independence and Connection to Other Men

According to Gilligan (1982), separation and independence are thought to be central to male development, which also includes identification with roles and positions, individual achievements, rational cognitions, and a sense of ethics based on principles of justice. "Coming to terms with one's loneliness, with one's isolation, with one's independence is part of becoming a man" (Moore et al., 1990, p. 281).

However, an important part of male development also involves connection to a group of other men. Western cultures have few formal initiation rites for a boy entering manhood. The Boy Scouts, military schools, and Little League baseball and other team sports are informal substitutes for initiation rites (Moore et al., 1990). Dougherty (1990) contended that until the mid-1950s, the U.S. armed forces were perhaps the most influential groups for most men, with their initiation ritual of boot camp and emphases on commitment, competition, and cooperation. Associations with other men in either formal or semiformal groups provide men with rules for behaving in relationships. Intimacy in such groups is usually indirect, often centering around working on another task (Moore et al., 1990).

☐ Indigenous Treatment Methods

Men's Groups

The Chicago Men's Gathering group, begun in the 1970s, was aimed at facilitating growth through awareness and consciousness-raising (Leafgren, 1990b). The study of men has developed more slowly than women's studies, however. Although many individual college courses about men exist, there are as yet no departments of men's studies anywhere in the United States (Femiano, 1990).

In the context of group counseling, men can learn about what is unique and special about being male (Dougherty, 1990). Men need this because they grow up in a world dominated by women, because women continue to be the primary caregivers and nurturers of children. The group may explore masculine ways of feeling and communicating and examine how these styles may be different from those of women. What it means to be a lover, husband, or father, powerful and dangerous aspects of manhood, need for control, fear of appearing feminine in the presence of other men, and physical contact among men also may be examined in a men's group (Dougherty, 1990; Wilcox & Forrest, 1992). These issues may perhaps be revealed in storytelling, which, according to Dougherty (1990), is men's primary mode of telling about themselves. Poetry, drawing, role playing, and other techniques also can be used in men's groups.

Mythopoetic Men's Movement

The mythopoetic men's movement draws extensively from Jungian psychology. As in goddess psychology, discussed in Chapter 11, archetypal images are a focus. The primary archetypes are the warrior, representing self-discipline and self-defense; the king, representing confidence, effective decision making, and executive organization; the lover, representing passion and creativity; and the magician, representing spirituality. According to mythopoetic thought, life is fully integrated when all four influences are expressed appropriately (Enns, 1994).

The philosophy behind this movement is similar to men's groups in that men have been taught to compete, win, achieve success, and equate economic success with their worth as human beings. However, the mythopoetic movement suggests that through isolation from their fathers, the loss of male initiation rites, and overidentification with the world of women, men learn to be passive followers, absorbing attacks from others.

Men's sense of patriarchy is built on immature masculinity, abuse of power, and enactment of fantasies, and their behavior wavers from passivity and weakness to abuse and intimidation (Enns, 1994; May, 1990). Men are victimized by performance expectations associated with work, sex, and war (Enns, 1994). Some men may develop fixed ego boundaries and deny feelings of vulnerability and dependence to protect themselves from the pain of separation from maternal influence (May, 1990).

The mythopoetic men's movement calls for a rediscovery of masculinity among men that is not defined in contrast to femininity. There is emphasis on initiation rites that mark the passage from immature masculinity and the world of women to the world of men. Some of these are rites that have been adapted from Native American tribal traditions. These rites are aimed at assisting men in opening up to their own feelings, including emptiness and loneliness, replacing false optimism with honesty, and replacing compulsive activities with self-exploration (Enns, 1994).

Perhaps the most important contributions of the mythopoetic men's movement are that it permits men to explore their inner experiences, promotes emotional closeness with other men, and de-emphasizes material and external satisfactions. However, four criticisms of the mythopoetic men's movement have been raised (Enns, 1994). The primary archetypes tend to reinforce traditional societal views of masculinity, overlooking qualities such as compassion, caring, and empathy. Another criticism is that men's pain is often blamed on women, particularly their mothers. Third, Native American tribal rituals are being co-opted. Finally, the movement proposes only individual solutions for societal problems. Enns (1994) wrote,

It is unlikely that images of warriors and wild men and experiences of fierceness will help men feel more positively about sharing power with women in the work world, become more comfortable with emotions related to vulnerability and responsiveness, or assume greater responsibility for providing emotional nourishment to the next generation. (p. 130)

The mythopoetic men's movement might be helpful to some male clients, but, as with goddess psychology, the counselor is again cautioned about using archetypes that magnify gender differences or restrict the client's behavior and emotions (Enns, 1994).

☐ Counseling Issues

Men are more likely than women to be diagnosed with substance abuse or antisocial personality disorder (May, 1990; Morrissey, 1995) and these conditions may be related to traditional gender roles. The traditional masculine role encourages hiding weakness, solving problems independently, keeping feelings to oneself, and taking action, and these values are in direct contrast to those of traditional counseling: revealing weakness, collaborative problem solving, disclosing feelings, and verbal dialogue (Wilcox & Forrest, 1992). Robertson and Fitzgerald (1992) found that men with more traditional opinions about masculinity were less willing to seek counseling. Along a similar line, Warren (1983) proposed that depressive symptoms are incompatible with the traditional male sex role, rendering men reluctant to admit to having problems or to seeking help from others. It is interesting that when men do receive mental health services, they spend more money, on average, than women (Morrissey, 1995). This difference could be an artifact of the kinds of treatment received; for example, more expensive inpatient substance abuse treatment compared to outpatient counseling.

Work

Taffel (1991) described the "work-identified man" (p. 53), who seems to define himself solely in terms of his work. The counselor working with such a client might inquire about work and emphasize the kind of relatedness to others required by the client's work environment. Whom the client respects, what he takes pride in, and whom he feels closest to on the job may prove helpful in understanding other problems in the client's life. Taffel maintained that exploring work often leads to family-of-origin issues, because a man's choice and manner of occupational relationship has its roots in his family of origin.

Violence

Many men who physically abuse their partners either witnessed violence between their parents or were themselves physically abused. This history contributes to the fact that some men view their behavior as normative rather than abusive. Male role socialization, another contributing factor, restricts the expression of feelings other than anger and discourages interpersonal conflict resolution modes that are not based on power (Grusznski & Bankovics, 1990).

Treatment for male batterers instructs the man to physically leave the situation when aggression is escalating. He is taught to identify physical cues, situational cues, self-statements, and feelings that occur prior to incidents of violence. Once his level of tension has decreased and he regains self-control, he learns to return to the situation and calmly discuss the issue. Grusznski and Bankovics (1990) asserted that helping men change their violent behavior involves teaching them to be assertive; release stress; decrease isolation; identify and express feelings, including remorse and shame; accept responsibility; recognize self-statements; and examine male roles, sex role stereotypes, attitudes toward women, and behavior learned in their family of origin.

Fathering

According to Levant's (1990) review of the literature, a man's family role is more significant to him than his paid work role. This means that multiple role strain is an issue for men as well as women involved in parenting. Lack of time, difficulty finding affordable, high-quality child care, inflexible workplace policies, and role-cycling (having to shift from one mode of functioning at work to another at home) all contribute to multiple role strain for working parents. Men may also face internal conflict over not adequately fulfilling their provider role (Levant, 1990).

There are few male models of childrearing available for men who wish to be involved parents. Training in listening and negotiation skills might be helpful, and a fatherhood course is one method of teaching these skills to men (Levant, 1990). The course is structured as an educational program for skill development, not counseling, and focuses on communication skills, awareness and expression of feelings, child development, and child management. Role plays, videotaped feedback, and homework exercises in addition to lectures are used.

Other Counseling Implications

Several authors have written about culturally consistent counseling approaches for counseling men. Silverberg (1986) suggested that the major goal in counseling men is the integration of traditional masculine and feminine components of the male role, that is, combining analytical, instrumental elements with emotional expressiveness, warmth, sensitivity, and tenderness. May (1990) reasoned that client trust in the counselor is critical in helping men explore their lives because many of the issues men face are unconscious and preverbal. He also warned that internalized homophobia is a primary obstacle in exploring emotions for many men. Taking into account male preferences for more personal space, counselors may want to position their chairs a little farther away from male clients than from female clients.

Ipsaro (1986) suggested that the counselor use more direct, analytical, educational techniques rather than ambiguous, emotionally laden interventions when counseling men. For example, Robertson and Fitzgerald (1992) suggested that using terms such as *classes, workshops,* or *seminars* rather than *personal counseling* may help encourage more traditional men to obtain counseling services. J. M. Sullivan (personal communication, June 14, 1998) sometimes "coaches" male clients. He notes the importance of respecting a male client and maintaining his dignity. Emphasis on time management, career development, and stress reduction through physical fitness may initially appeal to many men. Wilcox and Forrest (1992) suggested the use of cognitive, problem-solving, and action-oriented strategies. They mention the potential use of argument and debate as a productive technique in counseling as a parallel to engaging in competition. This suggests that rational–emotive therapy also may be a helpful theoretical approach with men.

In contrast, Heesacker and Prichard (1992) pointed out the importance of storytelling as a mode of communication by men as part of the counseling process. They also emphasized the recognition of silence as a crucial aspect of men's affective processes and the observation of actions, either from memories or in-session behavior, as a manner of accessing and integrating feelings. May (1990) recommended that an awareness of feelings can be developed through devices such as popular songs, artwork, old photographs, sentence completion and other structured exercises, and massage. May also maintained that including an element of social consciousness-raising in counseling to help men confront the societal attitudes that devalue women may be needed in order for men to permit themselves to develop their more feminine aspects.

An awareness of outcomes is particularly important when counseling men. Many men may be especially interested in making sure counseling sessions are productive, perhaps applying a value of competitive achievement to their time in counseling (Scher, 1979).

☐   Recommended Cultural Resources

Print Media

American Association for Counseling and Development, Committee on Men. (1990). Men's
issues: A bibliography. In D. Moore & F. Leafgren (Eds.), *Men in conflict* (pp. 313–356).
Alexandria, VA: American Association for Counseling and Development.
Majors, R., & Billson, J. (1993). *Cool pose*. New York: Simon & Schuster.

Multimedia

Spiking, B., Deeley, M., Cimino, M., & Peverall, J. (Producers). (1982). *The deer hunter*
[Videorecording]. Universal City, CA: MCA Videodisc.

13
CHAPTER

Counseling Gay Men and Lesbians

To be honest, gay persons are not just plain folk; we are quite extraordi-nary. . . . We are not—heaven forbid—"the same as" heterosexuals, but are uniquely different with our own positive and lasting contributions to humanity.

—Rictor Norton, writer (Judell, 1997, p. 23)

You understand that in homosexuality, just as in heterosexuality, there are all shades and degrees, from radiant health to sullen sickness, from simple expansiveness to all the refinements of vice.

—Andre Gide, writer (Judell, 1997, p. 25)

☐ Histories and Diversity

Estimates suggest that as many as 10%–20% of the United States population is gay, lesbian, or bisexual (Abbitt & Bennett, 1984; D'Andrea, 1994). However, in one survey only 2% of men acknowledged engaging in homosexual sex during the past decade, and in another survey only 2.8% of men and 1.4% of women identified themselves as homosexual ("Sex survey," 1994). In large cities, 10.2% of the men and 2.1% of the women reported that they had a sexual partner of their own sex in the past year, whereas in rural areas 1% of the men and 0.6% of the women reported the same behavior ("Sex survey," 1994). These differences may in part reflect the great difficulty this nation has with the cultural acceptance of people with a non-heterosexual orientation, even among people who are themselves gay, lesbian, or bisexual. In addition, 3 million male and female adolescents in the United States may have a homosexual orientation (O'Connor, 1992), although many of them may not have yet actually participated in sexual behavior consistent with their orientation.

Another source of confusion is the lack of agreement as to the definition of homosexuality, whether it is self-identification, sexual behavior, sexual desire, or a combination of these ("Sex survey," 1994). Sexual orientation has been described as a person's choice of sexual partners and could be heterosexual, homosexual, or bisexual (Patterson, 1995). However, researchers in the field have pointed out the need for workable definitions of *gay* (homosexual male), *lesbian* (homosexual female), and *bisexual* (DeAngelis, 1994b).

Recent research has strongly indicated that homosexuality is biological in origin and is not social or psychological (T. Adler, 1992). Differences between homosexual and heterosexual brain structures have been documented. Twin studies have indicated that the more genetically similar two brothers were, the more likely it was that the second brother would have the same sexual orientation as the first. The conclusion is that genetic and/or prenatal environmental factors largely determine sexual orientation.

Gay, lesbian, and bisexual people have long been subject to anti-gay bias, or *homophobia* (Weinberg, 1972). The majority of people in the United States perceive homosexuality as sick, immoral, or criminal (B. C. Murphy, 1992). Unfortunately, mental health professionals are not exempt from homophobia (B. C. Murphy, 1992; Weinberg, 1972). The Stonewall riots in 1969 signaled the birth of the gay liberation movement, and 4 years later homosexuality was declassified as a mental disorder. Homophobia continues to persist even though, aside from sexual orientation itself, there are no significant differences between gay men and lesbians and heterosexual men and women (DeAngelis, 1994b); for example, domestic violence is no less of a concern for lesbian couples, and perpetration of child sexual abuse is no less prevalent among straight men (Patterson, 1995).

Hate crimes against homosexuals are verbal and physical assaults motivated by the perception that the victim is gay, lesbian, or bisexual (Herek, 1989). The assaults may include verbal insults, taunts, threats, spitting, kicking, punching, throwing objects, vandalism, arson, attacks with weapons, rape, and murder. As many as 92% of gay men and lesbians have experienced anti-gay verbal abuse, and as many as 24% have experience physical violence. According to Bohn (cited in Bridgewater, 1992), attacks on gay men are most frequently carried out by an armed group, typically numbering four persons, who outnumber the victim or victims. Common victim reactions to antigay violence include resignation, shame, self-recrimination, guilt, numbness, despondency, depression, and anger, and Bridgewater (1992) recommended using cognitive techniques for initial crisis intervention with victims. Even a gay man who has not directly been victimized or does not personally know anyone who has experienced anti-gay violence, however, may still have been exposed to media coverage about anti-gay hate crimes and could be affected by the possibility of being physically attacked.

Gay men, lesbians, and bisexuals may themselves succumb to the antigay prejudices of our society, and this internalized homophobia has been associated with depression, low self-esteem, defensiveness, and impaired intimacy (Sleek, 1996). Frederick (Sleek, 1996) suggested that it may be helpful for the counselor to treat internalized homophobia by discussing the client's early experiences and ways that homosexual feelings were adapted to or repressed. Malyon (1982) recommended using cognitive restructuring and, if the counselor is gay, carefully considering the pros and cons of revealing this to the client.

There is much diversity within the gay, lesbian, and bisexual population in terms of the development and impact of sexual orientation on each individual's life. Sexual orientation has been described as multidimensional, situational, changeable, and contextual (Hersch, 1991), and any generalities about these groups may not necessarily represent the experience of a specific client.

The psychological experiences of gay men are in many ways similar to those of other men in this country. For example, the coming-out process for gay men has often included anonymous sex (Hersch, 1991), which is consistent with the object-oriented sexuality of many men in U.S. culture (Hawkins, 1992). (The coming-out process is an important issue in counseling and is discussed later in this chapter, in a separate section.) DeAngelis (1992) suggested that intimacy difficulties may arise because it may be easier for a gay man to have a sexual relationship with another man than to allow himself to love another man because of our culture's taboo against men expressing affection to each other. However, in other ways the experiences of gay men are different because of the effects of cultural discrimination. For example, Hawkins (1992) noted that when gay men are under stress, needs for validation, splitting behavior, or acting out may be frequent defenses for dealing with hostile, unsupportive environments and are not necessarily signs of personality disorders. Among undisclosed older gay men, career achievement has been one way to cope with the stigma of homosexuality (Adelman, 1990).

Lesbians endure the double effects of social oppression based on both gender and sexual orientation. They are at risk for depression, suicide, and substance abuse (Ritter, 1993; Rothblum, 1990) and are more closeted in the workplace compared to gay men (Ness, 1993). Between 30% and 35% of lesbians report excessive alcohol use, compared to 5% of heterosexual women (Rothblum, 1990). Depression is the most common reason lesbians seek counseling. Many lesbians are open to the counseling process. One survey (Bradford & Ryan, 1987, as cited in L. S. Brown, 1989) revealed that 78% of the lesbian respondents either were or had been in therapy, and lesbians frequently request lesbian-identified or lesbian-sensitive counselors (B. C. Murphy, 1992). As lesbians age, important counseling issues include the need to develop strong friendship ties, in essence, to create their own families; societal homophobia and internalized negative stereotypes about being old and a lesbian; and more general women's issues related to taking risks and pleasing others (Sang, 1992).

Unlike the majority of gay men and lesbians, most bisexual people eroticize heterosexually when they enter adulthood and later discover their homosexual interests (Wolf, 1992). Bisexuality may be more problematic for men than women because of society's more restrictive male sexuality expectations. It is not unusual for a bisexual client never to have known someone with similar feelings, talked to anyone, or read about bisexuality. Counseling may be helpful in terms of giving permission and information regarding bisexuality, helping build a support network, providing specific suggestions as to how and when to disclose bisexuality, and discussing how to deal with bisexuality within a relationship.

It has been noted that ethnic gay people face a "double indemnity" of race as well as sexual orientation and are more closeted in the workplace (Ness, 1993). Many gay men and lesbians of color must find a way to exist in three communities simultaneously: interacting with other gay people, with others of their ethnic group, and with the predominantly White heterosexual majority (Morales, 1992).

Several Native American tribes have historically accepted homosexual behavior without requiring a rigid classification of sexual orientation (Midnight Sun, 1988). For example, the Mohave and Navajo cultures had specific acceptable social roles for people who engaged in predominantly cross-gender behavior, including cross-dressing and same-sex sexual behavior. As tribal traditions have become diluted by majority culture, acceptance for gay Native Americans in some tribes is more difficult today than in the past.

Many African Americans still perceive *gay* or *lesbian* to be White terms tied to a White identity ("Sex survey," 1994). This is not surprising given that racial discrimination in advertising, employment, and admission to bars is reported to be just as prevalent in the gay community as in the rest of U.S. society (Gutierrez & Dworkin, 1992). Similarly, African Americans have supported anti-gay legislation in at least one state (J. M. Sullivan, personal communication, June 14, 1998). Many gay African Americans see themselves as African American first and gay or lesbian second, and therefore support from other African Americans is especially important (Riggs, 1989). Validation is an important adjustment theme for African American gay men and lesbians: validation within the African American community, validation within the gay and lesbian community, and the integration of these two identities (Loiacano, 1989). Gutierrez and Dworkin (1992) recommended that counselors do as much as they can to validate their gay African American clients and be aware of resources in both the African American and gay and lesbian communities.

Gay Latinos and Latinas may have difficulty being accepted in either Hispanic or gay communities. Morales (1992) noted that, in general, Hispanic communities are homophobic, and attitudes toward gay men and lesbians are negative; and that gay and lesbian communities have racist attitudes toward Latinos and Latinas. Many Latinos do not consider themselves to be gay if they take the active role in a same-sex sexual encounter. The incidence of AIDS is almost twice as high among Latinos and Latinas compared to the total U.S. population, and one of the contributing factors may be sex between men who do not identify with being gay because of cultural homophobia (Freiberg, 1991b).

Some gay Asian Americans may remain closeted within their ethnic community while being open about their sexual orientation in all other parts of their lives (C. S. Chan, 1992). Although they may need the support of other Asian Americans, the fear of rejection and stigmatization is too great. In a study by Chan (1989), 77% of gay Asian Americans reported that it was difficult to disclose their sexual orientation to other Asian Americans, and only 26% had come out to their parents. The most difficulty task for gay Asian Americans in the coming-out process, according to C. S. Chan (1992), is disclosing their sexual orientation to their parents, because they may expect a lack of understanding and fear rejection from their families. Additionally, issues of independence from sex role socialization also are relevant for Asian American lesbians. Some Asian American lesbians disclose their sexual orientation to their parents to dispel expectations for marriage and to assert that they are capable of being responsible for themselves.

☐ Cultural Values

Perhaps because of the invisible nature of sexual minority populations, cultural values for these groups are difficult to state. Sexual role equality is valued among many gay men and lesbians. Among lesbian couples, role flexibility is frequent, and a butch–femme pattern is rare (B. C. Murphy, 1992). Many lesbians place emphasis on power equality, intimacy, and communication.

Counselors need to be careful not to use language that is indicative of heterosexual bias. Examples include asking a lesbian couple which partner is in the "male" role or referring to sexual intimacy as "having sex," which describes heterosexual intercourse (B. C. Murphy, 1992). Nonheterosexist terms such as *significant other* or *partner* for couple relationships are best ("Lesbian, gay," 1996). Care in constructing informational forms is needed, because many questionnaires unwittingly presume that all respondents are heterosexual. For example, a question as to whether a client is sexually active is frequently followed with a question on the type of birth control used (Logan, 1997). This can be awkward for some gay clients, forcing disclosure, deceit, or discomfort.

☐ Indigenous Treatment Methods

Although there have been few reports of indigenous treatments developed by and for gay, lesbian, or bisexual people, those that exist seem to build on the strength of the community. Many gay men and lesbians develop families of choice and interlocking friendship networks that can be mobilized for treatment intervention. This "village" concept was first used during the AIDS crisis in the early 1980s (Logan, 1997). Gay men and lesbians from all walks of life came together to identify resources and allocate funds to provide support services such as food delivery, transportation, and "buddy" programs. Another positive outcome of these activities was that they provided an opportunity for many people to come out and live out, finding a sense of purpose and community with other people who were gay. A variation of the village concept comes from HIV-prevention research. Training gay community leaders to disseminate risk-reduction information resulted in a substantial reduction in unprotected anal intercourse among men who frequented gay bars (Azar, 1996c).

In Houston, a group of lesbians has developed the AssistHers program to serve lesbians with breast cancer, lupus, AIDS, other chronic illnesses, and mental health disorders (Logan, 1997). AssistHers provides services such as companionship, transportation, food delivery, and assessment and correction of environmental barriers. Volunteers are organized into treatment teams and meet monthly with a mental health professional for supervision and to process their feelings and issues about their clients. Through participation in the program volunteers gain increased insight into their own issues, self-esteem, and knowledge about the parameters of caregiving.

Among the complications of the village concept are issues of dual relationships, because in these groups individuals may have multiple roles. For example, friends may become clients, and romantic partners or former partners may become fellow helpers. Logan (1997) suggested that these complications urge counselors to move toward a redefinition of boundaries to permit the kind of complex relationships associated with traditional village life.

☐ Counseling Issues

Adolescence

Adolescence is an especially difficult period for many gay people. Between the ages of 12 and 14, many gay adolescents begin to realize that their attraction to members of their own sex could mean that they are part of a stigmatized minority group (D. Anderson, 1987). If they disclose their sexual feelings to their parents, the feelings often are denied as just being part of a phase the teen is going through (Zera, 1992). Other initial parent responses may be shock or anger. D. Anderson (1987) described parental reactions to their gay children as similar to a grief process that may include denial, anger, bargaining, and acknowledgment. If gay adolescents do not disclose their feelings to their family, awkward and inauthentic communication may result, leading to mutual isolation (B. C. Murphy, 1992). Indeed, in reviewing the literature, O'Connor (1992) noted that 20%–30% of gay adolescents attempt suicide, a rate two to three times higher than for other adolescents. Gay youths are also at risk for drug use, truancy, academic problems, dropping out of school, and running away from home. In addition, A. D. Martin and Hetrick (1988) found that 40% of gay adolescents had experienced violence perpetrated by family members or others. However, the adolescents themselves rated isolation and family rejection as their most important problems. Along the same lines, Hunter and Schaecher (1987) reported that one out of five of the lesbian adolescents and half of the gay male adolescents in their sample had experienced either verbal harassment or physical assault at school because of their sexual orientation. Gay males under age 25 have one of the fastest growing HIV infection rates and have a higher than average incidence of mental health problems (Azar, 1996c). Many male adolescent prostitutes are gay male adolescents who have been expelled from their homes (Hetrick & Martin, 1987). Among lesbian adolescents, pregnancy may be a way of either denying or testing their sexual orientation (Zera, 1992).

All in all, 40% of gay adolescents do seek psychiatric help, but when they do so they do not necessarily disclose their sexual orientation (Remafedi, 1987). This suggests that there is much opportunity for counselors to be of help to gay adolescents. Counselors need to support and positively affirm the gay feelings an adolescent may be experiencing. Bringing up the topic when the client has not, and disclosure to and involvement of parents, are potentially complicated. J. M. Sullivan (personal communication, June 14, 1998) asks about who the client notices and inquires about the content of sexual fantasies during masturbation as possible clues to sexual orientation. Zera (1992) noted that gay adolescents need positive, visible role models and socialization with gay peers. D. Anderson (1987) suggested forming support groups for gay adolescents.

Coming Out

Unlike most ethnic minority, elderly, female, or physically disabled people, people who are gay, lesbian, or bisexual are part of a hidden or invisible minority, because their sexual orientation is not automatically visible to others. The experience of being a minority of 1 is common (O'Connor, 1992) and can contribute to a strong feeling of isolation. *Coming out* has been described as a developmental process in which gay people recognize their sexual orientation and make choices to integrate this knowledge into their lives (Zera, 1992). A gay person may choose to come out to certain people and in certain situations before others. Counselors need to assess more than whether the client is out. Many additional questions arise, including "to whom?", "What was their reaction?", "How is your current relationship with them?", "Whom have you not yet told?", and so on.

Coming out is difficult for many reasons. Because of the homophobic nature of our society, coming out means risking the loss of interpersonal relationships, economic hardship, and physical danger due to prejudice and discrimination. Bridgewater (1992) noted that periodic regression to previous stages of identity develoment is a natural part of the coming-out process when homophobia is confronted. Coming out also is psychologically painful, because the gay person's old sense of self must be grieved before a new sense of self can emerge (Ritter, 1993). Coming out is complicated also because gay men and lesbians by and large must be bicultural, living concurrently in both heterosexual and homosexual cultures (L. S. Brown, 1989). Coming-out issues may also re-emerge when a gay couple takes steps toward additional intimacy, such as moving in together or deciding to parent (Ariel & Stearns, 1992; B. C. Murphy, 1992).

Coming out is positively correlated with mental health and with relationship satisfaction (Berger, 1990; DeAngelis, 1994b). The coming-out process is easier for some than for others. For example, level of education is strongly related to self-identification as a gay person, especially among women ("Sex survey," 1994). For a counselor working with a client who is dealing with coming out, the use of role play has been recommended to practice disclosure (B. C. Murphy, 1992). Bibliotherapy also can be useful, as well as participation in a support group with other gay people.

Career Concerns

Sexual orientation may affect the work life of many gay people in several potential areas, among them career choice, workplace benefits and stresses, and career advancement. For example, when compared to other female college students, lesbian students tended to decide on their career paths later, chose less traditional careers, and planned to have fewer children (Azar, 1996b). Also, lesbians who took their sexual orientation into account in making career decisions have more often chosen to work in the helping professions. They tended to be more open about their sexual orientation and accepted their gayness earlier than other lesbians. These findings suggest that sexual orientation and level of sexual identity formation both have an impact on career decisions. Orzek (1992) recommended that, when engaging in career planning with a gay client, the counselor identify the client's level of identity formation and accept the client's sexual orientation as viewed from within the client's own frame of reference.

Gay adults are frequently aware of being different, according to Zera (1992), and this difference is made salient in the workplace. Gay workers are often not able to integrate their personal lives into the workplace as freely as their heterosexual colleagues do, in simple actions such as displaying a photo of their partner or talking about a new home (Ness, 1993). Corporate nondiscrimination policies, including those concerning sexual orientation, are becoming normative in some parts of the country, and there are a few large corporations (e.g., Apple, Levi Strauss, Microsoft) who grant full domestic-partner benefits to gay employees. The "lavender ceiling" is the biggest reason professional people who are gay, lesbian, or bisexual may choose not to disclose their sexual orientation at work (Ness, 1993). Gay people in middle management see almost no examples of disclosure among those at the highest executive levels. Counselors can help their gay clients handle the additional stress they may experience from not disclosing their sexual orientation in the workplace.

Relationship Issues

Gay couples have some unique relationship issues, because in our homophobic society they are denied most of the legal, religious, economic, and social benefits typically bestowed on heterosexual couples (B. C. Murphy, 1992). For example, a gay couple may feel sadness over not having a wedding shower, ceremony, or presents. Alternative legal signs of commitment for gay men and lesbians might include buying a house, making a will, or filing a power of attorney with the county clerk. Counselors can help gay couples anticipate and perhaps plan rituals or celebrations around changes in their relationships.

When two men build a relationship together, the double influence of male sex role socialization in terms of low interpersonal skills, aggression, independence, achievement, competition, and object-oriented sexuality may become problematic (Hawkins, 1992). In addition, when relationship difficulties arise, gay men may be more prone to seek isolation, a coping mechanism from childhood used to deal with gay feelings, which makes intimacy even more difficult. This can occur when one member of a gay male couple is HIV seropositive. The partners, especially the seronegative member, may tend to avoid facing their relationship problems, conflicts may escalate, and relationship satisfaction and support may decline (Murray, 1996). For HIV-mixed couples, group intervention designed to teach communication and problem-solving skills has been recommended as a means of affirming the validity of the relationship, increasing hope, reducing isolation, and improving communication.

Most lesbians have a previous history of relating to men; 95% have dated men, and between one fourth and one third of them have been married to a man (B. C. Murphy, 1992). However, when the relationship involves two women, couple issues more frequently concern difficulties with differentiation and maintaining a sense of self (Dupuy, 1993; B. C. Murphy, 1992). Indeed, feelings of merger and identity fusion may be a primary presenting problem (Dupuy, 1993). Roth (1989, as cited in Dupuy, 1993) suggested several ways to promote individual autonomy in lesbian couples: (a) encourage statements of individuality; (b) teach the couple the concepts of boundaries, triangling, and fusion; and (c) reframe undifferentiated caretaking as disrespectful.

Parenting Issues

Estimates suggest that there are 2 million–20 million lesbian mothers and gay fathers in the United States (Ariel & Stearns, 1992; Laster, 1993). The number of lesbian mothers purported to reside with their children ranges from 1.5 million to 5 million (Falk, 1989). The number of gay fathers living with their children is lower, partly because they are less likely to retain primary custody of their children (Ariel & Stearns, 1992). Lesbians and gay men can become parents in a multitude of ways, including adoption, alternative insemination by donor, heterosexual intercourse during marriage, heterosexual intercourse for the purpose of procreation, and foster parenting (Ariel & Stearns, 1992; Falk, 1989). For example, one family might consist of a lesbian couple with a child whose father is a gay man who is also part of a couple. Both couples may actively participate in childrearing, whether they choose to share a residence or live in close proximity (Laster, 1993).

Several legal issues are potential concerns for gay parents. Given the homophobic nature of our society and, hence, the legal system, gay parents may have realistic concerns about losing physical custody of their children, visitation restriction, and prohibitions against adoption (Abbitt & Bennett, 1984; Patterson, 1995). "Second-parent adoption," or legal adoption by a nonbiological parent without the original parent losing any rights, is legal in seven states (Laster, 1993). Without legal status defining family relationships, in the event of medical emergency, separation, or death unwanted complications may arise (Ariel & Stearns, 1992).

Much more is known about lesbian mothers than about gay fathers. According to a review of the literature by Patterson (1995), there are no major differences between lesbian and heterosexual women in terms of either their mental health or their approaches to childrearing. One of the family issues that might affect lesbian mothers is overparenting or competition for the primary parent role if both women identify with a maternal role (Ariel & Stearns, 1992). Another potential concern is whether to come out to children for fear of (a) psychological or physical harm to the child by peers; (b) the child's rejection of the parent; or (c) the child telling other people, which might lead to employment, social, or custody problems (Abbitt & Bennett, 1984).

There is considerable research evidence that children of gay parents are no different from children of homosexual parents in terms of gender identity development; sexual orientation; preferences in toys, activities, interests, or occupations; personal adjustment; or social relationships (Ariel & Stearns, 1992; Hersch, 1991; Laster, 1993; Patterson, 1995). The most difficult period for children of gay parents is early adolescence, when homophobia in general is high, and children who are told of parental gay, lesbian, or bisexual identity either in childhood or late adolescence find the news easier to handle (Laster, 1993; Patterson, 1995). Feelings of isolation also are a potential concern, as only 29% of young adult children of gay parents report ever having known anyone else with a gay, lesbian, or bisexual parent (Patterson, 1995).

General Treatment Implications

Ariel and Stearns (1992) aptly stated that "the legacy of secrecy and fear of losing close, familial relationships . . . is an integral part of the fabric of the gay and lesbian experience" in their discussion of gay and lesbian families. These themes are important and relevant to counseling many gay clients, whether in individual, relationship, or group counseling. Slater (1988) emphasized the effects of homophobic socialization on both client and counselor and the importance of bringing these into conscious awareness. Bibliotherapy is recommended to counter myths and stereotypes. To counteract homophobia, counselors need to be gay affirmative, which means actively affirming the validity of gay relationships (B. C. Murphy, 1992). Supervision is recommended to guard against sexism, homophobia, and heterosexism in counseling, and for gay male and lesbian counselors to prevent overidentification. Mosher (1991) further noted that heterosexual counselors must be committed to justice in order to be effective with gay, lesbian, or bisexual clients, who live in an unjust world. Crisis counselor and advocate roles may be appropriate at times (Bridgewater, 1992). Counselors need to be knowledgeable about safe sex practices and HIV/AIDS education and should assess clients for the possibility of grief issues or posttraumatic stress disorder due to multiple losses related to AIDS. Finally, counselors who work with gay clients need to familiarize themselves with common sexual practices and sex therapy for gay men and lesbians, legal and financial resources, activist organizations, gay newspapers and magazines, couple support groups, and gay professional organizations (B. C. Murphy, 1992).

☐ Recommended Cultural Resources

Print Media

Alexander, C. J. (Ed.). (1996). *Gay and lesbian mental health*. Binghamton, NY: Harrington Park Press.

American Psychological Association. (1995). *Lesbian and gay parenting: A resource for psychologists*. Washington, DC: Author.

Berzon, B. (1988). *Permanent partners*. New York: Plume Books.

Clark, D. H. (1987). *The new loving someone gay*. Berkeley, CA: Celestial Arts.

Dworkin, S. H., & Gutierrez, F. J. (1992). *Counseling gay men and lesbians: Journey to the end of the rainbow*. Alexandria, VA: American Counseling Association.

Garnets, L. D., & Kimmel, D. C. (Eds.). (1993). *Psychological perspectives of lesbian and gay male experiences*. New York: Columbia University Press.

Hwang, D. H. (1988). *M. Butterfly*. New York: New American Library.

Rasi, R. A., & Rodriguez-Nogues, L. (Eds.). (1995). *Out in the workplace*. Los Angeles: Alyson.

Multimedia

Cohen, H. S., & Chasnoff, D. (1996). *It's elementary: Talking about gay issues in school* [Videorecording]. San Francisco: Women's Educational Media.

Darron, M. (Producer). (1983). *La cage aux folles* [Videorecording]. Farmington Hills, MI: CBS/Fox Video.

Hope, T., Schamus, J., & Lee, A. (Producers). (1994). *The wedding banquet* [Videorecording]. Beverly Hills, CA: Fox Video.

Woolley, S. (Producer). (1992). *The crying game* [Videorecording]. Van Nuys, CA: Live Home Video.

Organizations

Association for Gay, Lesbian, and Bisexual Issues in Counseling (AGLBIC), P.O. Box 216, Jenkintown, PA 19046.

Association of Lesbian and Gay Psychologists (ALGP), 2336 Market Street, Number 8, San Francisco, CA 94114.

Collage: Children of Lesbians and Gays Everywhere, 2300 Market Street, Box 165, San Francisco, CA 94114.

Gay and Lesbian Parents Coalition International (GLPCI), P.O. Box 50360, Washington, DC 20091.

National Bisexual Network, 584 Castro Street, Number 422, San Francisco, CA 94114.

National Gay Youth Network, P.O. Box 846, San Francisco, CA 94101.

Parents, Families and Friends of Lesbians and Gays (PFLAG), 1101 14th Street NW, Washington, DC 20005.

14

CHAPTER

Counseling Older People

How good we all are, in theory, to the old; and how in fact we wish them to wander off like old dogs, die without bothering us, and bury themselves.

—Edgar Watson Howe (Ehrlich & DeBruhl, 1996, p. 475)

☐ Histories and Diversity

Almost 13% of the U.S. population is over age 65 (AARP, 1995). People in the United States live one fourth or more of their lives as older people, over age 60 (J. E. Myers & Schwiebert, 1996). Approximately 58% of older people are female, and as many as 40% did not complete high school (AARP, 1993). Most older people live in metropolitan areas and in the same geographical location where they lived in midlife (J. E. Myers & Schwiebert, 1996). People over age 80 are the most rapidly growing segment of the U.S. population (Human Capital Initiative, 1993). By age 80, one in four elderly people lives in a nursing home, and 45% of the rest need some help with everyday activities (Human Capital Initiative, 1993). By the age of 85, 25% have been diagnosed with Alzheimer's disease (N. F. Russo, 1990).

Ageism is a term first used by Butler (1969) to describe discrimination against older people and a tendency to view all older people similarly and negatively. Many psychiatrists, psychologists, rehabilitation counselors, and other health and mental health professionals view older people negatively (Gatz & Pearson, 1988; J. E. Myers & Schwiebert, 1996). Old age is viewed as an undesirable time full of physical and emotional decline and loss. Stereotypes of elderly people are that they are all sick or senile; poor; depressed; unproductive; unable to learn; asexual; and live alone or in institutions, although they would prefer to live with adult children (Friend, 1990; J. E. Myers & Schwiebert, 1996). Many older people do not receive help for treatable depression because depression is mistakenly viewed as a normal part of aging. In fact, statistics dispute the stereotypes. Although 86% of elderly people do experience physical conditions that limit their daily activities in some way, 80% are able to continue living independently. Only 4%–5% of older people must live in a long-term care setting at any one time. Almost half of those over 65 see or talk to their children daily, and elderly parents tend to move closer to their children (Lefrancois, 1993). In general, older adults have lower diagnostic rates for mental disorders, except for cognitive impairment, than other age groups (J. K. Myers et al., 1984). There are many theories of later life development and aging that may be relevant to counseling older people (J. E. Myers & Schwiebert, 1996), and social breakdown theory, described by Kuypers and Bengtson (1973), is particularly relevant from a cultural perspective. This theory suggests that being old in U.S. society creates a predisposition toward vulnerability. Negative external social messages about incapacity and age become internalized and bring about decreased self-esteem and increased feelings of vulnerability, which may interact in a continuing downward spiral, eventually contributing to the untimely death of the older person.

The Older Americans Act, enacted in 1965, was one of the first steps taken on a national level to combat ageism. Its general purpose was to help older people live independently for as long as possible. The 1978 Age Discrimination in Employment Act protects people aged 40–70 from ageism in the workplace. The Older Women's League is a national political action organization that addresses the issues of older women (J. E. Myers & Schwiebert, 1996).

J. E. Myers and Schwiebert (1996, pp. 23–24) suggested that counselors of older clients ask themselves several questions that may increase their self-awareness about aging:

• Why do I want to work with older people?

• What have been my experiences with older people in my family?

• What are the characteristics of older people I consider to be desirable?

- How do I view the aging of my parents?

- Have I come to terms with the eventual death of my parents?

- How do I feel about my own eventual death?

- What signs of aging have I seen in myself physically, psychologically, and socially?

- How do other people react toward me as a result of these signs or changes?

- How do I feel about the reactions of other people toward my aging?

Old age is a different experience for men than for women. There are five times more widows than widowers, and bereaved men are five times more likely to remarry than women are. Thus elderly men are more likely to live with their spouse in a family environment, whereas elderly women are more likely to live alone. Older women are at risk for loneliness and poverty (J. E. Myers & Schwiebert, 1996). According to a National Institute for Mental Health report (Eichler & Parron, 1987), 26% of White women, 48% of Hispanic women, and 60% of Black women aged 65 and older who live alone have incomes below the established national poverty level. These conditions are particularly notable because, on average, a woman in the United States can expect to be a widow for 25 years (Special Committee on Aging, 1983). Old age affects women in a second major way as well: Seventy-two percent of the 2.2 million unpaid caregivers of older people are women (Eichler & Parron, 1987).

Older people of color tend to be poorer, less well educated, have fewer and lower quality housing choices, more illness, earlier death, and a generally lower quality of life (Baruth & Manning, 1991). Their numbers are increasing at a faster rate than those of older people in general (Human Capital Initiative, 1993).

Older Native Americans have the highest illiteracy rate of all ethnic groups in the United States, and their average life expectancy is 8 years less than that of Anglo American older people.

Older African Americans are more likely to be separated, divorced, or widowed compared to Anglo Americans, and they are more likely to live in an urban area with an adult child (Baruth & Manning, 1991; J. E. Myers & Schwiebert, 1996). They tend to rely on extended family, church, and other informal support instead of available public services. Hospital stays for older African Americans are longer and more frequent, perhaps because they have a high rate of multiple chronic diseases. Among African

Americans aged 65–74, one in four has diabetes (Pouliot, 1996). With respect to counseling, Vontress (1976) noted that some older African Americans may loudly verbalize the opposite of their real feelings or "play it cool" to avoid revealing their true emotions.

Older Latinos and Latinas have the least education of all older people of color, with only 19% having completed high school (Barrow & Smith, 1979). They frequently were employed as unskilled laborers or farmworkers, jobs that did not offer retirement benefits, and tend to remain in the workforce many years after most other older people have retired. More older Latinos and Latinas are seeking work because unemployment among Hispanic elders is nearly double that of Anglo elders. Sources suggest that Latinos and Latinas treat old age as beginning earlier, at age 60, compared to Blacks, at age 65, and Whites, at age 70 (Baruth & Manning, 1991). These conditions may contribute to the lower levels of life satisfaction expressed by older Latinos and Latinas when compared to African American and White older people (F. Johnson et al., 1988). Many older Latinos and Latinas have poor mental health and/or poor physical health, in terms of chronic illness, activity limitations, and days spent in bed (AARP, 1986; F. Johnson et al., 1988). Twice as many older Latinos and Latinas than Anglos are hospitalized in state mental institutions (Baruth & Manning, 1991). Many Latino and Latina elders are cared for at home, and 85% of those living outside of nursing homes have at least one chronic illness (AARP, 1986; Baruth & Manning, 1991). For example, 33% of Latinos and Latinas aged 65–74 have diabetes (Pouliot, 1996).

Older Asian Americans also are more likely to continue working, with 16% remaining in the workforce after age 75 (Baruth & Manning, 1991). Many Asian American elders never learned English, and many live in poverty. For example, among Chinese elders the incidence of poverty is higher than among Black or Spanish-speaking elders (Office of Special Concerns, 1974). Although hypertension and other health matters are also a concern, intergenerational family issues are the most frequent reason older Asian Americans come to counseling (Baruth & Manning, 1991). Generational differences in the United States have a major effect on older Asian Americans, because many of them believe and expect that younger family members will take care of them, and this does not always happen (Baruth & Manning, 1991). Counselors may also need to assess older Asian American clients for suicide potential, because the suicide rate for Asian American older people is three times the national average. Older Asian American men without families are especially vulnerable.

There are 1.75 million older gay men and lesbians in the United States (Berger, 1984). According to an over-40 homosexual, "young gays feel about old gays the same way I felt about them when I was young . They are relics" (Berger, 1984, p. 60). Several factors that contribute to the psychological health of older gay men are their level of connection with the gay community, their identification with homosexuality, their lower concern with concealing their sexual orientation, and their satisfactory sex life (Berger, 1980).

Cultural Values

Little information is available to guide counselors in regard to the specific values of older people. Even the information that is available may change, as the values of one elderly cohort, who grew up with the impact of certain historical events (e.g., the Great Depression or the world wars), may differ substantially from those of the next generation of older people.

According to J. E. Myers and Schwiebert (1996), older people in the United States value their ability to function independently. This makes an event such as the loss of the capacity to drive particularly difficult, symbolizing the beginning of loss of independence. Similarly, many older people may prefer to live on their own and not be dependent on or a burden to their adult children.

Keeping things to oneself or "not airing one's dirty laundry in public" is another commonly held value among older people (J. E. Myers & Schwiebert, 1996). This may contribute to their reluctance to seek counseling (Waxman, Carner, & Klein, 1984) and difficulty with self-disclosure during the counseling process (J. E. Myers & Schwiebert, 1996). Older people may lack a comfortable vocabulary for discussing their feelings, which may lead them to report emotional concerns in terms of physical difficulties.

Perhaps because of an increased awareness of their vulnerability, many older people express great concern over crime, even though statistics indicate that they are less likely than younger people to be victimized by crime (J. E. Myers & Schwiebert, 1996). Counselors can help older clients determine which of their fears are realistic and which are exaggerated.

Indigenous Treatment Methods

Although there are no published accounts of specific treatments that have been developed by and for older people, the process of life review seems to be a culturally compatible technique that has gained widespread use in counseling older people. Life review involves asking the client to look back over his or her life and recall life events and experiences—essentially "tell stories" about his or her life—with a goal of assessing and internalizing the client's life goals (J. E. Myers & Schwiebert, 1996). The counselor may ask the client to reflect on a certain period or specific life events to evoke memories for discussion and review. Written or taped autobiographies, reunions, genealogies, scrapbooks, diaries, photographs, and other material can be used as stimuli for the life review process (Malde, 1988; J. E. Myers & Schwiebert, 1996). Life review is particularly useful in resolving Erikson's (1963) adult development stage of ego integrity versus despair. The counselor can help the client identify events that are remembered negatively and reframe them in a more positive fashion.

☐ Counseling Issues

Age and Diagnosis

Depression, organic brain syndromes, and dementias are the most frequent psychiatric diagnoses given to older people (Eichler & Parron, 1987). Roughly 22% of people aged 65 and older have some form of mental disorder (Gatz & Smyer, 1992). It is important that the diagnosis be accurate, because although the observed symptoms may be similar in older people, treatment and prognosis are very different for depression versus dementia or Alzheimer's disease (Fry, 1986).

Diagnosis is complicated, however, because up to one third of older people with a medical disorder may also have depressive symptoms (Butler & Lewis, 1995). Among the most common physical conditions that may complicate fully understanding and appropriately counseling older people are arthritis, hypertension, hearing impairment, heart disease, arteriosclerosis, visual impairment, and diabetes (J. E. Myers & Schwiebert, 1996). Medications are a further complication. Many older people take several medications, and these are often prescribed by different physicians, filled at different pharmacies, or both. Symptoms could be due to either side effects or drug interactions. S. M. Wolfe, Fugate, Hulstrand, and Kamimoto (1988) found that more than two out of every three older people take some form of drugs. The average was two prescription and two over-the-counter drugs every day plus two social drugs (i.e., alcohol, nicotine). Older men averaged 7.5 drugs per day, and older women averaged 4.7 drugs per day. People over age 80 are most likely not to take their medication properly (Human Capital Initiative, 1993).

Depression

Depression is the most common mental health concern in older people (J. E. Myers & Schwiebert, 1996). Almost 5 million older people in the United States experience significant symptoms of depression, and more than 1 million have major depression (Human Capital Initiative, 1993). It is important to keep in mind, however, that the prevalence of depression in older people is lower than among young adults aged 25–44 (Robins et al., 1984). Unfortunately, most people seek treatment for their depression from a primary care physician rather than a mental health professional, and in roughly half the instances their depression is undiagnosed (Human Capital Initiative, 1993, Sturm & Wells, 1995). Depression in older people manifests itself somewhat differently than in other adults (J. E. Myers & Schwiebert, 1996). Older people report more physical symptoms of depression, which may include lack of appetite, constipation, fatigue, headaches, and difficulty breathing. Although women in general are more likely to be depressed, men are more frequently depressed among people who have lived more than 80 years.

Older men and women commit suicide more frequently than the average U.S. citizen; this is especially true for White men over age 80 (Butler & Lewis, 1995; Human Capital Initiative, 1993). Suicide rates may actually be underestimated, because the statistics do not include less obvious means, such as not eating or taking medication, delaying treatment, or taking unnecessary physical risks (Butler & Lewis, 1995). Older people who attempt suicide also tend to do so more successfully (Osgood, 1985). They may give fewer warning signals prior to their attempts. The most dangerous time for suicide in severely depressed older people may be 2–4 weeks after medical treatment for depression begins, when energy levels increase to the point where they are able to attempt suicide (J. E. Myers & Schwiebert, 1996).

Suicide in older people is perhaps best prevented by diagnosing and treating depression early. Cognitive and behavioral treatments are most successful with depressed older people, and few do not respond to treatment. Primary prevention of depression might include reducing isolation through participation in community center activities, involvement in church, wearing prescribed hearing aids, continuing physical exercise, increasing social and communication skills, and doing volunteer work (Human Capital Initiative, 1993; J. E. Myers & Schwiebert, 1996).

Grief and Loss

Among the major sources of stress for older people are losses: loss of income, loss of role and status, loss of a spouse, loss of cognitive functioning, and loss of physical health (Cox, 1988). Loss has been described as the predominant theme in the lives of older people (McDougall, 1993). Kubler-Ross (1969) described several stages of grief (e.g., shock, numbness, denial, and acceptance) that people may experience to varying degrees after a loss. Grief over the loss of a spouse may take up to 2 years to be resolved, but pathological grief might be indicated by either the persistence of severe grief symptoms 8–10 weeks following a loss (J. E. Myers & Schwiebert, 1996) or severe interference with daily functioning (Butler & Lewis, 1995). People who lose a spouse must often also learn to cope with a change in income, spending time alone, or acquiring household skills (Teachers Insurance and Annuity Association–College Retirement Equities Fund [TIAA-CREF], 1996). A counselor can assist an older client in preparing for his or her own or a loved one's death by helping resolve conflicts with family and significant others, discussing the client's feelings about death and the perception of death as the final stage of life, helping the client make final legal and other arrangements, and helping him or her review his or her life (J. E. Myers & Schwiebert, 1996).

Alzheimer's Disease and Other Chronic Illnesses

Illnesses in older people tend to be chronic, progressive, and multiple (J. E. Myers & Schwiebert, 1996). Chronic illness may lead to grief over changes in body image, physical limitations, and increasing dependence on others. Counselors can help older clients who are dealing with chronic illness plan their day-to-day activities, manage their medications, and modify their homes for safety purposes. Counselors also can help family members learn to differentiate between normal changes accompanying age and changes that are caused by ongoing physical illness.

A specific chronic illness that affects many older people is Alzheimer's disease, an organic brain syndrome discovered by Alois Alzheimer in 1907 (J. E. Myers & Schwiebert, 1996). Alzheimer's disease is very difficult to diagnose. Only after all other organic brain syndromes have been ruled out is a diagnosis of Alzheimer's disease given (American Psychiatric Association, 1994). Gradual onset, usually after age 65, a genetic history of Alzheimer's, and an absence of physical illness tend to indicate the disease. Approximately 10% of people over age 65, and 47% of those over age 85, have a probable diagnosis of Alzheimer's disease (Baruth &

Manning, 1991). However, the presence of plaques and tangles during postmortem examination of the brain is currently the definitive diagnostic test for Alzheimer's disease, and no certain cause or cure is known (J. E. Myers & Schwiebert, 1996).

Alzheimer's is progressive, with most people living 8–10 years with the disease after its onset. Memory loss and an inability to recognize family members are characteristic of the disease. J. E. Myers and Schwiebert suggested that counselors educate clients with Alzheimer's about the nature and course of the disease, help them express their feelings, and aid them in getting their personal affairs in order while their cognitive functioning is less impaired.

Work and Leisure

Retirement is an important transition for older people. Financial assets are a major predictor of voluntary early retirement, and health is a major predictor of involuntary retirement (Human Capital Initiative, 1993). In addition to a decrease in income, a retired person may lose his or her sense of identity and personal worth as well as experience a shrinking of his or her social network (J. E. Myers & Schwiebert, 1996). Older people who continue to work have to deal with myths that older workers are inflexible, slow, and unable to meet physical demands even though research studies have shown that older people make reliable employees who tend to have high job satisfaction (Human Capital Initiative, 1993), low absentee rates, high motivation, and an excellent work ethic (J. E. Myers, 1994). Counselors can assist clients who are considering retirement in planning for future finances, housing, lifestyle, family interactions, socialization, medical care, nutrition, exercise, relationships, recreation, education, and re-employment once they retire (J. E. Myers & Schwiebert, 1996). Regular exercise before and after retirement, continued contact with younger people, beginning retirement planning before age 40, and sufficient funds contributed to a satisfactory retirement, according to a 1995 survey of 1,851 older people receiving annuities (TIAA-CREF, 1996). Two thirds of those surveyed also either moved or considered moving, and those who moved did so to be closer to family or friends or for a better climate. Counselors who work with older people should inform themselves about specific laws and regulations relevant to this population. For example, there is a limit to the amount a retired person may earn before his or her Social Security benefits are reduced. Also, there are often lower tuition fees for older people who attend college as well as other recreation, transportation, and housing benefits.

Caretaking and Elder Abuse

Approximately 80% of all care provided to older people is done by the family (J. E. Myers & Schwiebert, 1996). One person usually is the primary caregiver, typically either a spouse or an adult child, most often a daughter. The stress of giving care to a parent can bring about uncomfortable feelings as caretaking roles are reversed or earlier unresolved conflicts resurface.

Stress, lack of respite care, inadequate emotional support for caregivers, and lack of resources all contribute to elder abuse. Approximately 1 in 10 older people is affected by elder abuse, whether it be in family, home, or institutional care (J. E. Myers & Schwiebert, 1996). The mistreatment may include physical abuse, psychological abuse, financial/material abuse, or neglect. Psychological abuse in terms of verbal assault, isolation, lack of affection, and so on, occurs most frequently, followed by financial abuse, neglect, and physical abuse (Reis, Nahmiash, & Shrier, 1993). Elder abuse is reported less frequently than child abuse. The actual rate of elder abuse is probably higher than statistics indicate, because many older people are reluctant to report abuse received while living with an adult child for fear that the alternative—institutionalization—would be even worse. Both victims and abusers are not likely to voluntarily seek treatment.

Successful interventions for elder abuse have emphasized education and counseling for the caregiver and concrete assistance such as nursing, homemaking, or bath care, for the care receiver (Reis & Nahmiash, 1995). Empowerment groups in which abused older people can vent their feelings, support each other, and raise self-esteem are another, less frequently used treatment option. Counselors should become familiar with symptoms of elder abuse—for example, by using the Brief Abuse Screen for the Elderly (Reis et al., 1993)—and their individual state's laws regarding mandatory reporting of suspected elder abuse.

☐ Other Counseling Implications

In 1983, J. E. Myers reported that only 36% of counselor education programs offered a course on working with older people and that only 1%–4% of older people receive outpatient mental health services. Low use of mental health services has been attributed to negative attitudes on the part of both clients and counselors and to a lack of specialized training for mental health practitioners (J. E. Myers & Schwiebert, 1996). Other factors that affect use of mental health services may include real or perceived costs of treatment, and a lack of attention to indigenous values and development of counseling techniques consistent with those values.

Gerontological counseling has evolved into a specialization within the field of counseling. Many counselor education programs now offer a training specialization in gerontological counseling (J. E. Myers & Schwiebert, 1996). Counselors who work with older clients rated their most important roles as those of pre-retirement counselor and educator, bereavement counselor, family counselor, and in-service counselor educator (R. P. Johnson & Riker, 1982). The American Counseling Association has developed 10 minimum essential gerontological competencies for all counselors (see text box on pages 170–171) and 16 minimum essential competencies for gerontological counseling specialists (J. E. Myers & Sweeney, 1990). The minimum competencies for all counselors primarily focus on counselor attitudes and knowledge, and the competencies for gerontological counseling specialists emphasize skills.

Group work with older clients is a popular form of counseling, particularly in inpatient settings. There are many specific considerations for group counseling with older people, as suggested by J. E. Myers and Schwiebert (1966):

1. Groups composed of older people take longer to develop trust, and more introductory ice-breakers and other structured activities are recommended in early sessions.

2. Information- and discussion-type groups tend to be more successful. Some specific topics for groups are grandparenting roles, relationships with adult children, widowhood, retirement, life review or reminiscence, music or art therapy, health concerns (Alzheimer's or Parkinson's caregiver support), and grief.

3. Poor candidates for group membership are people who are severely mentally or hearing impaired, incontinent, psychotic, or extremely depressed.

4. Small groups—for example, 4–6 members—give older people enough time to "tell their story" and make close seating easier to accommodate any sensory deficits.

5. Group leaders need to take active-directive roles: giving information, answering questions, and self-disclosing, while avoiding use of slang and quick or unclear speech, which may be difficult for older people to understand.

Minimum Essential Gerontological Competencies

1. Exhibits positive, wellness-enhancing attitudes toward older people, including respect for the intellectual, emotional, social, vocational, physical, and spiritual needs of older individuals and the older population as a whole.

2. Exhibits sensitivity to sensory and physical limitations of older people through appropriate environmental modifications to facilitate helping relationships.

3. Demonstrates knowledge of the unique considerations in establishing and maintaining helping relationships with older people.

4. Demonstrates knowledge of human development for older people, including major psychological theories of aging, physiological aspects of "normal" aging, and dysfunctional behaviors of older people.

5. Demonstrates knowledge of social and cultural foundations for older people, including common positive and negative societal attitudes, major causes of stress, needs of family caregivers, and the implications of major demographic characteristics of the older population (e.g., numbers of women, widows, increasing numbers of older minorities).

6. Demonstrates knowledge of special considerations and techniques for group work with older people.

7. Demonstrates knowledge of lifestyle and career development concerns of older people, including the effects of age-related physical, psychological, and social changes on vocational development, factors affecting the retirement transition, and alternative careers and lifestyles for later life.

8. Demonstrates knowledge of the unique aspects of appraisal with older people, including psychological, social, and physical factors which may affect assessment, and ethical implications of using assessment techniques.

continued on next page

Minimum Essential Gerontological Competencies
continued from previous page

9. Demonstrates knowledge of sources of literature reporting research about older people and ethical issues in research with older subjects.

10. Demonstrates knowledge of formal and informal referral networks for helping older people and ethical behavior in working with other professionals to assist older people.

Note: From J. E. Myers and Sweeney (1990).

Some specific modes of group counseling for severely impaired older people in an inpatient setting that have been particularly effective are reality orientation, remotivation, and resocialization (J. E. Myers & Schwiebert, 1996). Reality orientation techniques include coordinated staff efforts to help residents maintain orientation to time, place, and person. Remotivation therapy involves structured inpatient groups that promote discussion of topics related to the "real" world and building relationships with other group members with the aim of lessening confusion and disorientation. Resocialization is akin to psychodynamic group therapy in that it focuses on interpersonal relationships and feelings. Touch can be an important affirmation of dignity and worth, especially for clients who live alone or in institutional settings, and, when touch seems appropriate, J. E. Myers and Schwiebert (1996) suggested asking the client if a hug would be all right.

Bibliotherapy is another approach worth considering with older clients. The counselor needs to assess the client's level of literacy and select reading material with a size of type appropriate for the client's eyesight. Some questions the counselor might ask to help process the meaning of the book or other material for the client (J. E. Myers & Schwiebert, 1996, p. 183) are:

- With which character did you most identify?
- How did the book make you feel?
- Whom did you like best or least in the book?
- What themes did you see in the book?

Another approach is to make use of *early recollections*. This is a technique adapted from Adlerian theory in which older clients are asked to remember and recount their earliest memories (Sweeney & Myers, 1991). The themes and patterns the client generates reflect his or her guiding principles for living. Increasing awareness of a life script then allows the client the freedom to validate or change underlying themes.

Many other specific approaches and techniques have been suggested for counseling older people, among them biofeedback and other behavioral techniques for pain (Human Capital Initiative, 1993), family therapy, peer counseling, art therapies, making therapeutic use of pets or horticulture, guided imagery, and self-hypnosis (J. E. Myers & Schwiebert, 1996). However, more research and development of counseling techniques that are culturally consistent or indigenous to older clients are needed, and the recent advances toward developing gerontological counseling specializations and essential competencies offer hope that this will occur.

In addition to becoming familiar with counseling methods and issues relevant to older people, counselors also need to educate themselves about community resources, such as Meals on Wheels, home health care, personal care, respite services, and hospice programs (J. E. Myers & Schwiebert, 1996). Information about local senior centers; assisted living; retirement; nursing facilities; and laws related to wills, trusts, and conservatorships also would be useful.

☐ Recommended Cultural Resources

Print Media

Baruth, L. G., & Manning, M. L. (1991). *Multicultural counseling and psychotherapy*. New York: Merrill.

Martz, S. H. (Ed.). (1987). *When I am an old woman, I shall wear purple*. Watsonville, CA: Papier Mache Press.

Myers, J. E., & Schwiebert, V. L. (1996). *Competencies for gerontological counseling*. Alexandria, VA: American Counseling Association.

Multimedia

Gilbert, B. (Producer). (1982). *On golden pond* [Videorecording]. Farmington Hills, MI: Twentieth Century-Fox Video.

Hoffmann, D. (1995). *Complaints of a dutiful daughter* [Videorecording]. New York: Women Make Movies.

Zanuck, R., & Zanuch, L. F. (Producers). (1989). *Driving Miss Daisy* [Film]. Burbank, CA: Warner.

Organizations

American Association of Retired Persons (AARP), 601 E St. NW, Washington, DC 20049. Phone: (202) 434-2277.

Grey Panthers, 2025 Pennsylvania Ave. NW, Suite 821, Washington, DC 20006-1813. Phone: (800) 280-5362.

Older Women's League (OWL), 666 11th St. NW, Suite 700, Washington, DC 20001. Phone: (202) 783-6686.

15

Counseling People
With Disabilities

*Disability only becomes a tragedy for me when society fails to provide the things we
need to live our lives; job opportunities or barrier free buildings for examples. It is
not a tragedy for me that I'm living in a wheelchair.*

—Judy Heumann, disability activist and Assistant Secretary
for the Office of Special Education and Rehabilitative Services
(Tainter, Compisi, & Richards, 1995, p. 31)

*For me, "physically challenged" or "differently abled" do not capture the serious-
ness and depth of our pain and struggle. A friend of mine who is visibly disabled
described her daily struggle as being "center stage but invisible"—stared at but
avoided. I want to be appreciated, and appreciate myself, for what I really deal
with. From that I derive pride and self-esteem.*

—Ricki Boden, Marriage, Family, Child Counselor
(Boden, 1992, p. 157)

☐ Histories and Diversity

People with disabilities are the nation's largest minority group, numbering 49 million (Foster, 1996a; Tainter et al., 1995). It is estimated that one in six people in the United States has limited abilities to perform some major life activity (D. M. Murphy & Murphy, 1997). Among children, 5% may experience some degree of disability (Tomes, 1992). Approximately 2 million people with disabilities are inpatients in some type of institutional setting (Tomes, 1992). This is the only minority group that any person may become a member of at any time (Foster, 1996a).

People with disabilities constitute a very diverse group. The Americans With Disabilities Act (ADA; 1990) defines people with disabilities as anyone possessing a physical or mental impairment that substantially limits one or more major life activities, or a person on record or regarded by others as having such an impairment. Caring for oneself, performing manual tasks, walking, seeing, hearing, speaking, breathing, learning, and working are all among the major life activities whose performance may be impaired. Some of the many disabling conditions included are orthopedic, visual, speech, and hearing impairments; cerebral palsy; epilepsy; muscular dystrophy; multiple sclerosis; cancer; heart disease; diabetes; mental retardation; emotional illness; specific learning disabilities; HIV disease; tuberculosis; drug addiction; and alcoholism.

In addition to variations in the specific nature of their disabilities, people with disabilities also vary in terms of the age of onset of the disability; the severity of the condition; the extent to which they identify with their disability status; and the degree to which their specific condition is accepted by others (M. Vernon & Andrews, 1989); in addition to diversity in age, sex, ethnicity, sexual orientation, and socioeconomic status. Given the amazing diversity among people grouped together because they have disabilities, it is imperative that counselors fully assess their clients and refrain from presumptive stereotyping based solely on one aspect of their client—for example, the nature of the disability. To present an overview of some of the conditions included, some general information regarding specific disabilities follows, but the possibility of overgeneralization must again be noted.

According to the 1991–1992 census, approximately 15 million people in the United States have some hearing loss (D. M. Murphy & Murphy, 1997). Forty-six percent to 60% of the deaf population deals with unemployment, substance abuse, criminal behavior, or poor mental health (J. Vernon, 1995). In one study, 53% of the deaf mothers whose children had been referred to Child Protective Service had problems with substance abuse (Moser & Rendon, 1992). Although an estimated 40,000 deaf people in this country may have substantial psychopathology, only 1 in 50 receives the mental health services he or she needs (Pollard, 1996). There is only one inpatient substance abuse program, in St. Paul, Minnesota, that is specifically designed to meet the needs of deaf patients, and fewer than half of the states have any inpatient mental health units for deaf people at all (J. Vernon, 1995).

Among people with a visual impairment there is great variability within the population based on degree of impairment alone, because 70%–80% of all legally blind people in the United States have some sight (D. M. Murphy & Murphy, 1997). For someone with a visual impairment, just getting to the counselor's office can be daunting. During the initial phone contact it would help to give very thorough and explicit directions to the office, including the size and shape of the building; the number of buildings, driveways, or pathways from the nearest cross street; the location of the door; the layout of the floor plan and furniture; a description of the waiting area; and so on (Harsh, 1993).

A large subpopulation of people with mobility impairments are people with spinal cord injuries. Among people with spinal cord injuries, 82% are male, and the men tend to have more serious injuries than women (Page et al., 1987). Age of onset is highest in the 15- to 24-year-old group. No other disability affects sexual functioning as profoundly as spinal cord injury (Parker, 1983). The effects include difficulties with mobility, sexual performance, and forming and maintaining relationships with the opposite sex (Page et al., 1987). These difficulties may contribute to the erroneous myth that people with spinal cord injuries are asexual. Counselors can educate themselves about alternate sources of sexual arousal and gratification. Some recommendations for teaching students with mobility impairments that may apply to counseling as well are to make sure that the room is accessible, plan for unavoidable tardiness due to transportation delays, and understand and accommodate any absences caused by required medical treatment (D. M. Murphy & Murphy, 1997). If a client prefers later appointments, this may be due to anticipation of personal assistants being often tardy or unreliable and not to resistance to counseling.

Given that 15% of all adults report signs or symptoms of mental illness in the preceding month (Tomes, 1992), the number of people affected by emotional disabilities is enormous. The major impact of mental health problems as measured by life years lost is from depressive disorders, self-inflicted injuries, Alzheimer's disease or dementia, and alcohol dependence ("Disability from mental health problems," 1995). However, the full impact of emotional and cognitive disabilities may not be known, because people with learning disabilities or other hidden disabilities may not be included in reported statistics. Many adults who are now diagnosed with learning disabilities may not have known they had a disability for years because diagnostic testing was not easily available when they were in their youth. Also, children and adolescents with learning disabilities often develop low self-esteem or passive learning styles that later affect their productivity or ability to ask for help as adults (D. M. Murphy & Murphy, 1997; Palombo, 1979).

Like many other minority groups, people with disabilities have been subject to stereotypes and discrimination and these negative perceptions and actions have been described as *ablism* (Tainter et al., 1995). According to Riger (1992), people with disabilities have a personal and collective history of devaluation, marginalization, and exclusion. A 1985 Harris poll revealed that 74% of Americans with disabilities recognize a common identity with other disabled people, and 45% believe they are a "minority group in the same sense as African Americans and Hispanics" (Tainter et al., 1995). Stereotypes of people with disabilities portray them as abnormal; helpless; heroic and inspirational; invisible; childlike; in need of pity or charity; and as the smiling poster child, appreciative of even second-class status (Harsh, 1993; Murphy & Murphy, 1997; Tainter et al., 1995). The "spread phenomenon" refers to the mistaken belief that if one disability is present there must be others, such that a person with a physical disability is assumed to be impaired mentally or emotionally as well (D. M. Murphy & Murphy, 1997). There also is a medical model belief that having a disability means being less than whole and that therefore a person with a disability must want and need to be "cured." Examples of wanting to be cured are a person who prefers to try to walk painstakingly rather than make use of the greater mobility afforded by a wheelchair or another who struggles to lip read or speak when using an interpreter or a pad and pencil would actually yield better communication (Tainter et al., 1995; M. Vernon & Andrews, 1989).

A brief chronology of events relevant to people with disabilities (adapted from Pollard, 1996) is listed in the box on page 178. Although many of the events are specific to people with hearing impairments, they have implications for people with other disabilities and may be suggestive of political changes and legal rulings to come.

Native Americans have the highest proportion of people with disabilities among ethnic minority groups in the United States (Tomes, 1992). One urban study of Native Americans with disabilities found diabetes, followed by arthritis in women and substance abuse in men, to be the most frequent disabling condition (Marshall, 1996). Specific tribal beliefs may be attached to certain disabilities, which can complicate the counseling process. For example, the Dine'h have a legend that attributes seizures to incest between siblings, a belief that contributes to greater feelings of stigmatization and shame among Dine'h who are epileptic (Levy, 1987). Common barriers to rehabilitation services for Native Americans include lack

**A Brief Chronology of Events Relevant
to People With Disabilities**

1965   *Dictionary of American Sign Language* (Stokoe, Casterline,
& Croneberg, 1965) is published, showing that American Sign Language is a sophisticated, complex language
that is distinct from English.

1988   Deaf Freedom Day (March 13) redefined the focus and
qualifications for Gallaudet University's president and
board of trustees.

1990   Americans With Disabilities Act protects people with
disabilities from discrimination in employment, public
accommodations, transportation, and telecommunica-
tions.

1994   Tugg *v.* Towey ruling in U.S. district court decrees that
mental health services provided through sign language
interpreters are not equivalent to services hearing
people receive, thereby violating the Americans With
Disabilities Act.

of transportation, long distances to treatment centers, and lack of vocational training and employment opportunities (Marshall, 1996; W. E. Martin, 1988). Cultural barriers also hinder treatment, as evidenced by a survey of 332 vocational rehabilitation counselors who work with American
Indians (W. E. Martin, 1988). The counselors tended to rate clients who
were more acculturated to the dominant society as having more success
with the rehabilitation services they received and rated government rehabilitation services as more willing to support Native American healing practices for clients who lived on a reservation.

African American mothers of children with disabilities consistently
reported less stress, feeling less overwhelmed, and feeling less personally
burdened than other mothers in general, according to research reviewed
by Rogers-Dulan and Blacher (1995), who suggested that flexible family

roles, informal adoption, and help from extended family and the Black church all contribute to family support in making it easier to raise a child with a disability. African American family values that (a) all children are important, (b) the family is collectively responsible for raising children, (c) "fictive" kin and foster children are part of the family, and (d) family ties should be strong all help provide a buffer when a family member has a disability. Religion may have an influence on family adjustment as well, but its effects are not clearly known. Religious beliefs may facilitate accepting and finding meaning in the disability; however, religious implications of guilt, wrongdoing, or failure on the part of the parent could contribute to overprotectiveness and feelings of inadequacy. Rogers-Dulan and Blacker urged counselors and other service providers to coordinate their efforts to augment rather than replace the assistance exchange already present in many African American communities.

Cultural values may have an effect on how Latinos and Latinas deal with disabilities. Those clients who have an attitude of fatalism about their lives may be more difficult to motivate toward rehabilitation. An injured Latino or Latina who values family over work may be reluctant to relocate away from their extended family for better employment prospects elsewhere. For those men who place great importance on the integrity of their bodies, having to stay home "like a woman" because of a disability may contribute to depression or alcoholism. In contrast, other disabilities may receive little emphasis. Mild disabilities that do not impinge on a child's ability to form and maintain social relationships may not be considered disabilities at all (DeLaGarza, 1996).

Asian Americans have the lowest proportion of people with disabilities among the ethnic minority groups in the United States (Tomes, 1992). However, cultural beliefs may contribute to possibly inaccurate reporting rates. Some Asian cultures promote the belief that disabilities are the result of the actions of previous ancestors, making public knowledge of a disability a cause for family shame. For example, the Chinese are less positive toward people with disabilities than Whites are, and they are even less positive toward people with mental disabilities than they are toward people with physical disabilities. An attitude of acceptance of trauma or suffering as part of life may aid in psychological adjustment to disability but hinder rehabilitation efforts (F. Chan, Lam, Wong, Leung, & Fang, 1988).

Most caregivers are female, and this overlaps with women's issues of multiple role strain and making time for oneself. Disability may have additional effects on the lives of gay men and lesbians, because health insurance policies, legal wills, and other survivor preparations may be either unavailable or more complicated if someone in the family is homosexual (Roland, 1994).

☐ **Cultural Values**

Language

Language is an important concern when counseling some people with a disability. This is especially important with deaf clients. According to one estimate, only 30% of spoken English is understandable through lip reading ("Deaf culture," 1995), making American Sign Language (ASL) the primary language for full communication for most deaf people. ASL is a much different language from English, having its own vocabulary, syntax, grammar, homonyms, and pattern of discourse (Pollard, 1996). In addition, facial expressions, body movements, and space around the body may have specific semantic or grammatical functions, unlike in English. If a counselor is fluent in ASL it is important that he or she keep in mind that all hearing impaired people do not necessarily like to use ASL, and they do not all lip read. D. M. Murphy and Murphy (1997) made several recommendations for teachers that can also be applied to counselors: get the client's attention before talking; face the client, not an interpreter; speak slowly and clearly; use short sentences; make use of facial expressions and gestures; and ask the client to repeat or write down anything that you do not understand.

Disability Culture

Before the early 1980s, little was written about disability that was not clinical in nature, and even less was written by people with disabilities (Braunstein, 1997). Since then a "disability culture" of art, music, and literature has evolved. "Disability culture is disabled people talking about ourselves," according to writer and performance artist Cheryl Wade (Braunstein, 1997, p. 30). Disability culture implies a cultural identity based on a shared history of oppression. Steven Brown, cofounder of the Institute of Disability Culture (Braunstein, 1997, p. 30), states that "Most importantly, we are proud of ourselves as people with disabilities. We claim our disabilities with pride as part of our identity." Cultural transmission is difficult, because most disabled children are not born to disabled parents. There is a disability press, including publications such as *The Disability Rag*, and a weekly nationwide live radio show, "On a Roll."

Deaf Culture

More has been written about the cultural aspects of deafness than of any other disability. Most deaf people view themselves as part of a linguistic and cultural minority and not as disabled ("Deaf culture," 1995). People who identify with deafness as a minority group experience tend to capitalize the *D* in *Deaf* as an indication of cultural identification, whereas *deaf* with a small *d* refers to the physical condition of hearing impairment and is used more frequently among people who lost their hearing as adults. The solidarity and strength of Deaf culture is notable given that 90% of deaf people have hearing parents ("Deaf culture," 1995; Sudbury, 1993), and their language acquisition and introduction to the culture are primarily through peers.

Schools for the deaf, often boarding schools that provide a sense of "home," and Deaf clubs, social organizations owned and operated by Deaf people, are vital institutions that help to pass on Deaf cultural traditions (Bienvenue & Colonomous, 1988). For example, Deaf culture tends to value direct communication more than hearing culture does (Sudbury, 1993). This has many implications for counseling with respect to how humor, assertiveness, and family communications are perceived between Deaf and hearing people.

Deaf culture values deaf children. Deaf adults may make special efforts to spend time with them in order to help the children develop positive attitudes and self-acceptance (Bienvenue & Colonomous, 1988). Mainstreaming deaf children may make it more difficult for them to make connections with the Deaf community. The likelihood that a deaf child will be improperly evaluated or treated by a professional who has had no training in deafness is also greatly increased (J. Vernon, 1995).

Cochlear implantation, a medical procedure that may enable a deaf person to hear, is a controversial issue. Deaf people who view deafness as a cultural minority status oppose the more medical view of deafness as an undesirable disability that must be remedied (Pollard, 1996). The cultural view has been adopted by the American Deafness and Rehabilitation Association, a multidisciplinary network of professionals who work with the Deaf, which uses the acronym *ADARA* in order to de-emphasize the negative connotation of "rehabilitation" in its name. Pollard (1996) noted that cross-cultural legitimacy and ASL fluency are achievable only through consistent interaction with deaf people above and beyond the service provider's professional training.

☐ Counseling Issues

Career

Although two out of three people with a disability want to work, only half of disabled people are employed because of hiring discrimination or a lack of transportation (Tainter et al., 1995). Underemployment is also a significant problem. For example, many deaf clients feel stuck in their jobs yet do not assert themselves because they feel lucky to even have a job (Marino, 1996).

Employment discrimination is difficult to eliminate. The ADA does not allow employers to collect health or mental health histories, ask whether an applicant has a disability, test for disabilities, or require a pre-employment medical exam (ADA, 1990; Romei, 1991; Youngstrom, 1992a). The ADA does allow employers to ask about abilities needed to perform a job. But although the ADA prohibits overt discrimination, Foster (1996a) asserted that more subtle bias still remains. This occurs even though accommodations for disabled workers are relatively inexpensive. A U.S. Department of Labor (1982) survey of federal contractors who made efforts to hire workers with disabilities reported that 81% of the respondents spent $500 or less on accommodations. Also, turnover is low among employees with disabilities, so companies can easily justify any accommodation costs (Romei, 1991). When appropriate, highly skilled workers are more often provided environmental adaptations or special equipment, whereas less skilled workers more often receive job redesign, retraining, or selective placement as accommodations (U.S. Department of Labor, 1982).

The career counseling considerations for a client with a disability depend greatly on the specific nature of the disability. For example, for people with autism, the social aspects of work may be the most problematic, and certain occupations may decrease the likelihood of social problems (Grandin, 1996). Grandin noted that some freelance businesses—such as piano tuning, automobile repair, computer programming, and graphic arts—require skills that many autistic people possess, such as perfect pitch, mechanical ability, or artistic talent.

Using nontraditional job-seeking strategies, such as networking, and avoiding personnel departments, has been recommended for people with autism, who may not interview well (Grandin, 1996). This may also be helpful advice for clients with other emotional or communicative disabilities. Harsh (1993) suggested that a counselor of a visually impaired client become knowledgeable of the types of skills he or she can acquire though rehabilitation training, and this kind of knowledge would be useful with respect to many other disabilities as well.

Family

The effects of disability on family functioning may in part depend upon which phase the family is in in terms of dealing with disability. Roland (1994) described three phases: crisis, chronic, and terminal.

The *crisis* phase includes the symptoms the family must deal with prior to obtaining a diagnosis, when receiving the diagnosis, and during the period of initial adjustment after diagnosis. The primary issue during this phase is managing change and determining what must change and what can stay the same in the family's and the individual's senses of identity. The family's and the individual's histories of dealing with change are relevant here (Roland, 1994). Feelings of shock, denial, anger, and depression, which are typical of the grief process, may permeate the initial adjustment to disability.

The *chronic* phase involves day-to-day coping and stamina in dealing with a condition that may be permanent or last for many years. The family's history of dealing with constant stressors can give an indication of its strengths and help anticipate problems that may arise (Roland, 1994). The magnitude of daily stress that the client experiences needs to be understood from the client's own perspective. For example, Riger (1992) noted that the continual frustration architectural barriers present to some people with disabilities can instill feelings of shame, alienation, victimization, hurt, and outrage that can be as strong as the emotions resulting from physical or sexual assault.

The *terminal* phase includes preterminal preparation, death, and grief. Emotions are especially significant in this phase, along with attitudes toward hospice, death, and the culturally normative rituals that surround death (Roland, 1994).

Wright (1983) described overprotectiveness as a primary issue for families of children with disabilities. The counselor can work directly with the parents to help dissipate their feelings of guilt or urge them to participate in a parent discussion group, which can be useful in setting realistic expectations. Cultural reactions to disability may provide secondary gains for the client or family, which may help or hinder the adjustment process. Responsibilities and expectations of the client or family may be temporarily suspended in some cultures. The counselor may also want to explore the role of a patient in the client's culture (Roland, 1994).

Abuse

A counselor should be particularly watchful for signs of physical or sexual abuse when working with a client with a disability. Research has indicated that disabled children are more likely to have been physically or sexually abused than their peers (Courtois, 1988). Women with disabilities who are abused may not report the abuse because they may have no accessible shelter to go to and no alternatives for long-term help if the abuse is perpetrated by a care provider.

☐ Treatment Implications

When working with a client with a disability, a helpful general approach may be to offer assistance rather than to automatically provide it (D. M. Murphy & Murphy, 1997). For example, Harsh (1993) suggested that the easiest way to determine the level of assistance required by a person with a visual impairment is to ask, "Would you like to take my arm?" This kind of helpful but flexible stance addresses the great diversity among people with disabilities in terms of level of impairment and their degree of identification with having a disability. Counselors also should be willing to expand their role to include coordination among community agencies and advocacy on behalf of their clients with disabilities when appropriate (Vacc & Clifford, 1995).

Counselors must be on their guard for countertransference issues that may inhibit empathy for their clients with disabilities. Michael Berube, an able-bodied man, wrote that "Understanding disability as an integral part of the human condition . . . means imagining ourselves in their places— and that may be too much of a psychological burden for us to bear" (Berube, 1997, p. 85).

Some frequent counseling themes when working with people who are dealing with disabilities are feelings of abandonment, inclusion and exclusion, anger, and specialness (Boden, 1992). Rehabilitation counseling is a specialization in its own right within the field of counseling, and it is beyond the scope of this book to try to cover all of the counseling issues that are relevant to people with disabilities. The reader is encouraged to take additional coursework related to rehabilitation counseling for more specific information about the psychological and physical adjustments that a client who is living with a disability must make.

☐ Recommended Cultural Resources

Print Media

Berube, M. (1998). *Life as we know it*. New York: Random House.

Davis, L. J. (1995). *Enforcing normalcy*. New York: Verso.

Dolnick, E. (1993, September). Deafness as culture. *Atlantic Monthly, 272,* 37–53.

Linton, S. (1998). *Claiming disability: Knowledge and identity*. New York: New York University Press.

Mairs, N. (1996). *Waist-high in the world: A life among the nondisabled*. Boston: Beacon Press.

Murphy, D. M., & Murphy, J. T. (1997). Enabling disabled students. *NEA Higher Education Journal, 13,* 41–52.

Shapiro, J. (1994). *No pity*. New York: Random House.

Sontag, S. (1989). *Illness as metaphor*. New York: Doubleday.

Thomson, R. G. (1997). *Extraordinary bodies*. New York: Columbia University Press.

Trent, J. W., Jr. (1995). *Inventing the feeble mind*. Berkeley: University of California Press.

Multimedia

Bienvenue, M., & Colonomous, B. (1988). *An introduction to American deaf culture* [Videotape]. Silver Spring, MD: Sign Media.

Cornfield, S. (Producer). (1981). *The elephant man* [Videorecording]. Hollywood, CA: Paramount Home Video.

Sugarman, B., & Palmer, P. (Producers). (1987). *Children of a lesser god* [Videorecording]. Hollywood, CA: Paramount Pictures Corporation.

Organizations

ADARA (American Deafness and Rehabilitation Association), P.O. Box 27, Roland, AR 72135. Phone: (501) 868-8850.

National Association of the Deaf (NAD), 814 Thayer Ave., Silver Spring, MD 20910. Phone: (310) 587-1788 and (310) 587-1789.

Developing Multicultural Counseling Competency

Becoming culturally skilled is an active process, that . . . is ongoing, and that . . . is a process that never reaches an end point. (D. W. Sue & Sue, 1990, p. 146)

The purpose of this book has been to introduce the reader to basic issues and concepts related to multicultural counseling and to develop awareness of and appreciation for the need for culture-specific knowledge in the counseling process. As multicultural awareness and knowledge increase, growth in multicultural counseling skills is the next step. Practical experience and ongoing interaction with diverse clients and their cultures are crucial to the development of multicultural skills. Developing skill in multicultural counseling will be an ongoing continuing-education need for counselors well into the 21st century as the population of the United States continues to diversify, especially in terms of ethnicity and age. This final chapter on the topic of multicultural counseling includes a review of current multicultural theory, the status of the movement toward establishing multicultural counseling competencies for all counselors, training issues with respect to multicultural counseling, and multiculturalism with the counseling profession.

☐ Multicultural Theory

As noted in Chapter 1, there is great need for more comprehensive theory development about the nature of multicultural counseling. The most substantial contributions to multicultural theory so far have been more limited in scope: cultural adaptation theories, identity development theories, application of internal–external locus-of-control theory to multicultural counseling (D. W. Sue & Sue, 1990), triad training models (Pedersen, 1977, 1978, 1994), and so on. The field would be unified by a broad conceptual framework for the process of multicultural counseling that incorporates the counselor's own level of cultural awareness; an individually tailored assessment of the client's cultural background, cultural adaptation processes, and cultural identity development; the sociopolitical influences on both client and counselor; the use of both traditional and indigenous counseling techniques; and the complex interaction among client, counselor, and the societal context surrounding them.

The most highly developed attempt at creating a comprehensive theory of multicultural counseling to date has been the book *A Theory of Multicultural Counseling and Therapy*, edited by Derald Sue, Allen Ivey, and Paul Pedersen (1996). These scholars, who have themselves made substantial contributions to the field of multicultural counseling (Wehrly, 1991), have criticized the narrow focus of earlier counseling theories on either feelings, thoughts, behaviors, or social systems while ignoring biological, spiritual, political, and cultural influences. The broad metatheory of multicultural counseling and therapy (MCT) that they propose has as a base six propositions and many ensuing corollaries. The first proposition states that MCT is a theory about theories and offers an organizational framework or alternative worldview. The second proposition recognizes the multiple levels of experience (individual, group, and universal) and contexts (individual, family, and cultural milieu) that affect both counselor and client and whose many interrelationships need to be central in treatment. Proposition 3 recognizes the importance of cultural identity development. The fourth proposition calls for using treatment goals and modalities that are culturally consistent for the client. According to W. M. Lee (1996), Propositions 5 and 6 are the most radical in comparison to traditional theories of counseling. Proposition 5 expands the counselor's role beyond direct treatment of the individual, family, or group to incorporate prevention and system intervention, and Proposition 6 refocuses the basic goal of counseling on the "liberation of consciousness" using both Western and non-European modes of helping.

Such efforts to elaborate and refine the nature of the multicultural counseling process may be part of a cataclysmic transformation that lies ahead for the entire field of counseling (W. M. Lee, 1996). The nature of the counseling process and what it means to be a counselor may be need to be transformed in order for the field of counseling to stay current with and relevant to the changing demographic makeup of the United States and other countries.

☐ Multicultural Competencies

Much work has been done in regard to specifying the competencies any counselor would need in order to function adequately in a multicultural counseling relationship. The seminal article on this topic is a position paper prepared by a group of counseling psychologists within the American Psychological Association (D. W. Sue et al., 1982). The paper described 11 characteristics of culturally skilled counseling psychologists in the broad areas of beliefs and attitudes, knowledge, and skills. This initial work was further developed by the Association for Multicultural Counseling and Development (1986; D. W. Sue et al., 1992a, 1992b). There are currently 31 proposed cross-cultural competencies and objectives in the broad areas of counselor awareness of their own cultural values and biases (9 competencies), their awareness of the client's worldview (7 competencies), and culturally appropriate intervention strategies (15 competencies). See Appendix B for the specific competencies.

Several instruments have been developed that attempt to measure multicultural competency. The four existing measures of multicultural counseling competency all were developed with respect to D. W. Sue et al.'s (1982) position paper (Ponterotto, Rieger, Barrett, & Sparks, 1994; Pope-Davis & Dings, 1995).

The Cross-Cultural Counseling Inventory–Revised (CCCI–R) (LaFromboise, Coleman, & Hernandez, 1991) is the only measure that is not a self-report instrument. It is filled out by a supervisor or other professional who rates the counselor on 20 Likert scale items. A coefficient alpha reliability of .95 and interrater reliability in the .78–.84 range have been reported for the CCCI–R, and it appears to measure one unidimensional factor (Ponterotto et al., 1994).

The other three measures are all self-report instruments using Likert scale ratings. The first measure, The Multicultural Awareness-Knowledge-Skills Survey (MAKSS; D'Andrea, Daniels, & Heck, 1991) consists of three 20-item scales designed to measure awareness, knowledge, and skills. There are reasonably high reliabilities, measured by Cronbach's alpha, for the three scales (.75, .90, and .96 for Awareness, Knowledge, and Skills, respectively), and there is some evidence of criterion validity in that post-test MAKSS scores for a group that was given multicultural training rose significantly (D'Andrea et al., 1991; Pope-Davis & Dings, 1995).

The second measure, the Multicultural Counseling Awareness Scale (MCAS-B; Ponterotto et al., 1994) contains two subscales: the 14-item Awareness scale and the 28-item Knowledge/Skills scale. As with the MAKSS, the Awareness scale has a lower coefficient alpha reliability of .78, whereas the Knowledge/Skills and overall reliabilities are .93 and .92, respectively. Research with the MCAS-B indicates Knowledge/Skills scale differences between people who have taken a workshop, seminar or course and people without such multicultural training, between non-White and White test takers, and between people with PhDs compared to those with master's or bachelor's-level educations (Pope-Davis & Dings, 1995). No differences on the Awareness scale were found for these same samples. These results suggest that the two scales do measure different aspects of multicultural competency, providing limited support for a two-factor multicultural competency model.

The third measure, the Multicultural Counseling Inventory (MCI; Sodowsky, Taffe, Gutkin, & Wise, 1994) was developed with the use of factor analysis. It measures four factors: Multicultural Counseling Skills (11 items), Multicultural Awareness (10 items), Multicultural Counseling Knowledge (11 items), and Multicultural Counseling Relationship (8 items). Cronbach's alpha reliability coefficients range from .67 (Relationship) to .80 or .81 for each of the other three scales (Pope-Davis & Dings, 1995). Significant increases were found on all scales except the relationship scale for respondents after they completed a multicultural course. The strength of the MCI is that its items are more descriptive of behaviors, whereas the MAKSS and the MCAS–B tend to focus more on attitudes. Another strength is its inclusion of a relationship scale (Ponterotto et al., 1994).

In their detailed review of the three self-report measures, Pope-Davis and Dings (1995) concluded that the MCI has the most convincing evidence to support its use. However, Ponterotto et al. (1994) concluded that no measure of multicultural competency currently has any practical utility because they all lack systematic, longitudinal validation data. Ponterotto et al. also concluded that factor analyses have provided little validation for a three-dimensional (awareness, knowledge, skill) conceptualization of multicultural competency. They also asserted that more study is needed of the relationship between scores on these measures and behavioral measures of counseling performance and counseling outcome measures. Indeed, S. Sue (1998) concluded that there has not been a single scientifically rigorous research study examining the efficacy of treatment for any ethnic minority population. He suggested that this may be due to the potentially controversial nature of ethnic minority research or to the practical, methodological, and conceptual problems in undertaking such research, which may discourage investigators from conducting multicultural studies. In any case, without more research, it is difficult to propose specific competencies on anything other than theoretical or ideological grounds.

S. Sue (1998) proposed an alternative model that also consists of three dimensions of cultural competency needed for counseling and psychotherapy. The first dimension, *scientific mindedness*, refers to the counselor's ability to carry out clinical hypothesis testing with respect to cultural and other client data. The second dimension, *dynamic sizing*, refers to a counselor's ability to know when to generalize and be inclusive and when to individualize and be exclusive with respect to a particular client. This quality allows a counselor to make use of cultural issues when relevant and to not overgeneralize or stereotype a client. The third dimension, *culture-specific expertise*, is similar to the cultural knowledge dimension included in the American Counseling Association's multicultural counseling competencies proposed and existing assessment measures. There is some research evidence that treating ethnic minority clients in ethnic-specific programs—which may include modifying therapeutic practices in consideration of cultural customs, employing bicultural–bilingual staff, culture-friendly agency procedures, and so on—has been related to lower dropout rates and longer lengths of treatment (Takeuchi, Sue, & Yeh, 1995; Yeh, Takeuchi, & Sue, 1994). However, effects on treatment outcome were unclear. This alternative model also requires further research support.

☐ Multicultural Training

Training Models

Several models have been suggested for programmatic multicultural counseling training. Ridley, Mendoza, and Kanitz (1994) described five different frameworks for approaching multicultural counseling:

1. A generic or etic framework assumes that counseling is universally applicable without empirical justification or cultural modification.

2. An emic framework may teach a general process for gathering and integrating culture-specific information at the risk of promoting stereotypes.

3. An idiographic framework uses the client as the primary data source and stresses client individuality in cultural matters.

4. An autoplastic approach requires that clients change themselves in order to fit into their cultural environment.

5. An alloplastic approach emphasizes the influences of the client's political, social, and economic environment in contributing to his or her problems and focuses on empowerment and advocacy for clients at the risk of victimization.

Counselor training programs have often taken an etic, idiographic, or autoplastic approach to multicultural counseling training, although the current emphasis in the field is toward more emic and alloplastic approaches. The former blurs the need for specific curricula related to multicultural counseling because cultural influences are viewed as no different from any other specific problem in living that an individual may face.

Wehrly (1991) described a five-stage developmental model for multicultural counselor preparation that builds on the work of Carney and Kahn (1984) and Sabnani et al. (1991). The first stage calls for a structured and supportive training environment to reduce student anxiety, encourages self-awareness through keeping a journal, and initiates cultural knowledge learning through ethnic–cultural novels and book reports. The second stage emphasizes seeking information about the student's own cultural origins and predominant values as well as researching a different ethnic culture, including circumstances of the group's entry into the United States, treatment (as immigrants, slaves, etc.), and historical help providers throughout the group's history in this country. The third stage incorporates deeper understanding of the student's personal involvement in the racism that is pervasive in the United States and stresses the importance of the counselor addressing racial–cultural differences between counselor and client during the first counseling session. The fourth and fifth stages involve direct experience working with culturally different clients in practicum and internship settings under trained supervisors.

Training Format

The two primary formats that counselor education programs have used for multicultural training are the single-course and the curriculum-infusion (Fouad, Manese, & Casas, 1992) approaches. Recent statistics indicate that 89% of doctoral programs in counseling require at least one multicultural course, and 58% infuse multicultural content throughout their coursework (Ponterotto, 1997). However, one survey of psychologists who received their degrees between 1985 and 1987 reported that only 34% of the respondents indicated that a course on diverse populations was available in their doctoral programs, only 25% had actually taken such a course during graduate school, and 46% felt that their graduate coursework had "infrequently" or "never" covered diversity (Allison, Crawford, Echemendia, Robinson, & Knepp, 1994). A single course related to multicultural counseling, the most common format for multicultural training, is often criticized. It is only a starting point for graduate students and lacks the depth needed to foster sufficient learning; has the potential to promote stereotyping; and does not allow for integration of awareness, knowledge, and skills (D'Andrea et al., 1991; Reynolds, 1995; Rooney, Flores, & Mercier, 1998). On the other hand, comprehensive infusion of multicultural content into coursework and field experience requires institutional commitment and resource allocation that many counselor training programs are either not willing or able to make (D'Andrea et al., 1991). Hills and Strozier (1992) noted that assistant and adjunct faculty are likely to be responsible for implementing multicultural training efforts. Faculty at these lower ranks generally have less knowledge of the institution, less power, and less influence in bringing about curricular change. Even when a program has made a stated commitment to include multicultural training in all its coursework, real compliance and outcomes are difficult to monitor. It is one thing to include some multicultural topics and references in course syllabi and another to truly integrate multicultural issues and perspectives into all lectures and discussions.

There are other possible formats for multicultural training in addition to single course or curriculum infusion formats. Preli and Bernard (1993) recommended contact with cultural minority people and counseling practica with minority clients as well as cultural awareness, knowledge, and skills. Enns (1993) noted that feminist therapists over the last 20 years have educated themselves by taking courses on counseling women or on feminist therapy, that most of their learning took place through personal study and research, professional workshops, informal conversations and study groups, and actual counseling experience with female clients. Multicultural training is a multifaceted, lifelong process.

In addition to the direct potential benefits of more effective treatment for multicultural clients that may result from multicultural training in counseling, other benefits are that students become more aware of multicultural issues in general, students come to believe that it is less desirable to ignore cultural differences, and students have a place to deal with their own feelings about racial issues instead of during the counseling process as countertransference reactions (Jordan, 1993). Both ethnic minority and majority counselors benefit from multicultural training. It should not be assumed that counselors from cultural minority groups are automatically able to relate to clients from the dominant culture (D. Brown, 1996). Training in multicultural counseling is also a professional licensure requirement for independent practice in at least one state (DeAngelis, 1994a). Although pre–post testing with multicultural counseling competency assessment measures suggests that single-course and workshop format multicultural counseling training results in perceived changes by participants (D'Andrea et al., 1991; Pope-Davis & Dings, 1995), research into the long-term effects of multicultural training is needed (Jordan, 1993).

A Model Training Curriculum

A model curriculum outlined in terms of awareness, knowledge, and skills is offered here that combines recommendations from several sources (Das, 1995; Enns, 1993; Fouad et al., 1992; Preli & Bernard, 1993; Ridley et al., 1994) as well my own. The elements of this model curriculum are outlined in the text box on pages 194–195, Multicultural Training Curriculum Content.

Some elements of this model curriculum are currently part of most counselor education programs (e.g., ethical knowledge, handling client resistance), many are not (e.g., second-language fluency, indigenous healing practices), and others expand the counselor's role in nontraditional directions (e.g., prevention issues, advocacy). There are substantial resources written in the area of cultural self-awareness (Katz, 1989; McIntosh, 1988), and the vast preponderance of multicultural counseling literature is concerned with culture-specific knowledge and its potential impact in counseling. However, the greatest challenge in multicultural counselor training currently is in the area of skills, "the pinpointing of specific counseling skills that would assist the counselor in making their work with an individual client culturally effective" (W. M. Lee, 1996, p. 2).

A model multicultural training program would put the curriculum content described into practice by providing opportunities for contact within the program and in the surrounding community with people from cultural minority backgrounds and by requiring practicum experience with cultural minority populations (McRae & Johnson, 1991; Preli & Bernard, 1993). Access to multicultural supervision and internship experiences relevant to diverse cases have been rated as the most effective multicultural training experiences (Allison et al., 1994). Unfortunate-

Text continues on page 196.

Multicultural Training Curriculum Content

Awareness

- Consciousness-raising with respect to issues of racism, sexism, homophobia, ageism, and ablism

- Cultural self-awareness of the counselor's own ethnic background(s) and potential reactions of clients and other implications for counseling

- Cultural self-awareness of the counselor's own gender, sexual orientation, age, and social class and potential reactions of clients and other implications for counseling

- Cultural self-awareness of the counselor's own physical and mental disabilities and potential reactions of clients and other implications for counseling

- Respecting cultural differences

Knowledge

- Sociopolitical context of counseling, including oppression, discrimination, and racism; barriers to service; and social causes of psychological distress

- Cultural and racial bias in testing issues

- Cultural identity development models

- Acculturation issues

- Cultural variations in family makeup, developmental patterns, client expectations, and views of health and illness

- Ability to critique existing theories for cultural relevance (worldview)

- Second-language fluency

- Cultural knowledge of normative characteristics of specific cultural groups

continued on next page

Multicultural Training Curriculum Content
continued from previous page

- Cultural knowledge of with in-group differences

- Indigenous healing practices

- Immigration regulations

- Laws regarding sexual harassment, hate crimes, and housing or employment discrimination

- Ethical knowledge and practice (e.g., ethical guidelines for use of indigenous techniques)

- Prevention issues

- Community resources

Skills

- Interview skills for talking about cultural differences

- Assessment of cultural background and issues

- Development of an individualized theoretical orientation

- Displaying culturally responsive behaviors

- Communicating empathy in a manner culturally recognized by the client

- Handling client resistance

- Consultation skills for communication with indigenous healers

- Case management skills

- Advocacy skills for influencing organizations

- Community outreach/organizational skills

- Group conflict resolution skills

- Teaching skills for community education

ly, only 35% of counseling doctoral programs currently offer opportunities to engage in multicultural fieldwork (Ponterotto, 1997), and 46% of psychologists surveyed felt that the supervision they received in graduate school "never" or "infrequently" addressed cultural issues (Allison et al., 1994).

Training Methods and Processes

A variety of instructional strategies have been used in multicultural training (Pedersen, 1977; Preli & Bernard, 1993; Ridley et al., 1994), including experiential self-awareness exercises (see Chapter 2 for several examples), games, and genograms, as well as didactic methods, videotape viewing, readings, writing assignments, modeling and observational learning, technology-assisted training (e.g., videotaping and reviewing counseling sessions), and supervised practice and internships. The multicultural training technique that has perhaps received the most attention is the triad role play model developed by Pedersen (1977, 1978, 1994). In this role play exercise, participants take the roles of counselor, client, and problem/anti-counselor and simulate a counseling session that may help in articulating cultural problems, anticipating resistance, diminishing counselor defensiveness, and teaching recovery skills. A modification of this exercise that substitutes a pro-counselor for the anti-counselor role gives the counselor a supportive ally and may be more helpful with beginning counselors (Neimeyer, Fukuyama, Bingham, Hall, & Mussenden, 1986) and in developing knowledge and skills (Sue, 1979, cited in McRae & Johnson, 1991). The original anti-counselor version seems more effective for developing sensitivity and awareness (Sue, 1979, cited in McRae & Johnson, 1991).

Multicultural counselor training is a complex process that combines personal growth with content learning and skill development. According to Das (1995, p. 47),

> The cognitive distance between the mental health service providers and the lower class and minority consumers can be bridged through didactic instruction, but the social and emotional distance can be reduced only through an intensive program of reeducation of the counselors, one aimed at changing their attitudes.

Effective multicultural trainers need to do more than convey information, they need to balance cognitive and emotional learning strategies and create a safe environment that nurtures personal risk-taking (Ponterotto, 1998). Effective multicultural training requires the trainer to possess many of the qualities of a good counselor as well as a good teacher. A trainer's ability to self-disclose his or her own developmental experiences with multicultural awareness has been stressed as an important characteristic of effective training (Ponterotto, 1998; Rooney et al., 1998). In addition, trainers must be cognizant of the individual cultural developmental backgrounds of their students. Each student's level of cultural identity development may vary with respect to race, gender, sexual orientation, aging, or disability dimensions (Rooney et al., 1998).

Reynolds (1995) recommended training counselor education faculty in cultural diversity content regarding specific cultural groups, how oppression works, group work, how multicultural issues affect counseling, and so on. There are good reasons for more White people to become multicultural trainers (Kiselica, 1998). White faculty who have developed multicultural expertise can be role models for White counselors who are grappling with their own cultural identity development. Lark and Paul (1998) asserted that some ethnic or cultural similarity to the trainer is important for both credibility and modeling.

☐ Multiculturalism Within the Counseling Profession

Current Status

It is estimated that by the year 2005, people with ethnic minority backgrounds will compose 27% of the nation's workforce (*Occupational Outlook Quarterly*, 1991). However, they currently represent only 11% of graduate students in the United States (Brazziel, 1987/1988). In psychology, ethnic minority students represent 20% of undergraduate psychology majors, 11% of entering graduate students, and 9% of people with doctorates, eventually resulting in only 5% of the nation's psychologists who are from ethnic minority backgrounds (Youngstrom, 1992b). Only 5% of psychology graduate students are Black, 2% are Hispanic American, 1% are Asian American, and less than 1% are Native American (Kohout, Wicherski, & Cooney, 1992). In counselor education programs, Black and Hispanic students have long been underrepresented (Atkinson, 1983). Even when ethnic minority students are enrolled in counselor education programs, they are less likely to be full-time students or in doctoral-level programs (Atkinson, 1983). There is a growing disparity between ethnic minority representation in psychology and the total ethnic minority population in the United States (Bernal, 1990).

Underrepresentation of ethnic minority people among psychology and counseling faculty also is evident. In 1994, ethnic minority faculty made up only 6.5% of psychology department faculty nationwide (DeAngelis, 1997). Ethnic minority representation is consistently lower among full-time faculty compared to part-time faculty, lower in PhD compared to master's-level departments, and lower in clinical compared to counseling psychology programs (Norcross, Hanych, & Terranova, 1996; Quintana & Bernal, 1995). Ethnic minority faculty are in positions of lower status, influence, and income. Bernal (1990) noted that the level of ethnic minority faculty in psychology graduate departments has remained relatively stable even though graduate student enrollment and doctorate-recipient figures have increased.

Representation of ethnic minorities among faculty who train service providers is somewhat better, with 8% of all full-time clinical, counseling and school psychology faculty reported as ethnic minority (Kohout et al., 1992), and specifically, 8.2% of clinical psychology and 9.9% counseling psychology faculty reported as ethnic minority (Quintana & Bernal, 1995). Ethnic minority representation among APA-approved counseling psychology faculty was 11% in another survey, with ethnic minority representation higher at lower faculty ranks (Hills & Strozier, 1992). The profession has apparently not changed dramatically since Atkinson's 1983 report indicating that ethnic minority faculty in counselor education programs are more likely to be part-time, nontenured instructors and that Asian Americans, Hispanic Americans, and Blacks were underrepresented. Ponterotto (1997) noted that only 29% of counseling doctoral programs reported having at least 30% faculty of color.

Representation issues for women are similar. Only 10% of full professors nationwide are female (Hoyt, 1989). In psychology, more full-time faculty women are employed in master's-level than doctoral-level psychology departments, and representation of women is consistently higher among part-time faculty than full-time faculty (Norcross et al., 1996). Statistics regarding representation of gay, lesbian, or bisexual faculty and faculty with disabilities are often not collected, but informal observation suggests that issues of underrepresentation are apparent for these cultural groups as well. Only 4.5% of APA members surveyed identified themselves as gay, lesbian, or bisexual, and only 2.1% reported experiencing sensory or motor impairment (Allison et al., 1994). The underrepresentation of cultural minority faculty is particularly detrimental in that an important contribution to multicultural training is facilitated by multicultural mentoring over time (Lark & Paul, 1998).

Barriers to Participation

Barriers that prevent cultural minorities from becoming counselors begin early in life and are continued throughout graduate training. These barriers are economic, social, and cultural.

Finances are a real barrier to ethnic minority graduate students. A National Science Foundation survey of doctoral recipients in psychology indicated that White students relied more on their families and teaching assistantships for financial support, Asian students relied most on teaching assistantships, and Black and Hispanic students relied most on university fellowships (Moses, 1992). A higher proportion of ethnic minority psychology graduate students enroll in doctoral-level as compared to master's-level programs, perhaps because of a greater availability of scholarships, teaching and research assistantships, and other sources of financial assistance in doctoral programs. Brazziel (1987/1988) asserted that the university itself is the most important source of money for graduate students in general but that jobs on campus seem to be more available to White graduate students. Indeed, most ethnic minority graduate students enroll on a part-time basis (Nettles, 1987), and financial constraints are a likely cause. In the 1980s an increase in loans and a decrease in grants as sources of funding began to affect minority graduate enrollment (Nettles, 1987). Extended-family responsibilities may be an extra financial stress for ethnic minority graduate students. Counselors of color reported feeling more stress in graduate school from contributing to the financial support of family members not living in their household than did White counselors (W. M. Lee, 1995).

Social isolation also is a barrier to more cultural minority students becoming counselors. Research has indicated that the number of ethnic minority students in a graduate department and contact with ethnic minority faculty outside of class are important variables and that ethnic minority students in more integrated departments were more likely to have higher grades, better adjustment, and self-perceptions that they were making good progress (DeFour & Hirsch, 1990). However, only 33% of counseling doctoral programs report having a critical mass of at least 30% ethnic minority students (Ponterotto, 1997). The majority of ethnic minority graduate students feel isolated from much of their academic environment, have few faculty mentors and, when they do have mentors, those mentors are White and usually male (DeFour & Hirsch, 1990; Leal & Menjivar, 1992). Among ethnic minority graduate students there also may be feelings of alienation from each other, little networking between cultural groups (e.g., Latinas and Latin American women; Leal & Menjivar, 1992), and few incentives for intergroup communication or cooperation.

Cultural barriers to minority graduate student success are formidable. Learning the language of academia and acclimating to professional jargon is a noted barrier to Native American women in graduate school (Macias, 1989). According to Sedlacek (Foster, 1996b) African American students on White campuses may experience verbal racial stereotyping; graffiti with racial slurs; and threats or violence in residence halls, fraternities, interracial dating, or campus athletics. The effects of institutional racism should not be underestimated. Counselors of color reported significantly more stress in graduate school from having personal experience with racial prejudice on campus and from contacts with White faculty and graduate students (W. M. Lee, 1995). Similar social and cultural barriers likely confront graduate students who are gay, lesbian, or bisexual; older; or have a disability.

Remedies

Many remedies to alleviate these barriers have been suggested on an individual level, including financial help, increased program flexibility, multimodal learning, strategies for organizing study, and mentoring (Macias, 1989; Youngstrom, 1992b). Other suggestions have been made at the institutional level. To increase ethnic minority enrollment, Ponterotto (1998) recommended that admissions criteria include experience with minority populations, multicultural research interest, experience with extensive travel or living abroad, and second-language linguistic competence. Establishing campus training institutes to offer basic, advanced, and topic-specific courses, and establishing a clearinghouse or registry of diversity consultants, college-wide multicultural curriculum committees, and an institutional multicultural awareness education program for faculty and staff are other organization-level remedies (D'Andrea & Daniels, 1991; Foster, 1996b). Multicultural competency can be included in tenure, reappointment, promotion, merit pay, and chair selection criteria and in evaluation instruments for all courses and practica (Ponterotto, 1998).

APPENDIX

Guidelines for Providers of Psychological Services to Ethnic, Linguistic, and Culturally Diverse Populations

Preamble: The Guidelines represent general principles that are intended to be aspirational in nature and are designed to provide suggestions to psychologists in working with ethnic, linguistic, and culturally diverse populations.

1. Psychologists educate their clients to the processes of psychological intervention, such as goals and expectations; the scope and, where appropriate, legal limits of confidentiality; and the psychologists' orientations.

    a. Whenever possible, psychologists provide information in writing along with oral explanations.

    b. Whenever possible, the written information is provided in the language understandable to the client.

2. Psychologists are cognizant of relevant research and practice issues as related to the population being served.

    a. Psychologists acknowledge that ethnicity and culture impacts on behavior and take those factors into account when working with various ethnic/racial groups.

    b. Psychologists seek out educational and training experiences to enhance their understanding to address the needs of these populations more appropriately and effectively. These experiences include cultural, social, psychological, political, economic, and historical material specific to the particular ethnic group being served.

    c. Psychologists recognize the limits of their competencies and expertise. Psychologists who do not possess knowledge and training about an ethnic group seek consultation with, and/or make referrals to, appropriate experts as necessary.

    d. Psychologists consider the validity of a given instrument or procedure and interpret resulting data, keeping in mind the cultural and linguistic characteristics of the person being assessed. Psychologists are aware of the test's reference population and possible limitations of such instruments with other populations.

3. Psychologists recognize ethnicity and culture as significant parameters in understanding psychological processes.

    a. Psychologists, regardless of ethnic/racial background, are aware of how their own cultural background/experiences, attitudes, values, and biases influence psychological processes. They make efforts to correct any prejudices and biases.

        Illustrative Statement: Psychologists might routinely ask themselves, 'Is it appropriate for me to view this client or organization any differently than I would if [he or she] were from my own ethnic or cultural group?'

    b. Psychologists' practice incorporates an understanding of the client's ethnic and cultural background. This includes the client's familiarity and comfort with the majority culture as well as ways in which the client's culture may add to or improve various aspects of the majority culture and/or of society at large.

Illustrative Statement: The kinds of mainstream social activities in which families participate may offer information about the level and quality of acculturation to American society. It is important to distinguish acculturation from length of stay in the United States, and not to assume that these issues are relevant only for new immigrants and refugees.

c.   Psychologists help clients increase their awareness of their own cultural values and norms, and they facilitate discovery of ways clients can apply this awareness to their own lives and to society at large.

Illustrative Statement: Psychologists may be able to help parents distinguish between generational conflict and culture gaps when problems arise between them and their children. In the process, psychologists could help both parents and children to appreciate their own distinguishing cultural values.

d.   Psychologists seek to help a client determine whether a "problem" stems from racism or bias in others so that the client does not inappropriately personalize problems.

Illustrative Statement: The concept of "healthy paranoia," whereby ethnic minorities may develop defensive behaviors in response to discrimination, illustrates this principle.

e.   Psychologists consider not only differential diagnostic issues but also cultural beliefs and values of the client and his/her community in providing intervention.

Illustrative Statement: There is a disorder among the traditional Navajo called "Moth Madness." Symptoms include seizure-like behaviors. The disorder is believed by the Navajo to be the supernatural result of incestuous thoughts or behaviors. Both differential diagnosis and intervention should take into consideration the traditional values of Moth Madness.

4.   Psychologists respect the roles of family members and community structures, hierarchies, values, and beliefs within the client's culture.

a.   Psychologists identify resources in the family and the larger community.

b.   Clarification of the role of the psychologist and the expectations of the client precede intervention. Psychologists seek to ensure that both the psychologist and client have a clear understanding of what services and roles are reasonable.

Illustrative Statement: It is not uncommon for an entire American Indian family to come into the clinic to provide support to the person in distress. Many of the healing practices found in American Indian communities are centered in the family and the whole community.

5.   Psychologists respect clients' religious and/or spiritual beliefs and values, including attributions and taboos, since they affect world view, psychosocial functioning, and expressions of distress.

a.   Part of working in minority communities is to become familiar with indigenous beliefs and practices and to respect them.

Illustrative Statement: Traditional healers (e.g., shamans, curanderos, espiritistas) have an important place in minority communities.

b.   Effective psychological intervention may be aided by consultation with and/or inclusion of religious/spiritual leaders/practitioners relevant to the client's cultural and belief systems.

6.   Psychologists interact in the language requested by the client and, if this is not feasible, make an appropriate referral.

a.   Problems may arise when the linguistic skills of the psychologist do not match the language of the client. In such a case, psychologists refer the client to a mental health professional who is competent to interact in the language of the client. If this is not possible, psychologists offer the client a translator with cultural knowledge and an appropriate professional background. When no translator is available, then a trained paraprofessional from the client's culture is used as a translator/culture broker.

b.   If translation is necessary, psychologists do not retain the services of translators/paraprofessionals that may have a dual role with the client to avoid jeopardizing the validity of evaluation or the effectiveness of intervention.

    c. Psychologists interpret and relate test data in terms understandable and relevant to the needs of those assessed.

7. Psychologists consider the impact of adverse social, environmental, and political factors in assessing problems and designing interventions.

    a. Types of intervention strategies to be used match to the client's level of need (e.g., Maslow's hierarchy of needs).

    Illustrative Statement: Low income may be associated with such stressors as malnutrition, substandard housing, and poor medical care; and rural residency may mean inaccessibility of services. Clients may resist treatment at government agencies because of previous experience (e.g., refugees' status may be associated with violent treatments by government officials and agencies).

    b. Psychologists work within the cultural setting to improve the welfare of all persons concerned, if there is a conflict between cultural values and human rights.

8. Psychologists attend to as well as work to eliminate biases, prejudices, and discriminatory practices.

    a. Psychologists acknowledge relevant discriminatory practices at the social and community level that may be affecting the psychological welfare of the population being served.

    Illustrative Statement: Depression may be associated with frustrated attempts to climb the corporate ladder in an organization that is dominated by a top echelon of White males.

    b. Psychologists are cognizant of sociopolitical contexts in conducting evaluations and providing interventions; they develop sensitivity to issues of oppression, sexism, elitism, and racism.

    Illustrative Statement: An upsurge in the public expression of rancor or even violence between two ethnic or cultural groups may increase anxiety baselines in any member of these groups. This baseline of anxiety would interact with prevailing symptomatology. At the organizational level, the community conflict may interfere with open communication among staff.

9.   Psychologists working with culturally diverse populations should document culturally and sociopolitically relevant factors in the records.

   a.   number of generations in the country

   b.   number of years in the country

   c.   fluency in English

   d.   extent of family support (or disintegration of family)

   e.   community resources

   f.   level of education

   g.   change in social status as a result of coming to this country (for immigrant or refugee)

   h.   intimate relationship with people of different backgrounds

   i.   level of stress related to acculturation

Proposed Cross-Cultural Competencies and Objectives

I. Counselor Awareness of Own Cultural Values and Biases

   A. Attitudes and Beliefs

   1. Culturally skilled counselors have moved from being cultur-ally unaware to being aware and sensitive to their own cul-tural heritage and to valuing and respecting differences.

   2. Culturally skilled counselors are aware of how their own cul-tural backgrounds and experiences and attitudes, values and biases influence psychological processes.

   3. Culturally skilled counselors are able to recognize the limits of their competencies and expertise.

   4. Culturally skilled counselors are comfortable with differences that exist between themselves and clients in terms of race, ethnicity, culture, and beliefs.

B. Knowledge

   1. Culturally skilled counselors have specific knowledge about their own racial and cultural heritage and how it personally and professionally affects their definitions about normality–abnormality and the process of counseling.

   2. Culturally skilled counselors possess knowledge and understanding about how oppression, racism, discrimination, and stereotyping affects them personally and in their work. This allows them to acknowledge their own racist attitudes, beliefs, and feelings. Although this standard applies to all groups, for White counselors it may mean that they understand how they may have directly or indirectly benefitted from individual, institutional, and cultural racism (White identity development models).

   3. Culturally skilled counselors possess knowledge about their social impact on others. They are knowledgeable about communication style differences, how their style may clash with or foster the counseling process with minority clients, and how to anticipate the impact it may have on others.

C. Skills

   1. Culturally skilled counselors seek out educational, consultative, and training experiences to improve their understanding and effectiveness in working with competencies, they (a) seek consultation, (b) seek further training or education, (c) refer out to more qualified individuals or resources, or (d) engage in a combination of these.

   2. Culturally skilled counselors are constantly seeking to understand themselves as racial and cultural beings and are actively seeking a nonracist identity.

II. Counselor Awareness of Client's Worldview

A. Attitudes and Beliefs

   1. Culturally skilled counselors are aware of their negative emotional reactions toward other racial and ethnic groups that may prove detrimental to their clients in counseling. They are will-

ing to contrast their own beliefs and attitudes with those of their culturally different clients in a nonjudgmental fashion.

2. Culturally skilled counselors are aware of their stereotypes and preconceived notions that they may hold toward other racial and ethnic minority groups.

B. Knowledge

1. Culturally skilled counselors possess specific knowledge and information about the particular group they are working with. They are aware of the life experiences, cultural heritage, and historical background of their culturally different clients. This particular competency is strongly linked to the "minority identity development models" available in the literature.

2. Culturally skilled counselors understand how race, culture, ethnicity, and so forth may affect personality formation, vocational choices, manifestation of psychological disorders, help-seeking behavior, and the appropriateness or inappropriateness of counseling approaches.

3. Culturally skilled counselors understand and have knowledge about sociopolitical influences that impinge upon the life of racial and ethnic minorities. Immigration issues, poverty, racism, stereotyping, and powerlessness all leave major scars that may influence the counseling process.

C. Skills

1. Culturally skilled counselors should familiarize themselves with relevant research and the latest findings regarding mental health and mental disorders of various ethnic and racial groups. They should actively seek out educational experiences that foster their cross-cultural counseling knowledge, understanding, and skills.

2. Culturally skilled counselors become actively involved with minority individuals outside of the counseling setting (community events, social and political functions, celebrations, friendships, neighborhood groups, and so forth) so that their perspective of minorities is more than an academic or helping exercise.

III. Culturally Appropriate Intervention Strategies

   A. Attitudes and Beliefs

      1. Culturally skilled counselors respect clients' religious and/or spiritual beliefs and values, including attributions and taboos, because they affect their worldviews, psychosocial functioning, and expressions of distress.

      2. Culturally skilled counselors respect indigenous helping practices and respect minority community intrinsic help-giving methods.

      3. Culturally skilled counselors value bilingualism and do not view another language as an impediment to counseling (monolingualism may be the culprit).

   B. Knowledge

      1. Culturally skilled counselors have a clear and explicit knowledge and understanding of the generic characteristics of counseling and therapy (culture bound, class bound, and monolingual) and how they may clash with the cultural values of various minority groups.

      2. Culturally skilled counselors are aware of institutional barriers that prevent minorities from using mental health services.

      3. Culturally skilled counselors have knowledge of the potential bias in assessment instruments and use procedures and interpret findings keeping in mind the cultural linguistic characteristics of the clients.

      4. Culturally skilled counselors have knowledge of minority family structures, hierarchies, values, and beliefs. They are knowledgeable about the community characteristics and the resources in the community as well as the family.

      5. Culturally skilled counselors should be aware of the relevant discriminatory practices at the social and community level that may be affecting the psychological welfare of the population being served.

C. Skills

1. Culturally skilled counselors are able to engage in a variety of verbal and nonverbal helping responses. They are able to send and receive both verbal and nonverbal messages accurately and appropriately. They are not tied down to only one method or approach to helping but recognize that helping styles and approaches may be culture bound. When they sense that their helping style is limited and potentially inappropriate, they can anticipate and ameliorate its negative impact.

2. Culturally skilled counselors are able to exercise institutional intervention skills on behalf of their clients. They can help clients determine whether a "problem" stems from racism or bias in others (the concept of health paranoia) so that clients do not inappropriately personalize problems.

3. Culturally skilled counselors are not averse to seeking consultation with traditional healers, religious and spiritual leaders, and practitioners in the treatment of culturally different clients when appropriate.

4. Culturally skilled counselors take responsibility for interacting in the language requested by the client and, if not feasible, make appropriate referral. A serious problem arises when the linguistic skills of a counselor do not match the language of the client. This being the case, counselors should (a) seek a translator with cultural knowledge and appropriate professional background and (b) refer to a knowledgeable and competent bilingual counselor.

5. Culturally skilled counselors have training and expertise in the use of traditional assessment and testing instruments. They not only understand the technical aspects of the instruments but are also aware of the cultural limitations. This allows them to use test instruments for the welfare of the diverse clients.

6. Culturally skilled counselors should attend to as well as work to eliminate biases, prejudices, and discriminatory practices. They should be cognizant of sociopolitical contexts in conducting evaluation and providing interventions and should develop sensitivity to issues of oppression, sexism, elitism, and racism.

7. Culturally skilled counselors take responsibility in educating their clients to the processes of psychological intervention, such as goals, expectations, legal rights, and the counselor's orientation.

Note: From "Multicultural Counseling Competencies and Standards: A Call to the Profession" by D. W. Sue., P. Arredondo, and R. J. McDavis, 1992, *Journal of Counseling and Development, 70,* 477-486. Copyright 1992 by the American Counseling Association. Reprinted by permission.

REFERENCES

Abbitt, D., & Bennett, B. (1984). Being a lesbian mother. In B. Berzon (Ed.), *Positively gay* (pp. 123–129). Los Angeles: Mediamix Associates.

Adelman, M. (1990). Stigma, gay lifestyles, and adjustment to aging: A study of later life gay men and lesbians. *Journal of Homosexuality, 20*(3/4), 7–32.

Adler, N. J. (1981). Re–entry: Managing cross–cultural transitions. *Group and Organization Studies, 6,* 341–356.

Adler, P. (1975). The transitional experience: An alternative view of culture shock. *Journal of Humanistic Psychology, 15*(4), 13–23.

Adler, T. (1990, January). Causes, cure of PMS still elude researchers. *APA Monitor, 21*(1), 10.

Adler, T. (1992, February). Study links genes to sexual orientation. *APA Monitor, 23*(2), 12–13.

Allison, K. W., Crawford, I., Echemendia, R., Robinson, L., & Knepp, D. (1994). Human diversity and professional competence. *American Psychologist, 49,* 792–796.

Allport, G. W. (1954). *The nature of prejudice*. Reading, MA: Addison–Wesley.

American Association of Retired Persons. (1986). *A portrait of older minorities*. Long Beach, CA: Author.

American Association of Retired Persons. (1993). *A profile of older Americans*. Washington, DC: Author.

American Association of Retired Persons. (1995). *A profile of older Americans*. Washington, DC: Author.

American Association of University Women. (1991). *Shortchanging girls, shortchanging America*. Washington, DC: Author.

American Psychological Association. (1991). *Guidelines for providers of psychological services to ethnic, linguistic and culturally diverse populations*. Washington, DC: Author.

American Psychological Association. (1992). Ethical principles of psychologists and code of conduct. *American Psychologist, 47,* 1597–1611.

American Psychiatric Association. (1987). *Diagnostic and statistical manual of mental disorders* (3rd ed., rev.). Washington, DC: Author.

American Psychiatric Association. (1994). *Diagnostic and statistical manual of mental disorders* (4th ed.). Washington, DC: Author.

Americans With Disabilities Act (1990). Washington, DC: Office on the Americans with Disabilities Act, U.S. Department of Justice.

Anderson, D. (1987). Family and peer relations of gay adolescents. *Adolescent Psychiatry, 14,* 162–178.

Anderson, M. J., & Ellis, R. (1995). On the reservation. In N. Vacc, S. DeVaney, & J. Wittmer (Eds.), *Experiencing and counseling multicultural and diverse populations* (pp. 179–198). Bristol, PA: Accelerated Development.

Anwar, M. S. (1995). Review of *The function of myth in Akan healing experience: A psychological inquiry into two traditional Akan healing communities. Journal of Cross–Cultural Psychology, 26,* 442–443.

Ariel, J., & Stearns, S. M. (1992). Challenges facing gay and lesbian families. In S. H. Dworkin & F. J. Gutierrez (Eds.), *Counseling gay men and lesbians: Journey to the end of the rainbow* (pp. 95–112). Alexandria, VA: American Counseling Association.

Arredondo, P. (1991). Counseling Latinas. In C. C. Lee & B. L. Richardson (Eds.), *Multicultural issues in counseling: New approaches to diversity* (pp. 143–156). Alexandria, VA: American Counseling Association.

Asante, M. K. (1987). *The Afrocentric idea.* Philadelphia: Temple University Press.

Ashby, M. R., Gilchrist, L. D., & Miramontez, A. (1987). Group treatment for sexually abused American Indian adolescents. *Social Work With Groups, 10,* 21–32.

Association for Multicultural Counseling and Development. (1986). *Multicultural skill competencies.* Alexandria, VA: Author.

Astin, A. W. (1982). *Minorities in American higher education.* San Francisco: Jossey-Bass.

Atkinson, D. R. (1983). Ethnic minority representation in counselor education. *Counselor Education and Supervision, 23,* 7–19.

Atkinson, D. R., Morten, G., & Sue, D. W. (1989). *Counseling American minorities: A cross-cultural perspective* (3rd ed.). Dubuque, IA: William C. Brown.

Attneave, C. (1969). Therapy in tribal settings and urban network intervention. *Family Process, 8,* 192–210.

Attneave, C. (1982). American Indian and Alaskan native families: Emigrants in their own homeland. In M. McGoldrick, J. Pearce, & J. Giordano (Eds.), *Ethnicity and family therapy* (pp. 55–83). New York: Guilford Press.

Avila, D. L., & Avila, A. L. (1995). Mexican–Americans. In N. Vacc, S. DeVaney, & J. Wittmer (Eds.), *Experiencing and counseling multicultural and diverse populations* (pp. 119–146). Bristol, PA: Accelerated Development.

Axelson, J. A. (1993). *Counseling and development in a multicultural society.* Pacific Grove, CA: Brooks/Cole.

Azar, B. (1996a, October). Intrusive thoughts proven to undermine our health. *APA Monitor, 27*(10), 34.

Azar, B. (1996b, October). Model compares heterosexual women, lesbians. *APA Monitor, 27*(10), 59.

Azar, B. (1996c, October). More money is needed for AIDS prevention efforts. *APA Monitor, 27*(10), 55.

Bachman, S. L. (1996, June 22). California leads nation in mixed–race marriages. *San Jose Mercury News,* p. 20A.

Backover, A. (1991, March). Wage gap poses dilemma for women and counselors. *Guidepost, 33*(13), 1, 8, 10.

Backover, A. (1992, August). Minority Ph.D.'s: Some groups make gains, others fall. *Guidepost, 35*(2), 1, 14.

Baldwin, J. A., & Bell, Y. R. (1985). The African Self–Consciousness Scale: An Africentric personality questionnaire. *Western Journal of Black Studies, 9*(2), 65–68.

Ballou, M., & Gabalac, N. (1984). *A feminist position on mental health.* Springfield, IL: Charles C. Thomas.

Baratz, S. S., & Baratz, J. C. (1970). Early childhood intervention: The social science base of institutional racism. *Harvard Educational Review, 40,* 29–50.

Barrow, G., & Smith, P. (1979). *Aging, ageism, and society.* St. Paul, MN: West.

Bartholomew, C. G., & Schnorr, D. L. (1994). Gender equity: Suggestions for broadening career options of female students. *The School Counselor, 41,* 245–255.

Bartlett, J. (1992). *Familiar quotations* (16th ed.). Boston: Little, Brown.

Baruth, L. G., & Manning, M. L. (1991). *Multicultural counseling and psychotherapy.* New York: Merrill.

Behrens, J. T. (1997). Does the White Racial Identity Attitude Scale measure racial identity? *Journal of Counseling Psychology, 44,* 3–12.

Behrens, J. T., & Rowe, W. (1997). Measuring White racial identity: A reply to Helms (1997). *Journal of Counseling Psychology, 44,* 17–19.

Berg, I. K., & Miller, S. D. (1992). Working with Asian American clients: One person at a time. *Families in Society: The Journal of Contemporary Human Services, 73,* 356–363.

Berger, R. M. (1980). Psychological adaptation of the older homosexual male. *Journal of Homosexuality, 5,* 161–175.

Berger, R. M. (1984). Realities of gay and lesbian aging. *Social Work, 29,* 57–62.

Berger, R. M. (1990). Passing: Impact on the quality of same–sex couple relationships. *Social Work, 35,* 328–332.

Bernal, M. E. (1990). Ethnic minority mental health training: Trends and issues. In F. C. Sarafica, A. I. Schwebel, R. K. Russell, P. D. Isaac, & L. B. Myers (Eds.), *Mental health of ethnic minorities* (pp. 249–274). New York: Praeger.

Berry, J. W. (1969). On cross–cultural comparability. *International Journal of Psychology, 4,* 119–128.

Berry, J. W., Kim, U., Minde, T., & Mok, D. (1987). Comparative studies of acculturative stress. *International Migration Review, 21,* 491–511.

Berube, M. (1997, May 30). The cultural representation of people with disabilities affects us all. *Chronicle of Higher Education,* pp. B4–B5.

Betz, N., & Fitzgerald, L. (1987). *Career psychology of women.* Orlando, FL: Academic Press.

Bienvenue, M., & Colonomous, B. (1988). *An introduction to American deaf culture* [Video-tape]. Silver Spring, MD: Sign Media.

Billingsley, A. (1992). *Climbing Jacob's ladder.* New York: Simon & Schuster.

Biggs, M. (1996). *Women's words.* New York: Columbia University Press.

Bishop, B. (1989, April). Great expectations: Cultural consultant Gay Tischbirek discusses intercultural marriages. *The Paris Free Voice, 12*(3), p. 3.

Black and White in America. (1988, March 7). *Newsweek,* pp. 18–23.

Block, C. B. (1981). Black Americans and the cross–cultural counseling and psychotherapy experience. In A. J. Marsella & P. B. Pedersen (Eds.), *Cross–cultural counseling and psychotherapy* (pp. 177–194). New York: Pergamon Press.

Boden, R. (1988). Countertransference responses to lesbians with physical disability and chronic illness. In M. Shernoff (Ed.), *The sourcebook on lesbian-gay health care.* Washington, DC: National Lesbian/Gay Health Foundation.

Boden, R. (1992). Psychotherapy with physically disabled lesbians. In S. H. Dworkin & F. J. Gutierrez (Eds.), *Counseling gay men and lesbians: Journey to the end of the rainbow* (pp. 157–174). Alexandria, VA: American Counseling Association.

Bowler, R.M. (1980). Expatriate in Saudi Arabia: Stress, social support, modernity and coping. *Dissertation Abstracts International, 41,* 405B.

Boyer, S. P., & Sedlacek, W. E. (1989). Noncognitive predictors of counseling center use by international students. *Journal of Counseling and Development, 67,* 404–407.

Brandell, J. R. (1988). Treatment of the biracial child: Theoretical and clinical issues. *Journal of Multicultural Counseling and Development, 16,* 176–187.

Braunstein, M. (1997, February). In search of disability culture. *New Mobility, 8*(41)29–31.

Brazziel, W. F. (1987/1988, Fall/Winter). Road blocks to graduate school: Black Americans are not achieving parity. *Educational Record, 68*(4) and *69*(1), 108–115.

Brice, J. (1982). West Indian families. In M. McGoldrick, J. Pearce, & J. Giordano (Eds.), *Ethnicity and family therapy* (pp. 123–133). New York: Guilford Press.

Bridgewater, D. (1992). A gay male survivor of antigay violence. In S. H. Dworkin & F. J. Gutierrez (Eds.), *Counseling gay men and lesbians: Journey to the end of the rainbow* (pp. 219–230). Alexandria, VA: American Counseling Association.

Brown, D. (1996, Winter). Reply to Derald Wind (sic) Sue. *ACES Spectrum, 57*(2), 3, 6.

Brown, J. F. (1993). Helping Black women build high self–esteem. *American Counselor, 2*(1), 9–11.

Brown, L. S. (1989). New voices, new visions: Toward a lesbian/gay paradigm for psychology. *Psychology of Women Quarterly, 13*, 445–458.

Burciaga, J. A. (1989, September 20). A Chicano is also Indian. *San Jose Mercury News*, p. 9B.

Burnette, E. (1995, September). The strengths of mixed–race relationships. *APA Monitor, 26*(9), pp. 41–42.

Burnette, E. (1996, October). Anger undercuts ethnic–minority women's health. *APA Monitor, 27*(10), p. 53.

Butler, R. N. (1969). Age–ism: Another form of bigotry. *The Gerontologist, 9*, 243–246.

Butler, R. N., & Lewis, M. I. (1995). Late–life depression: When and how to intervene. *Geriatrics, 50*(8), 44–55.

Carney, C. G., & Kahn, K. B. (1984). Building competencies for effective cross–cultural counseling: A developmental view. *The Counseling Psychologist, 12*(1), 111–119.

Carter, R. T. (1990). The relationship between racism and racial identity among White Americans: An exploratory investigation. *Journal of Counseling and Development, 69*, 46–50.

Carter, R. T., & Swanson, J. L. (1990). The validity of the Strong Interest Inventory with Black Americans: A review of the literature. *Journal of Vocational Behavior, 36*, 195–209.

Cass, V. C. (1979). Homosexual identity formation: A theoretical model. *Journal of Homosexuality, 4*, 219–235.

Cass, V. C. (1984). Homosexual identity formation: Testing a theoretical model. *Journal of Sex Research, 20*, 143–167.

Castillo, A. (1995). *My father was a Toltec and selected poems.* New York: W. W. Norton.

Cerhan, J. U. (1990). The Hmong in the United States: An overview for mental health professionals. *Journal of Counseling and Development, 69*, 88–92.

Chan, C. S. (1989). Issues of identity development among Asian American lesbians and gay men. *Journal of Counseling and Development, 68*, 16–20.

Chan, C. S. (1992). Cultural considerations in counseling Asian American lesbians and gay men. In S. H. Dworkin & F. J. Gutierrez (Eds.), *Counseling gay men and lesbians: Journey to the end of the rainbow* (pp. 115–124). Alexandria, VA: American Counseling Association.

Chan, F., Lam, C. S., Wong, D., Leung, P., & Fang, X. (1988). Counseling Chinese Americans with disabilities. *Journal of Applied Rehabilitation Counseling, 19*(4), 21–25.

Chance, P. (1981, October). The remedial thinker. *Psychology Today, 15*, 62–73.

Chavez, S. (1986). Ethnic minorities in higher education adapting to a new social system. *International Journal for the Advancement of Counseling, 9*, 381–384.

Cheatham, H. (1990). Empowering Black families. In H. Cheatham & J. Stewart (Eds.), *Black families* (pp. 373–393). New Brunswick, NJ: Transaction Press.

Chodorow, N. (1978). *The reproduction of mothering, psychoanalysis and the sociology of gender.* Berkeley: University of California Press.

Chojnacki, J. T., & Gelberg, S. (1995). The facilitation of a gay/lesbian/bisexual support–therapy group by heterosexual counselors. *Journal of Counseling and Development, 73*, 352–354.

Christensen, P. (1989). Cross–cultural awareness development: A conceptual model. *Counselor Education and Supervision, 28*, 270–289.

Chung, R. C., & Okazaki, S. (1991). Counseling Americans of Southeast Asian descent: The impact of the refugee experience. In C. C. Lee & B. L. Richardson (Eds.), *Multicultural issues in counseling: New approaches to diversity* (pp. 107–126). Alexandria, VA: American Counseling Association.

Church, A. (1982). Sojourner adjustment. *Psychological Bulletin, 91*, 540–572.

Cloninger, C. R., Reich, T., & Guze, S. B. (1975). The multifactorial model of disease transmission: II. Sex differences in the familial transmission of sociopathy (antisocial personality). *British Journal of Psychiatry, 127*, 11–22.

Comas–Diaz, L., & Greene, B. (1994). *Women of color: Integrating ethnic and gender identities in psychotherapy*. New York: Guilford Press.

Comas–Diaz, L., & Jacobsen, F. M. (1987). Ethnocultural identification in psychotherapy. *Psychiatry, 50*, 232–241.

Contin, M. (1996, June 22). Classifying by race gets tougher. *San Jose Mercury News*, pp. 1A, 20A.

Corey, G., Corey, M., & Callanan, P. (1988). *Issues and ethics in the helping professions* (3rd ed.). Pacific Grove, CA: Brooks/Cole.

Costantino, G., Malgady, R., & Rogler, L. (1986). Cuento therapy: A culturally sensitive modality for Puerto Rican children. *Journal of Consulting and Clinical Psychology, 54*, 639–645.

Council for Accreditation of Counseling and Related Educational Programs. (1988). *Accreditation procedures manual and application*. Alexandria, VA: Author.

Courtois, C. A. (1988). *Healing the incest wound*. New York: Norton.

Cox, H. G. (1988). *Later life: The realities of aging* (2nd ed.). Englewood Cliffs, NJ: Prentice Hall.

Cross, W. E. (1995). The psychology of Nigrescence: Revising the Cross model. In J. G. Ponterotto, J. M. Casas, L. A. Suzuki, & C. M. Alexander (Eds.), *Handbook of multicultural counseling* (pp. 93–122). Thousand Oaks, CA: Sage.

Cuellar, I., Harris, I. C., & Jasso, R. (1980). An acculturation scale for Mexican American normal and clinical populations. *Hispanic Journal of Behavioral Science, 2*, 199–217.

Curry, G. D., & Spergel, I. A. (1992). Gang involvement and delinquency among Hispanic and African–American adolescent males. *Journal of Research in Crime and Delinquency, 29*, 273–291.

Dahlstrom, W. G., Lachar, D., & Dahlstrom, L. E. (1986). *MMPI patterns of American minorities*. Minneapolis: University of Minnesota Press.

Dana, R. (1988). Culturally diverse groups and MMPI interpretation. *Professional Psychology: Research and Practice, 19*, 490–495.

Dana, R. (1993). *Multicultural assessment perspectives for professional psychology*. Boston: Allyn & Bacon.

D'Andrea, M. (1994, October). Promoting the dignity of gay, lesbian and bisexual students. *Counseling Today, 37*(4), 23.

D'Andrea, M., & Daniels, J. (1991). Exploring the different levels of multicultural counseling training in counselor education. *Journal of Counseling and Development, 70*, 78–85.

D'Andrea, M., Daniels, J., & Heck, R. (1991). Evaluating the impact of multicultural counseling training. *Journal of Counseling and Development, 70*, 143–150.

Darling, E. (1997, February 19). "We speak standard English." *Palo Alto Weekly*, pp. 28–31.

Das, A. K. (1987). Indigenous models of therapy in traditional Asian societies. *Journal of Multicultural Counseling and Development, 15*, 25–36.

Das, A. K. (1995). Rethinking multicultural counseling: Implications for counselor education. *Journal of Counseling and Development, 74*, 45–52.

D'Avanzo, C., Frye, B., & Froman, R. (1994). Stress in Cambodian refugee families. *IMAGE: Journal of Nursing Scholarship. 26,* 101–105.

Davenport, D. S., & Yurich, J. M. (1991). Multicultural gender issues. *Journal of Counseling and Development, 70,* 64–71.

Davidson, K. (1993, May 2). Doctors becoming versed in curses. *San Francisco Examiner,* pp. A1, A8.

Deaf culture. (1995, Fall). *The Source,* 1.

DeAngelis, T. (1992, November). Div. 38 conference explores ethnic–minority health issues. *APA Monitor, 23*(11), pp. 32–33.

DeAngelis, T. (1994a, March). Mass. now requires multicultural training. *APA Monitor, 25*(3), p. 41.

DeAngelis, T. (1994b, September). More research is needed on gay, lesbian concerns. *APA Monitor, 25*(9), p. 39.

DeAngelis, T. (1997, February). Plan will increase number of ethnic–minority students. *APA Monitor, 28*(2), p. 43.

DeFour, D. C. & Hirsch, B. J. (1990). The adaptation of Black graduate students: A social network approach. *American Journal of Community Psychology, 18,* 487–503.

DeLaGarza, D. V. (1996). Exploring the web: Hispanic women with visual impairments. In A. Leal–Idrogo, J. T. Gonzales–Calvo, & V. D. Krenz (Eds.), *Multicultural women: Health, disability, and rehabilitation* (pp. 259–292). Dubuque, IA: Kendall/Hunt.

DelVecchio, R. (1995, May 14). Showing their true colors. *San Francisco Examiner & Chronicle,* pp. Datebook 30–31.

Dent, H. E. (1995, December). Everything you thought was true about testing, but isn't. *Focus, 9*(2), 4–6.

Dillard, J. M. (1983). *Multicultural counseling.* Chicago: Nelson–Hall.

Dinges, N. G., Trimble, J. E., Manson, S. M., & Pasquale, F. L. (1981). Counseling and psychotherapy with American Indian and Alaskan Natives. In A. J. Marsella & P. B. Pedersen (Eds.), *Cross–cultural counseling and psychotherapy* (pp. 243–276). New York: Pergamon Press.

Disability from mental health problems. (1995, September). *Counseling Today, 38*(3), p. 41.

Dobbins, J. E., & Skillings, J. H. (1991). The utility of race labeling in understanding cultural identity: A conceptual tool for the social science practitioner. *Journal of Counseling and Development, 70,* 37–44.

Donnelly, K. (1994, April 1). Living in America. *San Jose Mercury News,* pp. C1,3.

Dougherty, P. (1990). A personal perspective on working with men in groups. In D. Moore & F. Leafgren (Eds.), *Men in conflict* (pp. 265–275). Alexandria, VA: American Association for Counseling and Development.

Downing, N. E., & Roush, K. L. (1985). From passive acceptance to active commitment: A model of feminist identity development for women. *The Counseling Psychologist, 13,* 695–709.

Dudley, J. I. E. (1992). *Choteau Creek: A Sioux reminiscence.* Lincoln, NE: University of Nebraska Press.

Dupuy, P. (1993). Women in intimate relationships. In E. P. Cook (Ed.), *Women, relationships, and power: Implications for counseling* (pp. 79–108). Alexandria, VA: American Counseling Association.

Edgerton, R. B., & Karno, M. (1971). Mexican–American bilingualism and the perception of mental illness. *Archives of General Psychiatry, 24,* 286–290.

Edwards, A., & Polite, C. K. (1992). *Children of the dream: The psychology of Black success.* New York: Doubleday.

Ehrlich, E., & DeBruhl, M. (1996). *International thesaurus of quotations.* New York: Harper Perennial.

Eichler, A., & Parron, D. L. (1987). *Women's mental health: Agenda for research.* Rockville, MD: National Institute of Mental Health.

Elman, M. R., & Gilbert, L. A. (1984). Coping strategies for role conflict in married professional women with children. *Family Relations, 33,* 317–337.

Emerson, G. (1985). *Some American men.* New York: Simon & Schuster.

Enns, C. Z. (1992). Self–esteem groups: A synthesis of consciousness–raising and assertiveness training. *Journal of Counseling and Development, 71,* 7–13.

Enns, C. Z. (1993). Twenty years of feminist counseling and therapy: From naming biases to implementing multifaceted practice. *The Counseling Psychologist, 21,* 3–87.

Enns, C. Z. (1994). Archetypes and gender: Goddesses, warriors, and psychological health. *Journal of Counseling and Development, 73,* 127–133.

Erickson, M., Rossi, E., & Rossi, S. (1976). *Hypnotic realities.* New York: Wiley.

Erikson, E. (1963). *Childhood and society.* New York: Norton.

Erikson, E. (1968). *Identity: Youth and crisis.* New York: Norton.

Fabrega, H., & Nutini, H. (1994). Tlaxcalan constructions of acute grief. *Culture, Medicine and Psychiatry, 18,* 405–431.

Falk, P. J. (1989). Lesbian mothers. *American Psychologist, 44,* 941–947.

Femiano, S. (1990). Developing a contemporary men's studies curriculum. In D. Moore & F. Leafgren (Eds.), *Men in conflict* (pp. 237–248). Alexandria, VA: American Association for Counseling and Development.

Fendel, N., Hurtado, S., Long, J., & Giraldo, Z. (1996). Affirmative action: Who does it help? Who does it hurt? *CFA Professor, 28*(2), 13–17.

Fernandez, R. (1989). *Five cities high school dropout study: Characteristics of Hispanic high school students.* Washington, DC: Aspira Association. (ERIC Document Reproduction Service No. ED 322 240)

Festinger, L. (1954). A theory of social comparison process. *Human Relations, 7,* 117–140.

Festinger, L. (1957). *A theory of cognitive dissonance.* Evanston, IL: Harper & Row.

Figueroa, A. (1996, October 23). Latinos at Silicon Graphics work to expand minority applicant pool. *San Jose Mercury News,* p. 1TCL.

Fontaine, C. M. (1983, March/April). International relocation: A comprehensive psychosocial approach. *EAP Digest, 3*(3)27–31.

Forrester, D. A. (1986). Myths of masculinity. *Nursing Clinics of North America, 21*(1), 15–23.

Foster, S. (1995a, August). Bridging the counseling gap between Native Americans and mainstream America. *Counseling Today, 38*(2), pp. 1, 26–27.

Foster, S. (1995b, September). Understanding Black rage. *Counseling Today, 38*(3), pp. 10, 22.

Foster, S. (1996a, October). October is National Disability Employment Awareness Month. *Counseling Today, 39*(4), p. 18.

Foster, S. (1996b, March). Tension running high in higher education. *Counseling Today, 38*(9), 10, 16, 21.

Fouad, N. A., & Carter, R. T. (1992). Gender and racial issues for new counseling psychologists in academia. *The Counseling Psychologist, 20,* 123–140.

Fouad, N. A., Manese, J., & Casas, J. M. (1992, August). Curricular and training approaches in implementing cross-cultural counseling competencies. In D. W. Sue (Chair), *Cross–cultural counseling competencies: Revision, expansion and implementation.* Symposium conducted at the 100th Annual Convention of the American Psychological Association, Washington, DC.

Frankl, V. E. (1978). *The unheard cry for meaning: Psychotherapy and humanism.* New York: Simon & Schuster.

Freiberg, P. (1991a, March). Black men may act cool to advertise masculinity. *APA Monitor, 22*(3), p. 30.

Freiberg, P. (1991b, February). Hispanics lack knowledge about AIDS. *APA Monitor, 22*(2), p. 31.

Friend, R. (1990). Lesbian and gay people: A theory of successful aging. *Journal of Homosexuality, 20*(3/4), 77–87.

Fry, P. S. (1986). *Depression, stress, and adaptations in the elderly.* Rockville, MD: Aspen.

Furnham, A., & Bochner, S. (1986). *Culture shock: Psychological reactions to unfamiliar environments.* New York: Methuen.

Garcia, M., & Lega, L. I. (1979). Development of a Cuban ethnic identity questionnaire. *Hispanic Journal of Behavioral Sciences, 1,* 247–261.

Garrett, J. T., & Garrett, M. W. (1994). The path of good medicine: Understanding and counseling Native American Indians. *Journal of Multicultural Counseling and Development, 22,* 134–144.

Gatz, M., & Pearson, C. G. (1988). Ageism revised and the provision of psychological services. *American Psychologist, 43,* 184–188.

Gatz, M., & Smyer, M. A. (1992). The mental health system and older adults in the 1900s. *American Psychologist, 47,* 741–751.

German heritage tops among the U.S. public. (1992, December 20). *San Jose Mercury News,* p. 2C.

Gibbs, J. T. (1987). Identity and marginality: Issues in the treatment of biracial adolescents. *American Journal of Orthopsychiatry, 57,* 265–278.

Gilligan, C. (1982). *In a different voice: Psychological theory and women's development.* Cambridge, MA: Harvard University Press.

Gong–Guy, E., Cravens, R. B., & Patterson, T. W. (1991). Clinical issues in mental health service delivery to refugees. *American Psychologist, 46,* 642–648.

Gonzales, R., & Ruiz, A. (1995). *My first book of proverbs (Mi primer libro de dichos).* San Francisco: Children's Book Press.

Gonzales, S. A. (1979). The Chicano perspective: A design for self–awareness. In A. D. Trejo (Ed.), *The Chicanos* (pp. 81–98). Tucson: University of Arizona Press.

Good, B., & Good, M. D. (1985). The cultural context of diagnosis and therapy: A view from medical anthropology. In M. Miranda & H. H. L. Kitano (Eds.), *Mental health research in minority communities: Development of culturally sensitive training programs* (pp. 1–27). Rockville, MD: National Institute of Mental Health.

Gottfredson, L. S. (1994). The science and politics of race–norming. *American Psychologist, 49,* 955–963.

Grandin, T. (1996). *Making the transition from the world of school into the world of work.* Unpublished manuscript, Colorado State University, Fort Collins.

Grieger, I., & Ponterotto, J. G. (1995). A framework for assessment in multicultural counseling. In J. G. Ponterotto, J. M. Casas, L. A. Suzuki, & C. M. Alexander (Eds.), *Handbook of multicultural counseling* (pp. 357–374). Thousand Oaks, CA: Sage.

Grusznski, R., & Bankovics, G. (1990). Treating men who batter: A group approach. In D. Moore & F. Leafgren (Eds.), *Men in conflict* (pp. 201–211). Alexandria, VA: American Association for Counseling and Development.

Gullahorn, J. E., & Gullahorn, J. T. (1963). An extension of the U–curve hypothesis. *Journal of Social Issues, 19*(3), 33–47.

Gutierrez, F. J. (1985). Bicultural personality development: A process model. In E. Garcia & R. Padilla (Eds.), *Advances in bilingual education research* (pp. 96–124). Tucson: University of Arizona Press.

Gutierrez, F. J., & Dworkin, S. H. (1992). Gay, lesbian and African American: Managing the integration of identities. In S. H. Dworkin & F. J. Gutierrez (Eds.), *Counseling gay men and lesbians: Journey to the end of the rainbow* (pp. 141–156). Alexandria, VA: American Counseling Association

Gwyn, F., & Kilpatrick, A. (1981). Family therapy with low–income Blacks: A tool or turn–off? *Social Casework, 62,* 259–266.

Haley, J. (1973). *Uncommon therapy.* New York: W. W. Norton.

Hall, C. C. I. (1980). *The ethnic identity of racially mixed people: A study of Black–Japanese.* Unpublished doctoral dissertation, University of California, Los Angeles.

Hamilton, J. A., Alagna, S. W., King, L. S., & Lloyd, C. (in press). The emotional consequences of gender–based abuse in the workplace: New counseling programs for sex discrimination. *Women and Therapy.*

Hamilton, M. (1984, February 15). The "superwoman" syndrome. *San Francisco Examiner,* p. E5.

Harsh, M. (1993). Women who are visually impaired or blind as psychotherapy clients: A personal and professional perspective. *Women and Therapy, 14*(3/4), 55–64.

Harvey, D. F. (1970). Cross–cultural stress and adaptation in global organizations. *Dissertation Abstracts International, 31,* 2958B–2959B.

Haviland, W. (1975). *Cultural anthropology.* New York: Holt, Rinehart & Winston.

Havinghurst, R. J., & Neugarten, B. L. (1968). Social class differences. In E. M. Lloyd–Jones & N. Rosenau (Eds.), *Social and cultural foundations of guidance* (pp. 363–372). New York: Holt, Rinehart & Winston.

Hawkins, R. L. (1992). Therapy with the male couple. In S. H. Dworkin & F. J. Gutierrez (Eds.), *Counseling gay men and lesbians: Journey to the end of the rainbow* (pp. 81–94). Alexandria, VA: American Counseling Association.

Heesacker, M., & Prichard, S. (1992). In a different voice revisited: Men, women, and emotion. *Journal of Mental Health Counseling, 14,* 274–290.

Heinrich, R. K., Corbine, J. L., & Thomas, K. R. (1990). Counseling Native Americans. *Journal of Counseling and Development, 69,* 128–133.

Heitner, K. (1995, Fall). Backtalk. *Psychology of Women, 22*(4), 9.

Helms, J. E. (1984). Toward a theoretical explanation of the effects of race on counseling: A Black and White model. *The Counseling Psychologist, 12,* 153–165.

Helms, J. E. (1995). An update of Helms's White and people of color racial identity models. In J. G. Ponterotto, J. M. Casas, L. A. Suzuki, & C. M. Alexander (Eds.), *Handbook of multicultural counseling* (pp. 181–198). Thousand Oaks, CA: Sage.

Helms, J. E. (1997). Implications of Behrens (1997) for the validity of the White Racial Identity Attitude Scale. *Journal of Counseling Psychology, 44,* 13–16.

Helms, J. E., & Carter, R. T. (1990). Development of the White Racial Identity Inventory. In J. E. Helms (Ed.), *Black and White racial identity: Theory, research and practice* (pp. 67–80). Westport, CT: Greenwood Press.

Herek, G. M. (1989). Hate crimes against lesbians and gay men: Issues for research and policy. *American Psychologist, 44,* 948–955.

Herring, R. D. (1991). Counseling Native American youth. In C. C. Lee & B. L. Richardson (Eds.), *Multicultural issues in counseling: New approaches to diversity* (pp. 37–47). Alexandria, VA: American Counseling Association.

Herrnstein, R. J., & Murray, C. (1994). *The bell curve: Intelligence and class structure in American life.* New York: Free Press.

Hersch, P. (1991, January/February). Secret lives. *Family Therapy Networker, 15*(1), 37–43.

Herz, F. M., & Rosen, E. J. (1982). Jewish families. In M. McGoldrick, J. Pearce, & J. Giordano (Eds.), *Ethnicity and family therapy* (pp. 364–392). New York: Guilford Press.

Hetrick, E. S., & Martin, A. D. (1987). Developmental issues and their resolution for gay and lesbian adolescents. *Journal of Homosexuality, 14,* 25–43.

Hiegel, J. P. (1983). Collaboration with traditional healers: Experience in refugees' mental care. *International Journal of Mental Health, 12*(3), 30–43.

Hill, R. (1993). *Research on the African–American family.* Westport, CT: Auburn House.

Hills, H. I., & Strozier, A. L. (1992). Multicultural training in APA–approved counseling psychology programs: A survey. *Professional Psychology, 23,* 43–51.

Hines, P., & Boyd–Franklin, N. (1982). Black families. In M. McGoldrick, J. Pearce, & J. Giordano (Eds.), *Ethnicity and family therapy* (pp. 84–99). New York: Guilford Press.

Ho, L. (1990). *Cross–cultural swinging: A handbook for self–awareness and multicultural living!* (Available from Liang Ho, 2238 Kaala Way, Honolulu, HI 96822)

Ho, M. K. (1987). *Family therapy with ethnic minorities.* Newbury Park, CA: Sage.

Hoffman, L. (1991). A reflexive stance for family therapy. *Journal of Strategic and Systemic Therapies, 10*(3/4), 4–17.

Hoffman, T., Dana, R. H., & Bolton, B. (1985). Measured acculturation and MMPI–168 performance of Native American adults. *Journal of Cross-Cultural Psychology, 16,* 243–256.

Holmes, T. H., & Rahe, R. H. (1967). The Social Readjustment Rating Scale. *Journal of Psychosomatic Research, 11,* 213–218.

Homma–True, R. (1990). Psychotherapeutic issues with Asian American women. *Sex Roles, 22,* 477–486.

Hopkins, R. S. (1982). Defining and predicting overseas effectiveness for adolescent exchange students. *Dissertation Abstracts International, 42,* 5052A–5053A.

Horner, M. (1972). Toward an understanding of achievement–related conflicts in women. *Journal of Social Issues, 28,* 129–156.

How affirmative action should work. (1995, Spring). *Stanford Observer, 29*(3), pp. 1, 20.

Howe Chief, E. (1940). An assimilation study of Indian girls. *Journal of Social Psychology, 11,* 19–30.

Hoyt, K. B. (1989). The career status of women and minority persons: A 20–year retrospective. *Career Development Quarterly, 37,* 202–212.

Huang, L. (1994). An integrative approach to clinical assessment and intervention with Asian–American adolescents. *Journal of Clinical Child Psychology, 23*(1), 21–31.

Human Capital Initiative. (1993). *Vitality for life: Psychological research for productive aging.* Washington, DC: American Psychological Association.

Hunter, J., & Schaecher, R. (1987). Stresses on lesbian and gay adolescents in schools. *Social Work In Education, 9,* 180–190.

Ibrahim, F. A., & Kahn, H. (1984). *Scale to assess world views (SAWV).* Unpublished manuscript, University of Connecticut.

In–country refugees at record levels. (1995, November 15). *San Francisco Examiner,* p. C20.

Ipsaro, A. J. (1986). Male client–male therapist: Issues in a therapeutic alliance. *Psychotherapy, 23,* 257–266.

Ishiyama, F. I. (1990). A Japanese perspective on client inaction: Removing attitudinal blocks through Morita therapy. *Journal of Counseling and Development, 68,* 566–570.

Ivey, A. E., Ivey, M. B., & Simek–Morgan, K. (1993). *Counseling and psychotherapy: A multicultural perspective.* Boston: Allyn & Bacon.

Jackson, M. L. (1995, April). The demise of multiculturalism in America and the counseling profession. *Counseling Today, 37*(10), pp. 30–31.

Jacobs, J. H. (1992). Identity development in biracial children. In M. P. Root (Ed.), *Racially mixed people in America* (pp. 190–206). Newbury Park, CA: Sage.

Jaynes, G. D., & Williams, R. M. (1989). *A common destiny: Blacks and American society.* Washington, DC: National Academic Press.

Jensen, A. (1969). How much can we boost IQ and school achievement? *Harvard Educational Review, 39,* 1–123.

Johnson, C. L. (1985). *Growing up and growing old in Italian American families.* New Brunswick, NJ: Rutgers University Press.

Johnson, D. (1994, July 3). In bleak area in South Dakota, Indians put hopes in classroom. *New York Times,* p. 19.

Johnson, F., Foxall, M., Kelleher, E., Kentopp, E., Mannlein, E., & Cook, E. (1988). Comparison of mental health and life satisfaction of five elderly ethnic groups. *Western Journal of Nursing Research, 10,* 613–628.

Johnson, F. A., & Marsella, A. J. (1978). Differential attitudes toward verbal behavior in students of Japanese and European ancestry. *Genetic Psychology Monographs, 97,* 43–76.

Johnson, R. P., & Riker, H. C. (1982). Counselors' goals and roles in assisting older persons. *Journal of Mental Health Counseling, 4,* 30–40.

Joint Committee on Testing Practices. (1988). *Code of fair testing practices in education.* Washington, DC: Author.

Jones, R. L. (1975). Intercultural education for overseas managers of multinational corporations. *Dissertation Abstracts International, 36,* 1982A.

Jordan, M. B. (1993). Diversity issues concerning therapists: Diagnosis and training. *Independent Practitioner, 13,* 216–218.

Judell, B. (1997). *The gay quote book.* New York: Dutton.

Kamin, L. J. (1974) *The science and politics of I.Q.* New York: Wiley.

Katz, J. H. (1989). *White awareness* (6th ed.). Norman: University of Oklahoma Press.

Katz, P. (1981). Psychotherapy with Native adolescents. *Canadian Journal of Psychiatry, 26,* 455–459.

Keerdoja, E. (1984, November 19). Children of the rainbow: New parent support groups help interracial kids cope. *Newsweek, 104*(22), 120–122.

Kemp, A. D. (1990). From matriculation to graduation: Focusing beyond minority retention. *Journal of Multicultural Counseling and Development, 18,* 144–149.

Kerwin, C. (1993). Issues in biracial identity development. *Focus, 7*(2), 12.

Kerwin, C., & Ponterotto, J. G. (1995). Biracial identity development: Theory and research. In J. G. Ponterotto, J. M. Casas, L. A. Suzuki, & C. M. Alexander (Eds.), *Handbook of multicultural counseling* (pp. 199–217). Thousand Oaks, CA: Sage.

Kiselica, M. S. (1998). Preparing Anglos for the challenges and joys of multiculturalism. *The Counseling Psychologist, 26,* 5–21.

Kitano, H. H. L. (1981). Counseling and psychotherapy with Japanese Americans. In A. J. Marsella & P. B. Pedersen (Eds.), *Cross-cultural counseling and psychotherapy* (pp. 228–242). New York: Pergamon Press.

Kitano, H. H. L. (1989). A model for counseling Asian Americans. In P. B. Pedersen, J. G. Draguns, W. J. Lonner, & J. E. Trimble (Eds.), *Counseling across cultures* (3rd ed., pp. 139–151). Honolulu: University of Hawaii Press.

Kluckhohn, F. R., & Strodtbeck, F. L. (1961). *Variations in value orientation.* New York: Harper & Row.

Koehler, N. (1980). Re-entry shock. *Ladycom, 12*(3), 38–40.

Kohatsu, E. L. (1996, Winter). Identity and racism: Applying racial identity theory to research on Asian American psychology. *Variability, 15*(1), 8, 14.

Kohout, J., Wicherski, M., & Cooney, B. (1992). *Characteristics of graduate departments of psychology: 1989–1990.* Washington, DC: American Psychological Association.

Koss, M. P. (1985). The hidden rape victim: Personality, attitudinal, and situational characteristics. *Psychology of Women Quarterly, 9,* 193–212.

Koss, M. P. (1990) Changed lives: The psychological impact of sexual harassment. In M. A. Paludi (Ed.), *Ivory power: Sexual harassment on campus* (pp. 73–92). Albany: State University of New York Press.

Kristof, N. D. (1996, February 11). Family values, Japanese style. *San Jose Mercury News,* p. 17A.

Kroll, J., Habenicht, M., Mackenzie, T., Yang, M., Chan, S., Vang, T., Nguyen, T., Ly, M., Phommasouvanh, B., Nguyen, H., Vang, Y., Souvannasoth, L., & Cabugao, R. (1989). Depression and post-traumatic stress disorder in Southeast Asian refugees. *American Journal of Psychiatry, 146,* 1592–1597.

Kubler–Ross, E. (1969). *On death and dying.* New York: Macmillan.

Kuypers, J. A., & Bengtson, V. L. (1973). Competence and social breakdown: A social-psychological view of aging. *Human Development, 16,* 37–49.

LaFromboise, T. D. (1988). American Indian mental health policy. *American Psychologist, 43,* 388–397.

LaFromboise, T. D., Berman, J. S., & Sohi, B. K. (1994). American Indian women. In L. Comas–Diaz & B. Greene (Eds.), *Women of color: Integrating ethnic and gender identities in psychotherapy* (pp. 30–71). New York: Guilford Press.

LaFromboise, T. D., Coleman, H. L. K., & Hernandez, A. (1991). Development and factor sturcture of the Cross–Cultural Counseling Inventory–Revised. *Professional Psychology: Research and Practice, 22,* 380–388.

LaFromboise, T. D., Trimble, J., & Mohatt, G. (1990). Counseling intervention and American Indian tradition: An integrative approach. *The Counseling Psychologist, 18,* 628–654.

Lai, E. W. M., & Sodowsky, G. R. (1992, August). *Acculturation: An examination of theory, measurement, and sociocultural, mental health, and counseling variables.* Paper presented at the 100th Annual Convention of the American Psychological Association, Washington, DC.

Lambert, N. M. (1981). Psychological evidence in *Larry P. v. Wilson Riles:* An evaluation by a witness for the defense. *American Psychologist, 36,* 937–952.

Landrine, H. (1989). The politics of personality disorder. *Psychology of Women Quarterly, 13,* 325–339.

Langelier, R. (1982). French Canadian families. In M. McGoldrick, J. Pearce, & J. Giordano (Eds.), *Ethnicity and family therapy* (pp. 229–246). New York: Guilford Press.

Lappin, J., & Scott, S. (1982). Intervention in a Vietnamese refugee family. In M. McGoldrick, J. Pearce, & J. Giordano (Eds.), *Ethnicity and family therapy* (pp. 483–491). New York: Guilford Press.

Lark, J. S., & Paul, B. D. (1998). Beyond multicultural training: Mentoring stories from two White American doctoral students. *The Counseling Psychologist, 26,* 33–42.

Laster, L. T. (1993, July). Another mother, a different dad: Lesbian and gay parenting in the '90s. *Peninsula Parent, 15,* 62.

Lazarus, P. (1982). Counseling the Native American child: A question of values. *Elementary School Guidance and Counseling, 17,* 83–88.

Le, P. (1996, February 11). Students from Asia flock to Cupertino. *San Jose Mercury News,* pp. 1A, 6A.

Leafgren, F. (1990a). Being a man can be hazardous to your health: Life–style issues. In D. Moore & F. Leafgren (Eds.), *Men in conflict* (pp. 265–275). Alexandria, VA: American Association for Counseling and Development.

Leafgren, F. (1990b). Men on a journey. In D. Moore & F. Leafgren (Eds.), *Men in conflict* (pp. 3–10). Alexandria, VA: American Association for Counseling and Development.

Leal, A., & Menjivar, C. (1992). Xenophobia or xenophilia? Hispanic women in higher education. In L. B. Welch (Ed.), *Perspectives on minority women in higher education* (pp. 93–103). New York: Praeger.

Lee, C. C. (1990). Black male development: Counseling the "native son." In D. Moore & F. Leafgren (Eds.), *Men in conflict* (pp. 125–137). Alexandria, VA: American Association for Counseling and Development.

Lee, C. C. (1994). Pioneers of multicultural counseling: A conversation with Clemmont E. Vontress. *Journal of Multicultural Counseling and Development, 22,* 66–78.

Lee, C. C., & Armstrong, K. L. (1995). Indigenous models of mental health intervention: Lessons from traditional healers. In J. G. Ponterotto, J. M. Casas, L. A. Suzuki, & C. M. Alexander (Eds.), *Handbook of multicultural counseling* (pp. 441–456). Thousand Oaks, CA: Sage.

Lee, C. C., & Richardson, B. L. (1991). *Multicultural issues in counseling: New approaches to diversity.* Alexandria, VA: American Counseling Association.

Lee, M. W. (Producer). (1994). *The color of fear* [Film]. Oakland, CA: Stir–Fry Productions.

Lee, W. M. (1995, April). *Counselors of color: Graduate school and early career experiences.* Presentation at the annual meeting of the American Counselors Association, Denver, CO.

Lee, W. M. (1996). New directions in multicultural counseling. *Counseling and Human Development, 29*(2), 1–11.

Lee, W. M., & Mixson, R. J. (1995). Asian and Caucasian client perceptions of the effectiveness of counseling. *Journal of Multicultural Counseling and Development, 23,* 48–56.

Lee, W. M., & Nakagawa, J. Y. (1996). Ethnic and gender issues in making a work disability assessment for Southeast Asian women. In A. Leal–Idrogo, J. T. Gonzales–Calvo, & V. D. Krenz (Eds.), *Multicultural women: Health, disability, and rehabilitation* (pp. 319–329). Dubuque, IA: Kendall/Hunt.

Lefley, H. P. (1989). Counseling refugees: The North American experience. In P. Pedersen, J. G. Draguns, W. J. Lonner, & J. E. Trimble (Eds.), *Counseling across cultures* (3rd ed., pp. 205–241). Honolulu: University of Hawaii Press.

Lefrancois, G. R. (1993). *The lifespan* (4th ed.). Belmont, CA: Wadsworth.

Leong, F. T. (1985). Career development of Asian Americans. *Journal of College Student Personnel, 26,* 539–546.

Leong, F. T. (1991). Career development attributes and occupational values of Asian American and White American college students. *Career Development Quarterly, 39,* 221–230.

Lesbian, gay, bisexual issues and counselor awareness. (1996, Winter). *ACES Spectrum, 57*(2), 8, 15.

Levant, R. F. (1990). Coping with the new father role. In D. Moore & F. Leafgren (Eds.), *Men in conflict* (pp. 81–94). Alexandria, VA: American Association for Counseling and Development.

Levers, L. L., & Maki, D. R. (1995). African indigenous healing and cosmology: Toward a philosphy of ethnorehabilitation. *Rehabilitation Education, 9,* 127–145.

Le Vine, P. (1993). Morita–based therapy and its use across cultures in the treatment of bulimia nervosa. *Journal of Counseling and Development, 72,* 82–90.

Levy, J. (1987). Psychological and social problems of epileptic children in four Southwestern Indian tribes. *Journal of Community Psychology, 15,* 307–315.

Lieberg, C. (1996). *Calling the Midwest home.* Berkeley, CA: Wildcat Canyon Press.

Lijtmaer, R. M. (1993). Bilingual–bicultural difficulties in the therapeutic process with the Hispanic patient. *Independent Practitioner, 13,* 215–216.

Locke, D. C. (1995). Counseling interventions with African American youth. In C. C. Lee (Ed.), *Counseling for diversity: A guide for school counselors and related professionals* (pp. 21–40). Boston: Allyn & Bacon.

Logan, C. R. (1997, March). It takes a village to care for a lesbian. *Counseling Today, 39*(9), pp. 29, 35, 55.

Loiacano, D. (1989). Gay identity issues among Black Americans: Racism, homophobia, and the need for validation. *Journal of Counseling and Development, 68,* 21–25.

Lopez, S. (1988). The empirical basis of ethnocultural and linguistic bias in mental health evaluations of Hispanics. *American Psychologist, 43,* 1095–1097.

Lorion, R. P. (1974). Patient and therapist variables in the treatment of low income patients. *Psychological Bulletin, 81,* 344–354.

Lowrey, L. (1983). Bridging a culture in counseling. *Journal of Applied Rehabilitation Counseling, 14,* 69–73.

Lum, D. (1986). *Social work practice and people of color: A process–stage approach.* Monterey, CA: Brooks/Cole.

Lyon, J. M., Henggeler, S., & Hall, J. A. (1992). The family relations, peer relations, and criminal activities of Caucasian and Hispanic American gang members. *Journal of Abnormal Child Psychology, 29,* 439–449.

Lysgaard, S. (1955). Adjustment in a foreign society: Norwegian Fulbright grantees visiting the United States. *International Social Science Bulletin, 7,* 45–51.

Macias, C. J. (1989). American Indian academic success: The role of indigenous learning strategies. *Journal of American Indian Education, 28,* 43–52.

Malde, S. (1988). Guided autobiography: A counseling tool for older adults. *Journal of Counseling and Development, 66,* 290–293.

Malgady, R. G., Rogler, L. H., & Costantino, G. (1990). Culturally sensitive psychotherapy for Puerto Rican children and adolescents: A program of treatment outcome research. *Journal of Consulting and Clinical Psychology, 58,* 704–712.

Malyon, A. K. (1982). Psychotherapeutic implications of internalized homophobia in gay men. *Journal of Homosexuality, 7*(2/3), 59–69.

Marcos, L. R. (1979). Effects of interpreters on the evaluation of psychopathology in non–English–speaking patients. *American Journal of Psychiatry, 136,* 171–174.

Marin, G., Sabogal, F., VanOss Marin, B., Otero–Sabogal, R., & Perez–Stable, E. J. (1987). Development of a short acculturation scale for Hispanics. *Hispanic Journal of Behavioral Science, 9,* 183–205.

Marino, T. W. (1995, December). Mixed couples get mixed reactions. *Counseling Today, 38*(6), pp. 21, 26.

Marino, T. (1996). Career counselor offers unique bilingual skills. *Counseling Today, 38*(9), pp. 24–26.

Marshall, C. A. (1996). The power of inquiry as regards American Indian women with disabilities: Divisive manipulation or clinical necessity? In A. Leal–Idrogo, J. T. Gonzales–Calvo, & V. D. Krenz (Eds.), *Multicultural women: Health, disability, and rehabilitation* (pp. 293–308). Dubuque, IA: Kendall/Hunt.

Martin, A. D., & Hetrick, E. S. (1988). The stigmatization of the gay and lesbian adolescent. *Journal of Homosexuality, 15*(1/2), 163–183.

Martin, W. E., Jr., Frank, L. W., Minkler, S., & Johnson, M. (1988). A survey of vocational rehabilitation counselors who work with American Indians. *Journal of Applied Rehabilitation Counseling, 19*(4), 29–34.

Martinez, R., Norman, R. D., & Delaney, H. D. (1984). A Children's Hispanic background scale. *Hispanic Journal of Behavioral Sciences, 6,* 103–112.

Masuda, M., Matsumoto, G. H., & Meredith, G. M. (1970). Ethnic identity in three generations of Japanese Americans. *Journal of Social Psychology, 81,* 199–207.

Matheson, L. (1986). If you are not an Indian, how do you treat an Indian? In H. Lefley (Ed.), *Cross–cultural training for mental health professionals* (pp. 115–130). Springfield, IL: Charles C Thomas.

Mattox, C., Sanchez, F., Ulsh, S., & Valero, M. (1982). *Repatriation: A study of dual viewpoints.* Unpublished manuscript, University of Miami.

Mattson, S. (1993). Mental health of Southeast Asian refugee women: An overview. *Health Care for Women International, 14,* 155–165.

May, R. (1990). Finding ourselves: Self–esteem, self–disclosure, and self–acceptance. In D. Moore & F. Leafgren (Eds.), *Men in conflict* (pp. 11–21). Alexandria, VA: American Association for Counseling and Development.

Mayo, J. (1974). The significance of sociocultural variables in the psychiatric treatment of Black outpatients. *Comprehensive Psychiatry, 15,* 471–482.

McDavis, R. J., Parker, W. M., & Parker, W. J. (1995). Counseling African Americans. In N. Vacc, S. DeVaney, & J. Wittmer, (Eds.), *Experiencing and counseling multicultural and diverse populations* (pp. 217–250). Bristol, PA: Accelerated Development.

McDougall, J.G. (1993). Therapeutic issues with gay and lesbian elders. *Clinical Gerontologist, 14*, 45–57.

McGill, D., & Pearce, J. K. (1982). British families. In M. McGoldrick, J. Pearce, & J. Giordano (Eds.), *Ethnicity and family therapy* (pp. 457–479). New York: Guilford Press.

McGoldrick, M. (1982). Irish families. In M. McGoldrick, J. Pearce, & J. Giordano (Eds.), *Ethnicity and family therapy* (pp. 370–339). New York: Guilford Press.

McGoldrick, M., Giordano, J., & Pearce, J. K. (1996). *Ethnicity and family therapy* (2nd ed.). New York: Guilford Press.

McGowan, S. (1993, March). Equal job, equal pay: Women and minorities just aren't getting it. *Guidepost, 35*(10), 13–14.

McGrath, E., Keita, G. P., Strickland, B. R., & Russo, N. F. (1990). *Women and depression: Risk factors and treatment issues.* Washington, DC: American Psychological Association.

McGrath, P., & Axelson, J. A. (1993). *Accessing awareness and developing knowledge: Foundations for skill in a multicultural society.* Pacific Grove, CA: Brooks/Cole.

McIntosh, P. (1988). *White privilege and male privilege* (Working Paper No. 189). Wellesley, MA: Wellesley College Center for Research on Women.

McNair, L. D. (1992). African American women in therapy: An Afrocentric and feminist synthesis. *Women and Therapy, 12*(1/2), 5–19.

McRae, M. B., & Johnson, S. D., Jr. (1991). Toward training for competence in multicultural counselor education. *Journal of Counseling and Development, 70*, 131–135.

McRoy, R. G., & Oglesby, Z. (1984). Group work with Black adoptive applicants. *Social Work With Groups, 7*, 125–134.

Mercer, J. R. (1979). *SOMPA: Technical and conceptual manual.* New York: Psychological Corporation.

Midnight Sun. (1988). Sex/gender systems in native North America. In W. Roscoe (Ed.), *Living the spirit: A gay American Indian anthology* (pp. 32–47). New York: St. Martin's Press.

Miller, J. B. (1976). *Toward a new psychology of women.* New York: Beacon Press.

Milliones, J. (1980). Construction of a Black consciousness measure: Psychotherapeutic implications. *Psychotherapy: Theory, Research and Practice, 17*, 175–182.

Mintz, L. B., & Wright, D. M. (1993). Women and their bodies: Eating disorders and addictions. In E. P. Cook (Ed.), *Women, relationships, and power: Implications for counseling* (pp. 211–246). Alexandria, VA: American Counseling Association.

Mollica, R. F., Wyshak, G., & Lavelle, J. (1987). The psychosocial impact of war trauma and torture on Southeast Asian refugees. *American Journal of Psychiatry, 144*, 1567–1572.

Mondykowski, S. M. (1982). Polish families. In M. McGoldrick, J. Pearce, & J. Giordano (Eds.), *Ethnicity and family therapy* (pp. 393–411). New York: Guilford Press.

Moore, D., Parker, S., Thompson, T., & Dougherty, P. (1990). The journey continues. In D. Moore & F. Leafgren (Eds.), *Men in conflict* (pp. 277–283). Alexandria, VA: American Association for Counseling and Development.

Morales, E. S. (1992). Counseling Latino gays and Latina lesbians. In S. H. Dworkin & F. J. Gutierrez (Eds.), *Counseling gay men and lesbians: Journey to the end of the rainbow* (pp. 125–139). Alexandria, VA: American Counseling Association.

Mordkowitz, E. R., & Ginsburg, H. P. (1986, April). *The academic socialization of successful Asian American college students.* Paper presented at the meeting of the American Educational Research Association, San Francisco. (ERIC Document Reproduction Service No. ED 273 219)

Morganthau, T. (1994, October 24). IQ: Is it destiny? *Newsweek, 124*(17), 52–56.

Morrisey, M. (1995, October). Rising number of immigrants means new challenges for counselors. *Counseling Today, 38*(4), pp. 22, 28–29.

Morrison, A. M., & Von Glinow, M. A. (1990). Women and minorities in management. *American Psychologist, 45*, 200–208.

Morrissey, M. (1995, August). Report on women and mental health hopes to call attention to women's unique needs. *Counseling Today, 38*(2), pp. 22–23.

Moscicki, E. K., Rae, D. S., Regier, D. A., & Locke, B. Z. (1987). The Hispanic Health and Nutrition Examination Survey: Depression among Mexican Americans, Cuban Americans, Puerto Ricans. In M. Gaviria & J. D. Arana (Eds.), *Health and behavior: Research agenda for Hispanics* (pp. 145–159). Chicago: University of Illinois Press.

Moser, N., & Rendon, M. E. (1992). Alcohol and drug services: A jigsaw puzzle. *Journal of the American Deafness and Rehabilitation Association, 26*(2), 18–21.

Moses, S. (1992, February). Minority scholarships at risk. *APA Monitor, 23*(2), p. 9.

Mosher, D. L. (1991). Scared straight: Homosexual threat in heterosexual therapists. In C. Silverstein (Ed.), *Gays, lesbians, and their therapists: Studies in psychotherapy* (pp. 187–200). New York: W. W. Norton.

Murphy, B. C. (1992). Counseling lesbian couples: Sexism, heterosexism, and homophobia. In S. H. Dworkin & F. J. Gutierrez (Eds.), *Counseling gay men and lesbians: Journey to the end of the rainbow* (pp. 63–79). Alexandria, VA: American Counseling Association.

Murphy, D. M., & Murphy, J. T. (1997). Enabling disabled students. *NEA Higher Education Journal, 13*, 41–52.

Murphy, D. S. (1994, Spring). From multicultural infusion theory to multicultural infusion practice in a weekend! *MEI Center Connection, 2*(2), 3–5.

Murray, B. (1996, October). How does a couple cope when one partner is HIV+? *APA Monitor, 27*(10), p. 55.

Myers, J. E. (1983). A national survey of geriatric mental health services. *AMHCA Journal, 5*, 69–74.

Myers, J. E. (1994). Understanding the older worker: Physical and emotional factors. *Career Planning and Adult Development Journal, 10*(2), 4–9.

Myers, J. E., & Schwiebert, V. L. (1996). *Competencies for gerontological counseling.* Alexandria, VA: American Counseling Association.

Myers, J. E., & Sweeney, T. J. (1990). *Gerontological competencies for counselors and human development professionals.* Alexandria, VA: American Association for Counseling and Development.

Myers, J. K., Weissman, M. M., Tischler, G. L., Holzer, C. E., III, Leaf, P. J., Orvaschel, H., Anthony, J. C., Boyd, J. H., Burke, J. D., Jr., Kramer, M., & Stoltzman, R. (1984). Six–month prevalence of psychiatric disorders in three communities. *Archives of General Psychiatry, 41*, 959–967.

Nakao, S., & Lum, C. (1977). *Yellow is not white and white is not right: Counseling techniques for Japanese and Chinese clients.* Unpublished master's thesis, University of California, Los Angeles.

National Center for Educational Statistics. (1989). *Dropout rates in the U.S.: 1988.* Washington, DC: Author.

Neimeyer, G. J., Fukuyama, M. A., Bingham, R. P., Hall, L. E., & Mussenden, M. E. (1986). Training cross–cultural counselors: A comparison of the pro–counselor and the anti–counselor triad models. *Journal of Counseling and Development, 64*, 437–439.

Ness, C. (1993, October 10). The corporate closet. *San Francisco Examiner*, pp. A1, A12.

Nettles, M. (1987). *Financial aid and minority participation in graduate education: A research agenda for today.* Princeton, NJ: Graduate Record Examinations. (ERIC Document Reproduction Service No. ED 299 905)

Nishio, K., & Bilmes, M. (1987). Psychotherapy with Southeast Asian American clients. *Professional Psychology: Research and Practice, 18*, 342–346.

Nolen–Hoeksema, S. (1990). *Sex differences in depression.* Stanford, CA: Stanford University Press.

Norcross, J. C., Hanych, J. M., & Terranova, R. D. (1996). Graduate study in psychology: 1992–1993. *American Psychologist, 51*, 631–643.

Nwachuku, U. T., & Ivey, A. E. (1991). Culture-specific counseling: An alternative training model. *Journal of Counseling and Development, 70,* 106–111.

Oberg, K. (1960). Culture shock: Adjustment to new cultural environments. *Practical Anthropology, 7,* 177–182.

Occupational Outlook Quarterly. (1991, Fall). Washington, DC: U.S. Department of Labor.

O'Connor, M. F. (1992). Psychotherapy with gay and lesbian adolescents. In S. H. Dworkin & F. J. Gutierrez (Eds.), *Counseling gay men and lesbians: Journey to the end of the rainbow* (pp. 3–21). Alexandria, VA: American Counseling Association.

Office of Special Concerns. (1974). *A study of selected socioeconomic characteristics of ethnic minorities based on the 1970 census, Volume II: Asian–American.* Washington, DC: Department of Health, Education, and Welfare.

Okonogi, K. (1978). The Ajase complex of Japanese. *Japan Echo, 5,* 88–105.

O'Neil, J. M., & Egan, J. (1993). Abuses of power against women: Sexism, gender role conflict, and psychological violence. In E. P. Cook (Ed.), *Women, relationships, and power: Implications for counseling* (pp. 49–78). Alexandria, VA: American Counseling Association.

Orzek, A. M. (1992). Career counseling for the gay and lesbian community. In S. H. Dworkin & F. J. Gutierrez (Eds.), *Counseling gay men and lesbians: Journey to the end of the rainbow* (pp. 23–33). Alexandria, VA: American Counseling Association.

Osgood, N. (1985). *Suicide in the elderly.* Rockville, MD: Aspen.

O'Toole, K. (1988, February). American culture appears to reduce school grades. *Stanford Observer,* Stanford Center for the Study of Families, Children, and Youth supplement.

Oxford, R., & Nuby, J. F. (1998, January). *Racial differences in learning styles grades 9–12.* Paper presented at the meeting of the Multicultural Research Conference for Psychological Type and Culture, Honolulu, HI.

Padilla, A. M. (1981). Pluralistic counseling and psychotherapy for Hispanic Americans. In A. J. Marsella & P. B. Pedersen (Eds.), *Cross–cultural counseling and psychotherapy* (pp. 195–227). Elmsford, NY: Pergamon Press.

Page, R. C., Cheng, H., Pate, T. C., Mathus, B., Pryor, D., & Ko, J. (1987). The perceptions of spinal cord injured persons toward sex. *Sexuality and Disability, 8,* 112–132.

Palombo, J. (1979). Perceptual deficits and self–esteem in adolescence. *Clinical Social Work Journal, 7,* 34–61.

Pang, V. O., Mizokawa, D. T., Moishima, J. K., & Olstad, R. G. (1985). Self–concepts of Japanese–American children. *Journal of Cross–Cultural Psychology, 16,* 99–109.

Pania, T. (1992, May 10). Mother's Day brings no respite from worry about son. *San Jose Mercury News,* p. 17A.

Parham, T. A., & Helms, J. E. (1981). The influence of Black students' racial identity attitudes on preference for counselor's race. *Journal of Counseling Psychology, 28,* 250–257.

Parham, T. A., & McDavis, R. J. (1987). Black men, an endangered species: Who's really pulled the trigger? *Journal of Counseling and Development, 66,* 24–27.

Parker, W. D. (1983). The disabled and clinical sexuality. In S. F. Pariser, S. B. Levine, & M. L. Gardner (Eds.), *Clinical sexuality* (pp. 185–202). New York: Marcel Dekker.

Paster, V. S. (1985). Adapting psychotherapy for the depressed, unacculturated, acting-out, Black male adolescent. *Psychotherapy, 22,* 408–417.

Patterson, C. J. (1995). Summary of research findings. In American Psychological Association, *Lesbian and gay parenting: A resource for psychologists* (pp. 1–12). Washington, DC: Author.

Payer, L. (1989, March). Hell week. *Ms., 17*(9), 28, 30–31.

Pedersen, P. B. (1977). The triad model of cross–cultural counselor training. *Personnel and Guidance Journal, 56,* 94–100.

Pedersen, P. (1978). Four dimensions of cross–cultural counselor skill in counselor training. *Personnel and Guidance Journal, 56,* 480–484.

Pedersen, P. (1991). Counseling international students. *The Counseling Psychologist, 19*, 10–58.

Pedersen, P. B. (1994). *A handbook for developing multicultural awareness* (2nd ed.). Alexandria, VA: American Counseling Association.

Pedersen, P. (1995). *The five stages of culture shock*. Westport, CT: Greenwood Press.

Pedersen, P., Draguns, J. G., Lonner, W. J., & Trimble, J. E. (Eds.). (1996). *Counseling across cultures* (4th ed.). Thousand Oaks, CA: Sage.

Pedersen, P., Lonner, W. J., & Draguns, J. G. (Eds.). (1976). *Counseling across cultures*. Honolulu: University Press of Hawaii.

Phinney, J. (1990). Ethnic identity in adolescence and adulthood: A review of research. *Psychological Bulletin, 108*, 499–514.

Phinney, J. S. (1992). The Multigroup Ethnic Identity Measure. *Journal of Adolescent Research, 7*, 156–176.

Pinderhughes, E. (1982). Afro–American families and the victim system. In M. McGoldrick, J. Pearce, & J. Giordano (Eds.), *Ethnicity and family therapy* (pp. 108–122). New York: Guilford Press.

Pine, G. J., & Hilliard, A. G. (1990). Rx for racism: Imperatives for America's schools. *Phi Delta Kappan, 71*, 593–600.

Plas, J. M., & Bellet, W. (1983). Assessment of the value–attitude orientations of American Indian children. *Journal of School Psychology, 21*, 57–64.

PMS: A complex problem for many. (1989, Fall). *Health Scene*, 8.

Pollard, R. Q., Jr. (1996). Professional psychology and deaf people. *American Psychologist, 51*, 389–396.

Pomales, J., & Williams, V. (1989). Effects of level of acculturation and counseling style on Hispanic students' perceptions of counselor. *Journal of Counseling Psychology, 36*, 79–83.

Ponterotto, J. G. (1988). Racial consciousness development among white counselor trainees: A stage model. *Journal of Multicultural Counseling and Development, 16*, 146–156.

Ponterotto, J. G. (1997). Multicultural counseling training: A competency model and national survey. In D. B. Pope–Davis & H. L. K. Coleman (Eds.), *Multicultural counseling competencies: Assessment, education and training, and supervision* (pp. 111–130). Thousand Oaks, CA: Sage.

Ponterotto, J. G. (1998). Charting a course for research in multicultural counseling training. *The Counseling Psychologist, 26*, 43–68.

Ponterotto, J. G., & Casas, J. M. (1991). *Handbook of racial/ethnic minority counseling research*. Springfield, IL: Charles C Thomas.

Ponterotto, J. G., Rieger, B. P., Barrett, A., & Sparks, R. (1994). Assessing multicultural counseling competence: A review of instrumentation. *Journal of Counseling and Development, 72*, 316–322.

Pope-Davis, D. B., & Dings, J. G. (1995). The assessment of multicultural counseling competencies. In J. G. Ponterotto, J. M. Casas, L. A. Suzuki, & C. M. Alexander (Eds.), *Handbook of multicultural counseling* (pp. 287–311). Thousand Oaks, CA: Sage.

Pope-Davis, D. B., & Ottavi, T. M. (1994). The relationship between racism and racial identity among White Americans: A replication and extension. *Journal of Counseling and Development, 72*, 293–297.

Poston, W. S. C. (1990). The biracial identity development model: A needed addition. *Journal of Counseling and Development, 69*, 152–155.

Pouliot, J. S. (1996, June). Diabetes: Are you its type? *Better Homes and Gardens, 74*(6), 74, 76, 79.

Preli, R., & Bernard, J. M. (1993). Making multiculturalism relevant for majority culture graduate students. *Journal of Marital and Family Therapy, 19*, 5–16.

Pruitt, A. S., & Isaac, P. D. (1985). Discrimination in recruitment, admission, and retention of minority students. *Journal of Negro Education, 54*, 526–535.

Pudgett, T. (1988, December 5). Waking up to a nightmare: Hispanics confront the growing threat of AIDS. *Newsweek, 24,* 29.

Quintana, S. M., & Bernal, M. E. (1995). Ethnic minority training in counseling psychology: Comparisons with clinical psychology and proposed standards. *The Counseling Psychologist, 23,* 102–121.

Ramirez, M., III. (1984). Assessing and understanding biculturalism–multiculturalism in Mexican–American adults. In J. L. Martinez, Jr., & R. H. Mendoza (Eds.), *Chicano psychology* (pp. 77–94). Orlando, FL: Academic Press.

Raspberry, W. (1990, February 10). Asian Americans—Too successful? *The Washington Post,* p. A23.

Reid, P. T. (1993, Winter). Women of color have no "place." *Focus, 7*(1), 2–3.

Reis, M., & Nahmiash, D. (1995). When seniors are abused: An intervention model. *The Gerontologist, 35,* 666–671.

Reis, M., Nahmiash, D., & Shrier, R. (1993). *A Brief Abuse Screen for the Elderly (BASE): Its validity and use.* Paper presented at the 22nd annual scientific and educational meeting of the Canadian Association on Gerontology, Montreal, Quebec.

Remafedi, G. (1987). Homosexual youth: A challenge to contemporary society. *Journal of the American Medical Association, 258,* 222–225.

Reynolds, A. L. (1995). Challenges and strategies for teaching multicultural counseling courses. In J. G. Ponterotto, J. M. Casas, L. A. Suzuki, & C. M. Alexander (Eds.), *Handbook of multicultural counseling* (pp. 312–330). Thousand Oaks, CA: Sage.

Richardson, B. L. (1991). Utilizing the resources of the African American church: Strategies for counseling professionals. In C. C. Lee & B. L. Richardson (Eds.), *Multicultural issues in counseling: New approaches to diversity* (pp. 65–75). Alexandria, VA: American Counseling Association.

Richardson, E. H. (1981). Cultural and historical perspectives in counseling Indians. In D. W. Sue (Ed.), *Counseling the culturally different* (pp. 216–255). New York: Wiley.

Ridley, C. R. (1989). Racism in counseling as an adversive behavioral process. In P. B. Pedersen, J. G. Draguns, W. J. Lonner, & J. E. Trimble (Eds.), *Counseling across cultures* (3rd ed., pp. 55–77). Honolulu: University of Hawaii Press.

Ridley, C. R., Mendoza, D. W., & Kanitz, B. E. (1994). Multicultural training: Reexamination, operationalization, and integration. *The Counseling Psychologist, 22,* 227–289.

Riger, A. L. (1992). Disability issues stance tests our ethical integrity. *APA Monitor, 23*(11), p. 4.

Riggs, M. (1989). *Tongues untied.* New York: P.V.O.

Ritter, K. Y. (1993). Depression in women. In E. P. Cook (Ed.), *Women, relationships, and power: Implications for counseling* (pp. 139–178). Alexandria, VA: American Counseling Association.

Robertson, J. M., & Fitzgerald, L. F. (1992). Overcoming the masculine mystique: Preferences for alternative forms of assistance among men who avoid counseling. *Journal of Counseling Psychology, 39,* 240–246.

Robins, L. N., Helzer, J. E., Weissman, M. M., Orvaschel, H., Gruenberg, E., Burke, J. D., & Regier, D. A. (1984). Lifetime prevalence of specific psychiatric disorders in three sites. *Archives of General Psychiatry, 41,* 949–958.

Robinson, T. L., & Howard–Hamilton, M. (1994). An Afrocentric paradigm: Foundation for a healthy self–image and healthy interpersonal relationships. *Journal of Mental Health Counseling, 16,* 327–339.

Rodriguez–Nelson, M. (1993, Spring). Counseling Latino women. *Focus, 7*(2), 6, 16.

Rogers, C. R. (1951). *Client–centered therapy: Its current practice, implications, and theory.* Boston: Houghton Mifflin.

Rogers-Dulan, J., & Blacher, J. (1995). African American families, religion, and disability: A conceptual framework. *Mental Retardation, 33,* 226–238.

Rogler, L. H. (1994). International migrations: A framework for directing research. *American Psychologist, 49,* 701–708.

Rogler, L. H., Cortes, D. E., & Malgady, R. G. (1991). Acculturation and mental health status among Hispanics. *American Psychologist, 46,* 585–597.

Rogoff, B., & Chavajzy, P. (1995). What's become of research on the cultural basis of cognitive development? *American Psychologist, 50,* 859–877.

Roland, J. (1994). *Families, illness and disability.* New York: Basic Books.

Romei, L. K. (1991, September). No handicap to hiring: How the new law affects you. *Modern Office Technology, 36*(9), 88–90.

Rooney, S. C., Flores, L. Y., & Mercier, C. A. (1998). Making multicultural education effective for everyone. *The Counseling Psychologist, 26,* 22–32.

Rothblum, E. D. (1990). Depression among lesbians: An invisible and unresearched phenomenon. *Journal of Gay and Lesbian Psychotherapy, 1,* 67–87.

Rotunno, M., & McGoldrick, M. (1982). Italian families. In M. McGoldrick, J. Pearce, & J. Giordano (Eds.), *Ethnicity and family therapy* (pp. 340–363). New York: Guilford Press.

Row, W., Behrens, J. T., & Leach, M. M. (1995). Racial/ethnic identity and racial consciousness. In J. G. Ponterotto, J. M. Casas, L. A. Suzuki, & C. M. Alexander (Eds.), *Handbook of multicultural counseling* (pp. 218–235). Thousand Oaks, CA: Sage.

Ruiz, A. (1981). Cultural and historical perspectives in counseling Hispanics. In D. W. Sue (Ed.), *Counseling the culturally different: Theory and practice* (pp. 186–215). New York: Wiley.

Ruiz, A. S. (1990). Ethnic identity: Crisis and resolution. *Journal of Multicultural Counseling and Development, 18,* 29–40.

Ruiz, R. A., & Padilla, A. M. (1977). Counseling Latinos. *Personnel and Guidance Journal, 55,* 401–408.

Rumbaut, R. (1985). Mental health and the refugee experience: A comparative study of Southeast Asian refugees. In Tom Owan (Ed.), *Southeast Asian mental health: Treatment, prevention, services, training, and research* (pp. 433–456). Washington, DC: U.S. Department of Health and Human Services.

Russell, D. E. H. (1986). *Sexual exploitation: Rape, child sexual abuse and workplace harassment.* Beverly Hills, CA: Sage.

Russo, N. F. (1990). Forging research priorities for women's mental health. *American Psychologist, 45,* 368–373.

Saakvitne, K. W., & Pearlman, L. A. (1993). The impact of internalized misogyny and violence against women on feminine identity. In E. P. Cook (Ed.), *Women, relationships, and power: Implications for counseling* (pp. 247–274). Alexandria, VA: American Counseling Association.

Sabnani, H. B., Ponterotto, J. G., & Borodovsky, L. G. (1991). White racial identity development and cross–cultural counselor training: A stage model. *The Counseling Psychologist, 19,* 76–102.

Sabogal, F., Marin, G., Otero–Sabogal, R., Marin, B. V., & Perez–Stable, E. J. (1987). Hispanic familism and acculturation: What changes and what doesn't? *Hispanic Journal of Behavioral Sciences, 9,* 397–412.

Sackett, P. R., & Wilk, S. L. (1994). Within–group norming and other forms of score adjustment in preemployment testing. *American Psychologist, 49,* 929–954.

Sage, G. P. (1991). Counseling American Indian adults. In C. C. Lee & B. L. Richardson (Eds.), *Multicultural issues in counseling: New approaches to diversity* (pp. 23–35). Alexandria, VA: American Counseling Association.

Salgado de Snyder, V. N. (1987). Factors associated with acculturative stress and depressive symptomatology among married Mexican immigrant women. *Psychology of Women Quarterly, 11,* 475–488.

Salgado de Snyder, V. N., Cervantes, R. C., & Padilla, A. M. (1990). Gender and ethnic differences in psychosocial stress and generalized distress among Hispanics. *Sex Roles, 22,* 441–453.

Samuda, R. J. (1975). *Psychological testing of American minorities.* New York: Dodd, Mead.

Sanchez, A. R., & Atkinson, D. R. (1983). Mexican American cultural commitment, preference for counselor ethnicity, and willingness to use counseling. *Journal of Counseling Psychology, 30,* 215–220.

Sanders, D. (1987). Cultural conflicts: An important factor in the academic failures of American Indian students. *Journal of Multicultural Counseling and Development, 15,* 81–90.

Sandhu, D. S. (1993). Making the foreign familiar. *American Counselor, 2*(2), 22–25.

Sandoval, M. C. (1979). Santeria as a mental health care system: An historical overview. *Social Science and Medicine, 13B,* 137–151.

Sang, B. E. (1992). Counseling and psychotherapy with midlife and older lesbians. In S. H. Dworkin & F. J. Gutierrez (Eds.), *Counseling gay men and lesbians: Journey to the end of the rainbow* (pp. 35–48). Alexandria, VA: American Counseling Association.

Santiago–Rivera, A. L. (1995). Developing a culturally sensitive treatment modality for bilingual Spanish–speaking clients: Incorporating language and culture in counseling. *Journal of Counseling and Development, 74,* 12–17.

Scarr, S., Phillips, D., & McCartney, K. (1989). Working mothers and their families. *American Psychologist, 44,* 1402–1409.

Scher, M. (1979). On counseling men. *Personnel and Guidance Journal, 57,* 252–254.

Schoenfeld, P., Halevy–Martini, J., Hemley–Van der Velden, E., & Ruhf, L. (1985). Network therapy: An outcome study of twelve social networks. *Journal of Community Psychology, 13,* 281–287.

Scott, A. (1984, August 5). Prejudice awaits Japanese children returning from abroad. *San Francisco Examiner,* p. A14.

Scott–Blair, M. (1986, December 28). Ethnic background results in added pressure to do well. *The San Diego Union,* p. A10.

Scott-Jones, D. (1995, December). The *Bell Curve* critique. *Focus, 9*(2), 14–16.

Sex survey finds fewer gays and lesbians than many thought. (1994, October 19). *San Francisco Chronicle,* p. E3.

Shackford, K. (1984). Interracial children: Growing up healthy in an unhealthy society. *Interracial Books for Children Bulletin, 15,* 4–6.

Shibutani, T., & Kwan, K. M. (1965). *Ethnic stratification.* New York: Macmillan.

Shockley, W. (1971). Models, mathematics, and the moral obligation to diagnose the origin of Negro IQ deficits. *Review of Educational Research, 41,* 369–377.

Shore, J. (1975). American Indian suicide: Fact and fantasy. *Psychiatry, 8,* 86–91.

Siegel, A. (1992, February). Black professionals: A progress report. *Working Woman, 17*(2)24.

Silverberg, R. A. (1986). *Psychotherapy for men.* Springfield, IL: Charles C Thomas.

Sjogren, E. (1988, November). Growing up abroad. *TWA Ambassador, 52,* 78, 81–82.

Slater, B. R. (1988). Essential issues in working with lesbian and gay male youths. *Professional Psychology: Research and Practice, 19,* 226–235.

Sleek, S. (1995, September). Religion can play hidden role in relationships. *APA Monitor, 26*(9), p. 41.

Sleek, S. (1996, October). Research identifies causes of internal homophobia. *APA Monitor, 27*(10), p. 57.

Smart, J. F., & Smart, D. W. (1995). Acculturative stress of Hispanics: Loss and challenge. *Journal of Counseling and Development, 73,* 390–396.

Snyder, F. (1990, May). Women's health. *Ladies' Home Journal, 107*(5), 112, 114.

Sobie, J. (1986). The culture shock of coming home again. In C. N. Austin, (Ed.), *Cross cultural re-entry: A book of readings* (pp. 95–101). Abilene, TX: Abilene Christian University.

Sodowsky, G. R., Taffe, R. C., Gutkin, T. B., & Wise, S. L. (1994). Development of the Multicultural Counseling Inventory: A self–report measure of multicultural competencies. *Journal of Counseling Psychology, 41,* 137–148.

Special Committee on Aging. (1983). *Developments in aging: 1983* (Vol. 1). Washington, DC: U.S. Government Printing Office.

Srole, L., Langner, T., Michael, S., Opler, M. K., & Rennies, T. A. (1962). *Mental health in the metropolis: Midtown Manhattan study* (Vol. 1). New York: McGraw-Hill.

Starr, T. (1991). *The "natural inferiority" of women.* New York: Poseidon Press.

State of California Department of Mental Health. (1981a). *Asian/Pacific islander cultural strengths and stresses: Samoans in America.* Oakland, CA: Author.

State of California Department of Mental Health. (1981b). *Asian/Pacific islander cultural strengths and stresses: Vietnamese in America.* Oakland, CA: Author.

Stave, B. M., & Sutherland, J. F. (with Salerno, A.). (1994). *From the Old Country.* New York: Twayne.

Stokoe, W. C., Casterline, D. C., & Croneberg, C. G. (1965). *A dictionary of American Sign Language on linguistic principles.* Washington, DC: Gallaudet College Press.

Stoltz–Loike, M. (1992). The working family: Helping women balance the roles of wife, mother, and career woman. *Career Development Quarterly, 40,* 244–256.

Sturm, R., & Wells, K. B. (1995). How can care for depression become more cost–effective? *Journal of the American Medical Association, 273,* 51–58.

Sudbury, M. A. (1993). Cross cultural psychotherapy with deaf persons: A hearing, White, middle class, middle aged, non–gay, Jewish, male therapist's perspective. *Journal of the American Deafness and Rehabilitation Association, 26*(4), 43–55.

Sue, D. W. (1973). Asians are... *Personnel and Guidance Journal, 51,* 397–399.

Sue, D. (1990). Culture in transition: Counseling Asian–American men. In D. Moore & F. Leafgren (Eds.), *Men in conflict* (pp. 153–165). Alexandria, VA: American Association for Counseling and Development.

Sue, D. W., Arredondo, P., & McDavis, R. J. (1992a). Multicultural counseling competencies and standards: A call to the profession. *Journal of Counseling and Development, 70,* 477–486.

Sue, D. W., Arredondo, P., & McDavis, R. J. (1992b). Multicultural counseling competencies and standards: A call to the profession. *Journal of Multicultural Counseling and Development, 20,* 64–68.

Sue, D. W., Bernier, J. E., Durran, D., Feinberg, L., Pedersen, P. B., Smith, E. J., & Vasquez–Nuttall, E. (1982). Cross–cultural counseling competencies. *The Counseling Psychologist, 10,* 45–52.

Sue, D. W., Ivey, A. E., & Pedersen, P. B. (Eds.). (1996). *A theory of multicultural counseling and therapy.* Pacific Grove, CA: Brooks/Cole.

Sue, D., & Sue, S. (1987). Cultural factors in the clinical assessment of Asian Americans. *Journal of Consulting and Clinical Psychology, 55,* 479–487.

Sue, D. W., & Sue, D. (1990). *Counseling the culturally different: Theory and practice* (2nd ed.). New York: Wiley.

Sue, D., & Sue, D. M. (1995). Asian Americans. In N. Vacc, S. DeVaney, & J. Wittmer (Eds.), *Experiencing and counseling multicultural and diverse populations* (pp. 63–89). Bristol, PA: Accelerated Development.

Sue, S. (1994, August). *Psychopathology among Asian Americans: A model minority?* Paper presented at the meeting of the Asian American Psychological Association, Los Angeles.

Sue, S. (1998). In search of cultural competence in psychotherapy and counseling. *American Psychologist, 53,* 440–448.

Sue, S., & Sue, D. W. (1974). MMPI comparisons between Asian–American and non–Asian students utilizing a student health psychiatric clinic. *Journal of Counseling Psychology, 21,* 423–427.

Suinn, R. M., Rickard–Figueroa, K., Lew, S., & Vigil, S. (1987). The Suinn–Lew Asian Self-Identity Acculturation Scale: An initial report. *Educational and Psychological Measurement, 47,* 401–407.

Summit results in formation of spirituality competencies. (1995, December). *Counseling Today, 38*(6), 30.

Sutton, C. T., & Broken Nose, M. A. (1996). American Indian families: An overview. In M. McGoldrick, J. Giordano, & J. K. Pearce (Eds.), *Ethnicity and family therapy* (2nd ed., pp. 31–44). New York: Guilford Press.

Suzuki, L. A., & Kugler, J. F. (1995). Intelligence and personality assessment: Multicultural perspectives. In J. G. Ponterotto, J. M. Casas, L. A. Suzuki, & C. M. Alexander (Eds.), *Handbook of multicultural counseling* (pp. 493–515). Thousand Oaks, CA: Sage.

Swanson, J. L., & Tokar, D. M. (1991). Development and initial validation of the Career Barriers Inventory. *Journal of Vocational Behavior, 39,* 344–361.

Sweeney, T. J., & Myers, J. E. (1991). Early recollections: An Adlerian technique with older people. *The Clinical Gerontologist, 4*(4), 3–12.

Sweetland, R. C., & Keyser, D. J. (Eds.). (1983). *Tests.* Kansas City, MO: Test Corporation of America.

Taffel, R. (1991). Bringing the job home. *Family Therapy Networker, 15*(6), 46–54.

Tafoya, N., & Del Vecchio, A. D. (1996). Back to the future: An examination of the Native American holocaust experience. In M. McGoldrick, J. Giordano, & J. K. Pearce (Eds.), *Ethnicity and family therapy* (2nd ed., pp. 45–54). New York: Guilford Press.

Tainter, B., Compisi, C., & Richards, C. (1995). Embracing cultural diversity in the rehabilitation system. In S. Walker (Ed.), *Disability and diversity: New leadership for a new era* (pp. 28–32). Washington, DC: President's Committee on Employment of People With Disabilities and the Howard University Research and Training Center.

Tajfel, H. (1981). *Human groups and social categories.* New York: Cambridge University Press.

Takeuchi, D. T., Sue, S., & Yeh, M. (1995). Return rates and outcomes from ethnicity-specific mental health programs in Los Angeles. *American Journal of Public Health, 85,* 638–643.

Tannen, D. (1990). *You just don't understand: Women and men in conversation.* New York: William Morrow.

Tatum, B. D. (1993, Spring). Coming of age: Black youth in White communities. *Focus, 7*(2), 15–16.

Taylor, S. E., Wood, J. V., & Lichtman, R. R. (1983). It could be worse: Selective evaluation as a response to victimization. *Journal of Social Issues, 39,* 19–40.

Teachers Insurance and Annuity Association–College Retirement Equities Fund. (1996, August). Born to retire. *The Participant,* 8–13.

Tefft, S. K. (1967). Anomy, values and culture change among teen–age Indians: An exploratory study. *Sociology of Education, 40*(2), 145–157.

Thomas, K., & Althen, G. (1989). Counseling foreign students. In P. Pedersen, J. G. Draguns, W. J. Lonner, & J. E. Trimble (Eds.), *Counseling across cultures* (3rd ed., pp. 205–241). Honolulu: University of Hawaii Press.

Thomas, M. B., & Dansby, P. G. (1985). Black clients: Family structures, therapeutic issues, and strengths. *Psychotherapy, 22, 398*–407.

Thomason, T. C. (1995). Counseling Native American students. In C. C. Lee (Ed.), *Counseling for diversity: A guide for school counselors and related professionals* (pp. 109–126). Boston: Allyn & Bacon.

Tien, L. (1994). Southeast Asian American refugee women. In L. Comas–Diaz & B. Greene (Eds.), *Women of color: Integrating ethnic and gender identities in psychotherapy* (pp. 479–503). New York: Guilford Press.

Tomes, H. (1992, March). Disabilities are major public interest issue. *APA Monitor, 23*(3), p. 26.

Tomine, S. I. (1991). Counseling Japanese Americans: From internment to reparation. In C. C. Lee & B. L. Richardson (Eds.), *Multicultural issues in counseling: New approaches to diversity* (pp. 91–105). Alexandria, VA: American Counseling Association.

Trimble, J. E., & Fleming, C. M. (1989). Providing counseling services for Native American Indians: Client, counselor, and community characteristics. In P. B. Pedersen, J. G. Draguns, W. J. Lonner, & J. E. Trimble (Eds.), *Counseling across cultures* (3rd ed., pp. 177–204). Honolulu: University of Hawaii Press.

Troiden, R. R. (1989). The formation of homosexual identities. *Journal of Homosexuality, 17,* 43–73.

Tucker, M. B., & Mitchell–Kernan, C. (1990). New trends in Black–American interracial marriage: The social structural context. *Journal of Marriage and the Family, 52,* 209–218.

Uba, L. (1994). *Asian Americans: Personality patterns, identity, and mental health.* New York: Guilford Press.

U.S. Bureau of the Census. (1981). *Age, sex, race, and Spanish origin of the population by regions, divisions, and states: 1980.* Supplementary Reports: 1980 Census of the Population. Washington, DC: U.S. Government Printing Office.

U.S. Bureau of the Census. (1985). *American Indians, Eskimos and Aleuts on identified reservations and in the historic areas of Oklahoma (excluding urbanized areas): 1980 census of population.* (Subject Report PC80–2–1D, Part 1). Washington, DC: U.S. Department of Commerce.

U.S. Bureau of the Census (1986). *Statistical abstract of the United States: 1987* (107th ed.). Washington, DC: U.S. Government Printing Office.

U.S. Bureau of the Census. (1988). *The Hispanic population in the United States: March 1988.* Washington, DC: U.S. Government Printing Office.

U.S. Bureau of the Census. (1990a). *Census of population and housing summary* (Tape File 1C, CD–ROM). Washington, DC: U.S. Government Printing Office.

U.S. Bureau of the Census (1990b). *Marital status and living arrangements: March, 1990* (Current Population Reports, Series P–20, No. 450). Washington, DC: U.S. Government Printing Office.

U.S. Bureau of the Census. (1990c). *Statistical abstract of the United States.* Washington, DC: U.S. Government Printing Office.

U.S. Bureau of the Census. (1991). *Population profile of the United States: 1991* (Current Population Reports, Series P–23, No. 173). Washington, DC: U.S. Government Printing Office.

U.S. Bureau of the Census. (1992). *The Hispanic population in the United States: March 1991.* Washington, DC: U.S. Government Printing Office.

U.S. Bureau of the Census. (1993a). *Statistical abstract of the United States.* Washington, DC: U.S. Government Printing Office.

U.S. Bureau of the Census. (1993b, September). *We the first Americans.* Washington, DC: U.S. Government Printing Office.

U.S. Department of Labor (1982). *Accommodation can be reasonable: A study of accommodations provided to handicapped employees be federal contractors.* Washington, DC: Author.

U.S. General Accounting Office, Human Resources Division. (1990). *Asian Americans.* (Report No. GAO/HRD90-36FS). Washington, DC: Author.

U.S. Senate Select Committee on Indian Affairs. (1985). *Indian juvenile alcoholism and eligibility for BIA schools* (Senate Hearing 99–286). Washington, DC: U.S. Government Printing Office.

Useem, R. H. (1966). The American family in India. *The Annals, 368,* 132–145.

Vacc, N. A., & Clifford, K. (1995). Individuals with a physical disability. In N. Vacc, S. DeVaney, & J. Wittmer (Eds.), *Experiencing and counseling multicultural and diverse populations* (pp. 251–271). Bristol, PA: Accelerated Development.

Van Meter, M. J. S., & Agronow, S. J. (1982). The stress of multiple roles: The case for role strain among married college women. *Family Relations, 31,* 131–138.

Vasquez, M. J. T. (1982). Confronting barriers to participation of Mexican American women in higher education. *Hispanic Journal of Behavioral Sciences, 4,* 147–165.

Vasquez, M. J. T. (1994). Latinas. In L. Comas–Diaz & B. Greene (Eds.), *Women of color* (pp. 114–138). New York: Guilford Press.

Vernon, J. (1995). An historical perspective on psychology and deafness. *Journal of the American Deafness and Rehabilitation Association, 29*(2), 8–13.

Vernon, M., & Andrews, J. F. (1989). *The psychology of deafness: Understanding deaf and hard of hearing people.* New York: Longman.

Voices of diversity. (1993, March 7). *San Jose Mercury News West Magazine,* pp. 8–23.

Vontress, C. E. (1976). Counseling middle–aged and aging cultural minorities. *Personnel and Guidance Journal, 55,* 132–135.

Vontress, C. E. (1981). Racial and ethnic barriers in counseling. In P. B. Pedersen, J. G. Draguns, W. J. Lonner, & J. E. Trimble (Eds.), *Counseling across cultures* (2nd ed., pp. 87–107). Honolulu: University of Hawaii Press.

Walker, L. (1984). *The battered woman syndrome.* New York: Springer.

Wampold, B. E., Casas, J. M., & Atkinson, D. R. (1981). Ethnic bias in counseling: An information processing approach. *Journal of Counseling Psychology, 28,* 498–503.

Warren, L. W. (1983). Male intolerance of depression: A review with implications for psychotherapy. *Clinical Psychology Review, 3,* 147–156.

Watters, E. (1995, September 17). Claude Steele has scores to settle. *New York Times Magazine,* pp. 45–47.

Waxman, H. M., Carner, E. A., & Klein, M. A. (1984). Underutilization of mental health professionals by community elderly. *The Gerontologist, 24,* 23–30.

Webster's seventh new collegiate dictionary. (1969). Springfield, MA: G.&C. Merriam.

Webster's third new international dictionary of the English language, unabridged. (1981). Springfield, MA: Merriam–Webster.

Wehrly, B. (1991). Preparing multicultural counselors. *Counseling and Human Development, 24*(3), 1–24.

Weinberg, G. (1972). *Society and the healthy homosexual.* Garden City, NY: Anchor.

Weiss, D. E. (1991, March 31). Long and short of the division between the sexes. *San Jose Mercury News,* pp. 1L, 8L.

Welts, E. P. (1982). Greek families. In M. McGoldrick, J. Pearce, & J. Giordano (Eds.), *Ethnicity and family therapy* (pp. 269–288). New York: Guilford Press.

White, J. (1984). *The psychology of Blacks.* Englewood Cliffs, NJ: Prentice Hall.

White, J., & Parham, T. (1990). *The psychology of Blacks: An African–American perspective* (2nd ed.). Englewood Cliffs, NJ: Prentice Hall.

Wilcox, D. W., & Forrest, L. (1992). The problems of men and counseling: Gender bias or gender truth? *Journal of Mental Health Counseling, 14,* 291–304.

Wilkins, R. (1995, March 27). Racism has its privileges. *Nation, 260*(12), 409–410, 412, 414–416.

Williams, C. (1987). Issues surrounding psychological testing of minority patients. *Hospital and Community Psychiatry, 38,* 184–189.

Williams, C. L., & Berry, J. W. (1991). Primary prevention of acculturative stress among refugees. *American Psychologist, 46,* 632–641.

Willms, G. (1990). The application of Morita's principle to work with HIV–infected clients. *Journal of Morita Therapy, 1,* 233–235.

Wilson, L. L., & Stith, S. M. (1991). Culturally sensitive therapy with Black clients. *Journal of Multicultural Counseling and Development, 19,* 32–43.

Winawer–Steiner, H., & Wetzel, N. A. (1982). German families. In M. McGoldrick, J. Pearce, & J. Giordano (Eds.), *Ethnicity and family therapy* (pp. 247–268). New York: Guilford Press.

Wolf, T. J. (1992). Bisexuality: A counseling perspective In S. H. Dworkin & F. J. Gutierrez (Eds.), *Counseling gay men and lesbians: Journey to the end of the rainbow* (pp. 175–187). Alexandria, VA: American Counseling Association.

Wolfe, H. B. (1995). Women entering or reentering the work force. In N. Vacc, S. DeVaney, & J. Wittmer (Eds.), *Experiencing and counseling multicultural and diverse populations* (3rd ed., pp. 317–337). Bristol, PA: Accelerated Development.

Wolfe, S. M., Fugate, L., Hulstrand, E. P., & Kamimoto, L. E. (1988). *Worst pills, best pills: The older adult's guide to avoiding drug induced death or illness.* Washington, DC: Public Citizen Health Research Group.

Women narrow the paycheck gap. (1996, January 16). *San Jose Mercury News,* p. 3E.

Wrenn, G. (1962). The encapsulated counselor. *Harvard Educational Review, 32,* 444–449.

Wright, B. A. (1983). *Physical disability—A psychosocial approach* (2nd ed.). New York: Harper & Row.

Yamaguchi, S. (1995). Review of *Japanese sense of self. Journal of Cross-Cultural Psychology, 26,* 441–442.

Yamamoto, J., & Acosta, F. X. (1982). Treatment of Asian Americans and Hispanic Americans: Similarities and differences. *American Academy of Psychoanalysis, 10,* 585–607.

Yeh, M., Takeuchi, D. T., & Sue, S. (1994). Asian American children in the mental health system: A comparison of parallel and mainstream outpatient service centers. *Journal of Clinical Child Psychology, 23,* 5–12.

Youngstrom, N. (1992a, July). ADA is super advocate for those with disabilities. *APA Monitor, 23*(7), p. 26.

Youngstrom, N. (1992b, February). Adapt to diversity or risk irrelevance, field warned. *APA Monitor, 23*(2), p. 44.

Zapata, J. T. (1995). Counseling Hispanic children and youth. In C. C. Lee (Ed.), *Counseling for diversity: A guide for school counselors and related professionals* (pp. 85–108). Boston: Allyn & Bacon.

Zera, D. (1992). Coming of age in a heterosexist world: The development of gay and lesbian adolescents. *Adolescence, 27,* 849–854.

Ziegler, J. (1986, February 5). Doctors talk about race and mental illness. *San Francisco Examiner,* p. E2.

Zinick, G. (1985). Identity conflict or adaptive flexibility? Bisexuality reconsidered. *Journal of Homosexuality, 11,* 7–19.

Zuckerman, M. (1990). Some dubious premises in research and theory on racial differences. *American Psychologist, 45,* 1297–1303.

Zuniga, M. E. (1988). Assessment issues with Chicanas: Practice implications. *Psychotherapy, 25,* 288–293.

Zuniga, M. E. (1991). "Dichos" as metaphorical tools for Latino clients. *Psychotherapy, 28,* 480–483.

INDEX

9-to-5 Working Women Educational
Fund, 135

A

Abbitt, D., 145, 156
Ablism, 2, 13, 177
*Accessing Awareness and Developing
Knowledge* (McGrath & Axelson), 21
Acculturation Rating Scale for Mexican
Americans, 33
Acculturation Rating Scale for Puerto
Ricans, 33
Acculturation, 6, 30–32, 36–47
  Asian American men, 137
  counseling, 39–44
  culture shock, 38–39
  generational effects, 46–47
  group–specific measures, 33
  language, 97
  re–entry shock, 44–45
  social readjustment, 37–38
Acosta, F. X., 47
Acts of Congress
  Age Discrimination in Employment
    Act, 160
  Americans With Disabilities Act, 175,
    178, 182
  Civil Rights Act of 1964, 23–24, 75
  Civil Rights Act of 1991, 24
  Comprehensive Education Training
    Act, 124
  Dawes Act, 59
  Educational Amendments Act, 124
  Equal Pay Act of 1963, 123
  Immigration Act of 1965, 117

  Immigration Reform and Control Act
    of 1986, 99
  Indian Child Welfare Act, 59
  Indian Removal Act, 59
  Older Americans Act, 160
  Women's Educational Equity Act of
    1974, 123–124
Acupuncture, 107
Adara, 181, 185
Adelman, M., 147
Adler, A., 1, 172
Adler, N. J., 44–45
Adler, P., 39
Adler, T., 130, 147
Adolescents
  gay/lesbian, 147, 152–153
  Latino/Latina, 98
Adoption
  gays/lesbians, 156
  Native Americans, 59–60
Affirmative action
  and testing, 23–25
  brief history, 24
African American church, 76–77, 80, 137
African Americans, 1, 3, 5, 11–12, 73–87,
  121
  assessment devices, 33
  counselors, 197–200
  cultural resources, 87
  cultural values, 76–80
  disabled, 178–179
  ethnic identity, 49–52
  gays/lesbians, 149–150
  histories/diversity, 73–76
  indigenous treatment methods, 80–81
  IQ testing, 22–23, 27

job discrimination, 2
men, 137
Meyers–Briggs scores, 28
MMPI scores, 27–28
older, 161–162
proverbs, 79
Strong Interest Survey, 28
test bias, 26
treatment implications, 82–87
women, 124–125
African Self–Consciousness Scale, 33
Afrocentric worldview, 78–80
Ageism, 2, 13, 159–160
Agronow, S. J., 133
AIDS
gays, 151, 153, 157
Latinos/Latinas, 90, 93–94, 125
men, 137
women, 124
Ajase complex, 107
Alagna, S. W., 19
Alcoholism, 176
African American women, 124
lesbians, 149
Native Americans, 66, 68, 124
Alexander, C. J., 158
Allison, K. W., 192–193, 196, 198
Allport, G., 10, 17
Althen, G., 42
Alzheimer's disease, 159, 166–167, 176
American Association for Counseling and
Development, 145
American Association of Physical
Anthropologists, 12
American Association of Retired Persons,
60, 159, 162, 173
American Association of University
Women, 126
American Counseling Association, 169–
171
guidelines for multicultural counselors,
207–212
*Minimum Essential Gerontological
Competencies*, 170–171
American Deafness and Rehabilitation
Association, 181, 185
American Indian College Fund, 72
American Psychiatric Association, 34, 130,
166
Guidelines, 7, 201–206
American Psychological Association, 7,
14, 158, 188

American Sign Language, 178, 180
Anderson, D., 152–153
Anderson, M. J., 61, 65–66, 69
Andrews, J. F., 175, 177
Annie and the Old One (Miles), 72
Anwar, M. S., 80
Anxiety, 129
acculturation, 40
Appel, L., 102
Apple Computer Co., 154
Archetypes, 128–129, 140–141
Ariel, J., 154, 156–157
Armstrong, K. L., 107
Arredondo, P., 7, 89–92, 94, 99, 207–212
Asante, M. K., 78
Ashby, M. R., 65
Asian Americans, 1, 3, 9, 13, 43, 50–51,
102–113
assessment devices, 33–34
counseling issues, 108–113
counselors, 197–200
cultural resources, 113
cultural values, 104–106
disabled, 179
discrimination, 24
gay/lesbian, 150
generational acculturation, 46–47
histories/diversity, 102–104
indigenous treatment methods, 106–
108
men, 137
MMPI scores, 27–28
older, 162
women, 125
Assertiveness training, 127–128
Assessment, 6
bias, 25–30
culture–fair, 29–30
culture–specific, 30–32
historical influences, 22–25
multicultural, 32–35
AssistHers, 151–152
Association for Gay, Lesbian, and Bisexual
Issues in Counseling, 158
Association for Multicultural Counseling
and Development, 7–9, 188
Association for Spiritual, Ethical, and
Religious Value Issues in Counseling,
119
Association of Lesbian and Gay Psychologists, 158

Astin, A. W., 66
Atkinson, D. R., 49–50, 54, 99–100, 197–198
Atlantic Monthly, 185
Attneave, C., 58, 61–64, 69–70
The Autobiography of Malcolm X (Haley), 87
Avila, A. L., 90–91
Avila, D. L., 90–91
Axelson, J. A., 16, 21, 57–58, 61, 63, 65, 74–77, 81, 85, 115, 117
Azar, B., 133, 153–154

B

Bachman, S. L., 120
Backover, A., 83–84, 132
Baldwin, J. A., 33
Ballou, M., 127
Bankovics, G., 143
Baratz, J. C., 12
Baratz, S. S., 12
Barnes, M., 72
Barrett, A., 188
Bartholomew, C. G., 132
Bartlett, J., 22, 114
Baruth, L. G., 57, 58, 60–63, 65, 68, 71, 78, 83, 85, 89, 98, 110, 161–162, 166, 172
Bass, R., 113
Bay Mills Community College, 67
Behavior modification, 128, 173
Behrens, J. T., 32
Belgian Americans, 115
The Bell Curve (Herrnstein & Murray), 23
Bell, Y. R., 33
Bellet, W., 33
Bengtson, V. L., 160
Bennett, B., 146, 156
Berg, I. K., 112–113
Berger, R. M., 154, 162–163
Berman, J. S., 58
Bernal, M. E., 197–198
Bernard, J. M., 192–193, 196
Berry, J. W., 6, 40–42
Berube, M., 184–185
Berzon, B., 158
Betz, N., 133
The Bible, 123
Bibliotherapy, 154, 157, 171
Bicultural–Multicultural Experience Inventory, 33

Bienvenue, M., 181, 185
Biggs, M., 1
Bilingual education, 92
Billingsley, A., 76–78
Billson, J., 145
Bilmes, M., 106
Bingham, R. P., 196
Biofeedback, 173
Biracial identity development, 52–54
    marriage, 120–121
Bisexuals, 148–149
Bishop, B., 121
Blacher, J., 79, 178–179
The Black Church in the African American Experience (Lincoln & Mamiya), 87
Black colleges, 83–84
Black Is, Black Ain't (Riggs), 87
Black Racial Identity Scale, 33
Black rage, 82–83
Blackfeet Community College, 67
Block, C. B., 75, 82, 84–85
Bochner, S., 5, 39
Boden, R., 20, 174, 184
Body therapy, 128
Bolton, B., 33
Borodovsky, L. G., 52
Bowen family systems therapy, 87
Bowler, R. M., 40
Boy Scouts, 139
Boyd–Franklin, N., 74, 76–78, 80, 82, 85–87
Boyer, S. P., 41–42
Braunstein, M., 180
Brazziel, W. F., 197, 199
Brice, J., 76, 87
Bridgewater, D., 148, 153, 157
Brief Abuse Screen for the Elderly, 168
Brigham, C., 15
British Americans, 114–116, 118
Broken Nose, M. A., 60, 62–63, 69–71
Brown University, 24
Brown v. Board of Education, 75
Brown, D., 193
Brown, J. F., 125
Brown, L. S., 149, 154
Brown, S., 180
Buddhism, 104, 106–108
    Thervada, 108
    Zen, 107
Burciaga, J. A., 90–91
Bureau of Indian Affairs, 57, 59–60, 65

Burke, J. D., Jr.
Burnette, E., 53, 120–121, 124
Butler, R. N., 159–160, 164–166

C

Callanan, P., 3
Cambodian Americans, 102–103, 108
Career concerns
    Asian Americans, 110–111
    disabled people, 182
    gays/lesbians, 154
    Latinos/Latinas, 98–99
    men, 142
    older people, 167
    Pacific Islander Americans, 110–111
    women, 131–133
Carner, E. A., 163
Carney, C. G., 191
Carter, R. T. 28, 32–33, 115, 132
Casas, J. M., 57, 73, 75, 86, 100, 191
Cass, V. C., 54–55
Casterline, D. C., 179
Castillo, A., 88–89
Category fallacy, 34
Cattell's Culture-Fair Series, 29
Cerhan, J. U., 104, 106
Cervantes, R. C., 91
Chan, C. S., 150
Chan, F., 179
Chan, S., 44
Chance, P., 29
Chasnoff, D., 158
Chavajzy, P., 25–26
Chavez, C., 90
Chavez, S., 53, 56
Cheatham, H., 78
Cheyenne River Community College, 67
Chicago Men's Gathering, 140
Children of a Lesser God (Sugarman &
    Palmer), 185
Children of the Dream (Edwards & Polite),
    84
Children's Hispanic Background Scale, 33
Chinese Americans, 9, 46, 102–104, 179
    folk tales, 109
Chodorow, N., 126
Chojnacki, J. T., 55
Choteau Creek (Dudley), 72
Christensen, P., 52, 54
Chronic illness, 166–167

Chung, R. C., 107–109
Church, A., 38, 40–42
Cimino, M., 145
Claiming Disability (Linton), 185
Clark Atlanta College, 83
Clark, D. H., 158
Client-centered therapy, 86, 107–108,
    113
Clifford, K., 184
Cloninger, C. R., 84
Cochlear implantation, 181
Code of Fair Testing Practices in Educa-
    tion, 29–31
Cognitive behavioral therapy, 86, 100,
    113, 165
Cognitive dissonance theory, 13–14
Cohen, H. S., 158
Coleman, H.L.K., 188
Colesberry, R. F., 113
Collage: Children of Lesbians and Gays
    Everywhere, 158
College of the Menominee Nation, 67
Colleges/universities
    Black, 83–84
    Native American, 66–67
Colonomous, B., 181, 185
The Color of Fear (Lee), 17, 21
The Color Purple (Spielberg), 135
Comas-Diaz, L., 34, 56, 124, 135
Come See the Paradise (Colesberry), 113
Coming out, 148, 153–154
Compadrazgo, 92
Competencies for Gerontological Counseling
    (Myers & Schwiebert), 172
Compisi, C., 54, 174
Complaints of a Dutiful Daughter (Hoffman),
    172
Confrontational therapy, 113
Confucianism, 104, 108, 123
Constantino, G., 95
Constructive living, 107
Contin, M., 52
Cool Pose (Majors & Billson), 145
Cooney, B., 197
Coppola, F., 101
Corbine, J. L., 57–58
Corey, G., 3
Corey, M., 3
Cornfield, S., 185
Cortes, D. E., 40–41
Costner, K., 72

Council for Accreditation of Counseling and Related Education Programs (CACREP), 7
Counseling Across Cultures (Pedersen et al.), 5
Counseling Gay Men and Lesbians (Dworkin), 158
Counseling Interracial Individuals and Families (Wehrly), 122
Countertransference, 6, 15
Courtois, C. A., 184
Cox, H. G., 166
Cravens, R. B., 34
Crawford, I., 192
Croneberg, C. G., 178
Cross, W. E., 49, 51
Cross-cultural competencies and objectives, 207–212
Cross-Cultural Counseling Inventory–Revised, 188
Crownpoint Institute of Technology, 67
The Crying Game (Woolley), 158
Cuban Americans, 9, 91
    assessment devices, 33
Cuban Behavioral Identity Questionnaire, 33
Cuellar, I., 33
Cuentos, 95
Cultural ambivalence, 15
Cultural bias, 14–15
Cultural identity, 32, 48–56
    biracial identity, 52–53
    counseling implications, 56
    cultural resources, 56
    group-specific measures, 33
    racial/ethnic identity, 49–54
Cultural racism, 13–14, 43
Cultural resources, 21, 56, 72, 87, 101, 113, 122, 135, 145, 158, 163–164, 185
Cultural values, 2, 16
    African Americans, 76–80
    Asian Americans, 104–106
    disabled people, 180–181
    gays/lesbians, 151
    Latinos/Latinas, 92–95
    men, 137–139
    Native Americans, 60–63
    older people, 163
    Pacific Islander Americans, 104–106
    women, 126

Culture shock, 5, 38–39
    counseling, 40–44
    re-entry, 44–45
Culture transition, 2, 36–47
    counseling, 39–44
    culture shock, 38–39
    generational effects, 46–47
    re-entry shock, 44–45
    social readjustment, 37–38
Culture-specific testing, 30–32
Curry, G. D., 98

D

D'Andrea, M., 146, 188–18, 192–193, 200
D'Avanzo, C., 108
Dahlstrom, L. E., 28
Dahlstrom, W. G., 28
Dana, R., 28, 30, 32–34
Dances With Wolves (Costner & Wilson), 72
Daniels, J., 188–189, 200
Danish Americans, 115
Dansby, P. G., 78
Darling, E., 80
Darron, M., 158
Darwin, C., 4
Das, A. K., 1, 5, 6, 7, 107, 114, 116, 193, 196
Davenport, D. S., 124, 137
Davidson, K., 95
Davis, L. J., 185
Davis-Eells Games, 29
Deaf culture, 181
DeAngelis, T., 7, 63, 83, 85, 147–148, 154, 193, 198
DeBruhl, M., 36, 159
Decision making
    Asian Americans, 111
    Native American, 62
    Pacific Islander Americans, 111
    women, 128
Deeley, M., 145
The Deer Hunter (Spiking et al.), 145
DeFour, D. C., 199
Del Vecchio, A. D., 60, 66, 68
DeLaGarza, D. V., 179
Delaney, H. D., 33
DelVecchio, R., 17
Dent, H. E., 25–26
Depression
    acculturation, 40

African Americans, 81, 84, 124
Asian American women, 125
disabled people, 183
intercultural marriage, 121
Latinos/Latinas, 91
Native Americans, 68, 124
older people, 160, 164–165
women, 129
Developmental Inventory of Black
    Consciousness, 33
*Diagnostic and Statistical Manual of Mental
    Disorders, 4th Edition* (APA), 34, 130
*Diagnostic and Statistical Manual of Mental
    Disorders, 3rd Edition* (APA), 130
Diagnostic issues
    African Americans, 84–85
    age, 164
    women, 129–130
Dichos, 95–96
Dillard, J. M., 65
Dim Sum (Sternberg et al.), 113
Dine'h Americans, 177
Dinges, N. G., 59, 64
Dings, J. G., 188–189, 193
Disability culture, 180–181
The Disability Rag, 180
Disabled people, 3, 54, 174–185
    counseling issues, 182–184
    cultural resources, 185
    cultural values, 180–181
    histories/diversity, 175–179
    test bias, 28–29
    treatment implications, 184
Disclosure, 127, 139, 153
    African Americans, 85
    Native Americans, 69
Discrimination, 5–6, 10–11, 19–21, 73–87,
    91–92, 98, 111, 123–124, 159–160,
    182
    pay, 131–132
Dobbins, J. E., 74
Dolnick, E., 185
Donnelly, K., 41
Dornbusch, S., 46–47
Dougherty, P., 138–140
Downing, N. E., 54
D–Q University, 67
Draguns, J. G., 5
Driving Miss Daisy (Zanuck & Zanuck), 173
Dropout rates
    African Americans, 74

Latinos/Latinas, 89–90
Mexican Americans, 91
Native Americans, 60
Puerto Ricans, 91
Dudley, J.I.E., 57, 72
Dull Knife Memorial College, 67
Dupuy, P., 155
Dworkin, S. H., 150, 158

E

Early recollections, 172
Ebonics, 79–80
Echemendia, R., 192
Edgerton, R. B., 97
Educational concerns
    African Americans, 83–84
    Asian Americans, 108–110
    Native Americans, 65–66
Edwards, A., 74–75, 84
Egan, J., 139
Ehrlich, E., 36, 159
Eichler, A., 161, 164
El Norte (Thomas), 101
Elder abuse, 168
The Elephant Man (Cornfield), 185
Ellis, R., 1, 61, 65–66, 69
Elman, M. R., 133
Emerson, G., 136
Empowerment, 6, 44
Encapsulation, 15
Enforcing Normalcy (Davis), 185
Enns, C. Z., 123, 126–129, 132, 136, 140–
    141, 192–193
Enryo, 105
Equal Rights Amendment, 124
Erickson, M. 53, 62, 108
Erikson, E., 164
Esparza, M., 101
Esquivel, L., 101
*Ethical Principles of Psychologists and Code of
    Conduct* (APA), 7–8
Ethnic Identity Questionnaire, 33
Ethnic identity, 3, 32, 48–54
Ethnicity and Family Therapy (McGoldrick
    et al.), 115, 122
Eugenics Research Association, 14
European Americans, 1, 3, 9, 114–122
    assessment devices, 33
    counseling issues, 119–121
    cultural resources, 122

indigenous treatment methods, 118
Northern European, 115–116
Southern European, 116–118
Existential therapy, 107
Extraordinary Bodies (Thomson), 185

F

Fa'a aiga family unit process, 107–108
Fabrega, H., 94
Falk, P. J., 156
Family counseling
African Americans, 86–87
Asian Americans, 113
disabled people, 183
European Americans, 118
Latinos/Latinas, 100
Milan–style, 118
Native Americans, 71
Northern European Americans, 116
older people, 173
Pacific Islander Americans, 113
women, 134
Family structure
African Americans, 77–78
Asian Americans, 104–105, 108
disabled people, 183
gays/lesbians, 157
Latinos, 92–93
Native American, 62
Pacific Islander Americans, 108
Southern European Americans, 117–118
Fang, X., 179
Fear of success, 126
Feldman, E. S., 122
Femiano, S., 140
Feminist identity development model, 54
Feminist therapy, 126–128, 132
Fendel, N., 75, 110–111, 132, 137
Fernandez, R., 97
Festinger, L., 10, 13–14
Fetal alcohol syndrome, 65
Feuerstein, R., 29
Figueroa, A., 98
Filipino Americans, 9, 102–103
Finnish Americans, 115
Fisk University, 83
Fitzgerald, L., 133, 142, 144
Fleming, C. M., 57–58, 68–71
Flores, L. Y., 192

Florida A&M, 83
Folk tales
Chinese, 109
dichos, 95–96
Puerto Rican, 95
Fond du Lac Tribal and Community
College, 67
Fontaine, C. M., 39, 44
*For Colored Girls Who Have Considered
Suicide When the Rainbow Is Enuf*
(Shange), 87
Forrest, L., 139–140, 142, 144
Forrester, D. A., 138
Fort Belknap Community College, 67
Fort Berhold Community College, 67
Fort Peck Community College, 67
Foster, S., 68–70, 77, 82, 86, 175, 182,
200
Fouad, N. A., 132, 191, 193
France, A., 36
Frank, L. W., 28
Frankl, V. E., 107
Freiberg, P., 74, 83, 90, 93, 124–125, 150
French Americans, 115–116, 118
Freud, S., 1, 118
Friend, R., 160
Froman, R., 108
Fry, P. S., 164
Frye, B., 108
Fugate, L., 164
Fukuyama, M. A., 196
Furnham, A., 5, 39

G

Gabalac, N., 127
Gallaudet University, 178
Galton Society, 14
Galton, Sir. F., 3–4
Garcia, M., 33
Garnets, L. D., 158
Garrett, J. T., 61–63, 69–71
Garrett, M. W., 61–63, 69–71
Gathering Voices (Innu Nation), 72
Gatz, M., 160, 164
Gay and Lesbian Mental Health (Alexander),
158
Gay and Lesbian Parents Coalition
International, 158
Gays, 3, 54–55, 146–158
counseling issues, 152–157

counselors, 197–200
cultural resources, 158
cultural values, 151
disabled, 179
ethnic minorities, 149–150
histories/diversity, 146–150
identity development, 54–55
indigenous treatment methods, 151–152
Latinos, 93
older, 162–163
Gelberg, S., 55
Gender roles, 125, 136
African American families, 78
analysis, 127–128
Asian Americans, 104
intercultural marriage, 121
multiple role strain, 133–134
Generational acculturation, 46–47, 97, 105, 112
German Americans, 114–116, 119
Gestalt therapy, 113, 116, 127
Gibbs, J. T., 53
Gide, A., 146
Gilbert, B., 172
Gilbert, L. A., 133
Gilchrist, L. D., 65
Gilligan, C., 126, 139
Ginsburg, H. P., 110
Giordano, J., 3, 115, 122
Glass ceiling, 131–133
Goddard, H., 14–15
Goddess psychology, 128–129
Gong-Guy, E., 34
Gonzales, R., 95–96, 101
Gonzales, S. A., 93, 125
Good, B., 23
Good, M. D., 23
Gottfredson, L. S., 24–25
Graduate Record Exams, 12–13
Grand Canyon (Kasdan et al.), 21
Grandin, T., 182
Greek Americans, 117–118
Greek Orthodox Church, 120
Greene, B., 124, 135
Grey Panthers, 173
Grieger, I., 32
Griggs v. Duke Power Company, 24
Grillo, M., 21
Group counseling
African Americans, 86

Asian Americans, 107–108, 113
men, 140
Native Americans, 71
older people, 169, 171
Pacific Islander Americans, 113
Grusznski, R., 143
Guided imagery, 64, 127–128, 173
Guidelines for Providers of Psychological Services to Ethnic, Linguistic, and Culturally Diverse Populations (APA), 201–206
Gullahorn, J., 44
Gutierrez, F. J., 49, 52–53, 150, 158
Gutkin, T. B., 189
Guze, S. B., 84
Gwyn, F., 86

H

Haitian Americans, 75
Halevy-Martini, J., 64
Haley, A., 87
Haley, J., 108
Hall, C.C.I., 53, 66
Hall, J. A., 19, 98
Hall, L. E., 196
Hamilton, M., 130
Hampton Institute, 83
Hansen effect, 46
Hanych, J. M., 198
Harris, I. C., 33
Harsh, M., 176–177, 182, 184
Harvard University, 14, 24
Harvey, D. F., 44–45
Haskell Indian Nations University, 67
Haviland, W., 2
Havinghurst, R. J., 16
Hawkins, R. L., 148, 155
Hearing impairment, 175–176, 180–181
Heck, R., 188–189
Heesacker, M., 144
The Heidi Chronicles and Other Plays (Wasserstein), 135
Heinrich, R. K., 57–58, 64, 66, 69–70
Heitner, K., 123
Helms, J. E., 32–33, 49, 51–52
Hemley-Van der Velden, E., 64
Henggeler, S., 98
Herek, G. M., 147
Hernandez, A., 188
Herring, R. D., 57–58, 60–61, 64–66, 68–71

Herrnstein, R. J., 4, 23
Hersch, P., 148, 157
Herz, F. M., 117–118, 120
Heterosexism, 13, 157
Hetrick, E. S., 152–153
Heumann, J., 174
Hiegel, J. P., 107
Hill, R., 77
Hilliard, A. G., 11–12
Hills, H. I., 192, 198
Hinduism, 107
Hines, P., 74, 76–78, 80, 82, 85–87
Hirsch, B. J., 199
Hispanic Acculturation Scale, 33
Hispanic Journal of Behavioral Sciences, 101
Hmong Americans, 102–103, 106
Ho, L., 11, 12, 16, 18
Ho, M. K., 93, 100, 113
Hochschild, A., 135
Hoffman, D., 172
Hoffman, L. 49
Hoffman, T., 33
Holland's Self-Directed Search, 28
Holm, T., 72
Holmes, T. H., 36–38
Holzer, C. E., III
Homicide rates
    African Americans, 74
    men, 137
Homma-True, R., 104–107, 111–112, 125
Homophobia, 2, 93, 144, 147–148, 150, 157
Hope, T., 158
Hopkins, R. S., 40
Hospital, J. T., 1
Howard University, 83
Howard-Hamilton, M., 79, 81
Howe Chief, E., 33
Howe, E. W., 159
Hoyt, K. B., 5, 74–75, 123, 198
Huang, L., 104
Hulstrand, E. P., 164
Human Capital Initiative, 159, 161, 164–165, 167, 173
Hunter, J., 152
Hwang, D. H., 158

I

Ibrahim, F. A., 30
Identity

confusion, 40, 46–47
development, 6, 30–32
Illness as Metaphor (Sontag), 185
Immigrants, 5, 38
    culture shock, 42–44
    generational acculturation, 46–47
    test bias, 26
Indian Assimilation Scale, 33
Indian Health Service, 124
Indigenous counseling techniques, 7
    African Americans, 80–81
    Asian Americans, 106–108 Pacific
        Islander Americans, 106–108
    European Americans, 118
    gays/lesbians, 151–152
    Latinos/Latinas, 95–96
    men, 140–141
    Native Americans, 63–65
    older people, 163–164
    women, 126–129
Innu Nation, 72
Institute for American Indian Arts, 67
Institute of Disability Culture, 180
Institutionalized racism, 12–13, 20
Intercultural marriage, 52–54, 120–121
Internalized oppression, 11
International students, 5, 38, 41–42, 45
Interpreters, 34–35
Introduction to American Deaf Culture
    (Bienvenue & Colonomous), 185
Inventing the Feeble Mind (Trent), 185
Ipsaro, A. J., 144
IQ, 14–15
    and culture, 22–23
Irish Americans, 114–116, 118
Isaac, P. D., 83
Ishiyama, F. I., 107
Islam, 77, 107
It's Elementary (Cohen & Chasnoff), 158
Italian Americans, 117–119
Ivey, A. E., 9, 118, 127, 187
Ivey, M. B., 118

J

Jackson, M., 4–5, 82
Jacobs, J. H., 53
Jacobsen, F. M., 34, 56
James, H., 114
Japanese Americans, 9, 46, 102–104
Jasso, R., 33

Jaynes, G. D., 75
Jensen, A., 4, 22–23
Jewish Americans, 117–120
John C. Smith College, 83
Johnson, C. L., 117–119
Johnson, D., 66
Johnson, F., 47, 162
Johnson, M., 28
Johnson, R. P., 169
Johnson, S. D., Jr., 193, 196
Joint Committee on Testing Practices,
    29–31
Jones, R. L., 41
Jordan, M. B., 85, 192–193
Journal of Black Psychology, 87
Journal of Black Studies, 87
Journal of Counseling and Development, 212
The Joy Luck Club (Tan), 113
Jubilee (Walker), 87
Judell, B., 146
Jung, C., 1, 128–129, 140

K

Kahn, H., 30
Kahn, K. B., 191
Kamimoto, L. E., 164
Kamin, L. J., 14–15, 21
Kanitz, B. E., 190
Karenga, M., 81
Karno, M., 97
Kasdan, L., 21
Katz, J. H., 16, 21, 115, 193
Katz, P., 70
Keerdoja, E., 53
Keita, G. P., 124, 129
Kelly, N., 113
Kemp, A. D., 83–84
Kerwin, C., 53
Keyser, D. J., 28–29, 160
Kilpatrick, A., 86
Kim, E., 135
Kim, U., 40
Kimmel, D. C., 158
King, L. S., 19
Kingston, M. H., 113
Kiselica, M. S., 197
Kitano, H.H.L., 43, 46, 103–107, 113
Klein, M. A., 163
Kluckhohn, F. R., 30
Knepp, D., 192

Koehler, N., 45
Kohatsu, E. L., 51
Kohout, J., 197–198
Korean Americans, 9, 102–103
Koss, M. P., 19, 133
Kroll, J., 44
Kubler-Ross, E., 166
Kugler, J. F., 27, 32
Kwan, K. M., 3
Kwanzaa, 81

L

La Cage aux Folles (Darron), 158
Lac Courte Oreilles Ojibwa Community
    College, 67
Lachar, D., 28
LaFromboise, T. D., 58, 60–62, 66, 68,
    124, 137, 188
Lai, E.W.M., 32
Lam, C. S., 179
Lambert, N. M., 23
Landrine, H., 129, 130
Langelier, R., 116, 118, 120
Langner, T., 120
Language, 16, 65, 91, 112, 180
    assessment bias, 34–35
    culture shock, 39, 41
    discrimination, 92
    Ebonics, 79–80
    Latinos, 97
    test bias, 25–27
Laotian Americans, 102, 106, 108
Lappin, J., 46
Lark, J. S., 197–198
Larry *v.* Riles, 23
Laster, L. T., 156–157
Latin American Stress Inventory, 30
Latinos/Latinas, 1, 3, 9, 43, 51, 75, 88–
    101, 120
    assessment devices, 33
    counseling issues, 97–100
    counselors, 197–200
    cultural resources, 101
    cultural values, 92–95
    dichos, 95–96
    disabled, 179
    ethnic identity, 49–52
    gay/lesbian, 150
    histories/diversity, 89–92
    indigenous treatment methods, 95–96

IQ testing, 23, 27
job discrimination, 24
Meyers-Briggs scores, 28
older, 162
SAT scores, 26
women, 124–125
Lau v. Nichols, 92
Lavelle, J., 44
Lawson, W. B., 84
Lazarus, P., 70
Le, P., 110
Le Vine, P., 107
Leach, M. M., 32
Leaf, P. J.
Leafgren, F., 137–140
Leal, A., 91, 199
Leal-Idrogo, A., 92
Learning Potential Assessment Device, 29
Lee, A., 158
Lee, C. C., 6, 92–93, 107, 137
Lee, M. W., 17, 21
Lee, S., 87
Lee, W. M., 26, 34–35, 112, 187, 188,
    193, 199, 200
Leech Lake Tribal College, 67
Lefley, H. P., 42, 44, 46, 81
Lega, L. I., 33
Leiter's International Performance Scale,
    29
Leong, F. T., 111
Lesbian and Gay Parenting (APA), 158
Lesbians, 3, 20, 146–158
    counseling issues, 152–157
    counselors, 197–200
    cultural resources, 158
    cultural values, 151
    disabled, 179
    ethnic minorities, 149–150
    histories/diversity, 146–150
    identity development, 54–55
    indigenous treatment methods, 151–
        152
    older, 162–163
Leung, P., 197
Levant, R. F., 133, 139, 143
Levers, L. L., 80–81
Levi Strauss, Inc., 154
Levy, J., 177
Lew, S., 33
Lewis, M. I., 164–166
Licensure, 7–9

Lichtman, R. R., 19
Lieberg, C., 57
Life as We Know It (Berube), 185
Life expectancy
    men, 137
    Native Americans, 60
Life review, 164
Life scripting, 113, 127, 173
Lijtmaer, R. M., 97
Like Water for Chocolate (Esquivel), 101
Lincoln, C. E., 87
Linton, S., 185
Little Big Horn College, 67
Little Big Man (Millar), 72
Little Hoop Community College, 67
Lloyd, C., 19
Locke, B. Z., 83, 85–86, 91
Logan, C. R., 151–152
Loiacano, D. 150
The Long Walk of Fred Young (Barnes), 72
Lonner, W. J., 5
Lopez, S., 32
Lorion, R. P., 16
Loving v. Virginia Supreme Court, 120
Lowrey, L., 71
Lum, C., 113
Lyon, J. M., 98
Lysgaard, S., 40

M

M. Butterfly (Hwang), 158
Mabry, M., 56, 87
Machismo, 93–94
Macias, C. J., 200
Mairs, N., 185
Majors, R., 145
Maki, D. R., 80–81
Malay Americans, 102
Malcolm X (Worth & Lee), 87
Malde, S., 164
Malgady, R. G., 40–41, 95
Malyon, A. K., 148
Mamiya, L. H., 87
Manese, J., 191
Manning, M. L., 57–58, 60–63, 65, 68, 71,
    78, 83, 85, 89, 98, 110, 161–162,
    166, 172
Manson, S. M., 59
Marcos, L. R., 35
Margulies, S., 87

Marin, B. V., 92
Marin, G., 33, 92
Marino, T. W., 120–121, 182
Markey, P., 113
Marriage
    biracial, 52–54
    intercultural, 120–121
    interfaith, 120
Marsella, A. J., 47
Marshall, C. A., 177–178
Martin, A. D., 152–153
Martin, W. E., 28, 68, 70, 178
Martinez, R., 33
Martz, S. H., 172
Maslow, A., 205
Masuda, M., 33
Matheson, L., 61–62
Matsumoto, G. H., 33
Mattox, C., 45
Mattson, S., 104, 106, 113, 125
May, R., 137, 141–142, 144
Mayo, J., 85
McCartney, K., 133
McDavis, R. J., 7, 74–75, 78, 83, 85–86,
    137, 202–212
McDougall, J. G., 166
McGill, D., 116, 118–119
McGoldrick, M., 3, 115–118, 120, 122
McGowan, S., 132
McGrath, E., 124–125, 129
McGrath, P., 16, 21
McIntosh, P., 51, 193
McKay, J., 43
McNair, L. D., 86
McNeil, R., 66
McRae, M. B., 193, 196
McRoy, R. G., 86
Mead, M., 22
Men in Conflict (Moore & Leafgren), 145
Men, 136–145
    counseling issues, 142–144
    cultural resources, 145
    cultural values, 137–139
    gay, 146–158
    histories/diversity, 136–137
    indigenous treatment methods, 140–
    141
Men's groups, 140
Mendoza, D. W., 190
Menjivar, C., 91, 199
Mental illness, 176–177

Mercier, C. A., 192
Meredith, G. M., 33
Mexican Americans, 9, 30, 90–91, 97, 99
    assessment devices, 33
    Meyers-Briggs scores, 28
    women, 125
Meyers-Briggs Type Indicator, 28
Michael, S., 120
Microsoft, Inc., 154
Midnight Sun, 149
Mien Americans, 102
The Milagro Beanfield War (Redford &
    Esparza), 101
Milan-style family therapy, 118
Miles, M., 72
Military personnel, 38, 45
Millar, S., 72
Miller, J. B., 126
Miller, S. D., 112–113
Milliones, J., 33
Minde, T., 40
Minkler, S., 28
Minnesota Multiphasic Personality
    Inventory, 27–28
Mintz, L. B., 131
Miramontez, A., 65
Mirroring, 69
Mississippi Masala (Nozik & Nair), 21
Mitchell-Kernan, C., 120
Mixson, R. J., 112
Mizokawa, D. T., 50
Mobility impairments, 176
Model minority myth, 108–110
Mohatt, G., 68
Mohave Americans, 149
Moishima, J. K., 50
Mok, D., 40
Mollica, R. F., 44
Mondykowski, S. M., 117–118
Moore, D., 138–139
Morales, E. S., 55, 149–150
Mordkowitz, E. R., 110
Morehouse College, 83
Morgan State University, 83
Morganthau, T., 4
Morita therapy, 107, 112
Morita, S., 107
Morrison, A. M., 143
Morrissey, M., 42–44, 129, 134, 142
Morten, G., 49–50
Moscicki, E. K., 91

Moser, N., 175
Moses, S., 199
Mosher, D. L., 157
Multicultural Awareness–Knowledge–
    Skills Survey, 188–189
Multicultural counseling
    certification, 7–9
    competencies, 188–190, 207–212
    current issues, 5–9
    curriculum, 193–196
    guidelines, 201–206
    history, 3–5
    theory, 187–188
    training, 190–197
Multicultural Counseling and Psychotherapy
    (Baruth & Manning), 172
Multicultural Counseling Awareness
    Scale, 189
Multicultural Counseling Inventory, 189
Multicultural counselors, 197–200
    barriers to participation, 199–200
Multigroup Ethnic Identity Measure, 32
Multiple role strain, 133–134
Murphy, B. C., 126, 128, 147, 149, 151–
    152, 154–155, 157
Murphy, D. M., 175–177, 180, 184–185
Murphy, D. S., 18
Murphy, J. T., 175–177, 180–185
Murray, B., 155
Murray, C., 4, 23
Murray, P., 87
Musca, T., 101
Mushuan Innu Band Council, 72
Mussenden, M. E., 196
My Family Mi Familia (Coppola), 101
My First Book of Proverbs (Gonzales & Ruiz),
    101
Myers, J. E., 29, 159–161, 163–172
Myers, J. K., 160
Mythology, 128, 140–141
Mythopoetic men's movement, 140–141

N

Nahmiash, D., 168
Naikan therapy, 107–108
Nair, M., 21
Nakagawa, J. Y., 26, 34–35
Nakao, S., 113
Nation of Islam, 77
National Association of the Deaf, 185

National Bisexual Network, 158
National Center for Educational Statistics,
    65
National Committee on Pay Equity, 131
National Gay Youth Network, 158
National Institute for Mental Health, 161
National Science Foundation, 199
Native American Value-Attitude Scale, 33
Native Americans, 1, 3, 57–72
    assessment devices, 33
    counseling issues, 68–71
    counselors, 197–200
    cultural values, 60–63
    disabled, 177–178
    gays/lesbians, 149
    histories/diversity, 57–60
    indigenous treatment methods, 63–65
    IQ testing, 23, 27
    men, 137
    Meyers-Briggs scores, 28
    older, 161
    resources, 72
    test bias, 28
    traditions, 141
    treatment implications, 65–67
    women, 124
Navajo Americans, 58, 65, 124, 149
Navajo Community College, 67
NEA Higher Education Journal, 185
Nebraska Indian Community College, 67
Neimeyer, G. J., 196
Ness, C., 149, 154–155
Nettles, M., 199
Network therapy, 63–64
Neugarten, B. L., 16
New Loving Someone Gay, The (Clark), 158
Nishio, K., 106
No Pity (Shapiro), 185
Nolen-Hoeksema, S., 131, 133
Nonverbal behavior
    Latinos/Latinas, 99
    Native Americans, 69
Norcross, J. C., 198
Norman, R. D., 33
North Carolina Central College, 83
Northern European Americans, 115–116
Northwest Indian College, 67
Norton, R., 146
Norwegian Americans, 115
Nozik, M., 21
Nuby, J. F., 28

Nutini, H., 94
Nwachuku, U. T., 127

O

O'Connor, M. F., 147, 153
O'Neil, J. M., 139
O'Toole, K., 46–47
Oberg, K., 38–39
Occupational Outlook Quarterly, 197
Office of Special Concerns, 162
Oglala Lakota College, 67
Oglesby, Z., 86
Okazai, S., 107–109
Okonogi, K., 107
Okun, C., 21
Older people, 3, 159–173
    counseling issues, 164–172
    cultural resources, 172–173
    cultural values, 163
    histories/diversity, 159–163
    indigenous treatment methods, 163–
        164
    test bias, 29
Older Women's League, 160, 173
Olstad, R. G., 50
"On a Roll," 180
On Golden Pond (Gilbert), 172
Opler, M. K., 120
Ordinary People (Schwary), 122
Orzek, A. M., 154
Osgood, N., 165
Otero-Sabogal, R., 33, 92
Ottavi, T. M., 32, 115
Out in the Workplace (Rasi & Rodriguez–
    Nogues), 158
Oxford, R., 28

P

Pacific Islander Americans, 102–113
    counseling issues, 108–113
    cultural resources, 113
    cultural values, 104–106
    histories/diversity, 102–104
    indigenous treatment methods, 106–
        108
Padilla, A. M., 91, 94, 100
Page, R. C., 176
Palmer, P., 185
Palombo, J., 177

Pang, V. O., 50
Pania, T., 74–75
Parenting issues
    fathering, 143
    gays/lesbians, 156–157
Parents, Families, and Friends of Lesbians
    and Gays, 158
Parham, T. A., 33, 79, 137
Parker, S., 138
Parker, W. D., 176
Parker, W. J., 74
Parker, W. M., 74
Parron, D. L., 161, 164
Pasquale, F. L., 59
Paster, V. S., 86
Patterson, C. J., 147, 156–157
Patterson, T. W., 34
Paul, B. D., 197–198
Payer, L., 130
Peace Corps, 4, 38
Pearce, J. K., 3, 115–116, 118–119, 122
Pearlman, L. A., 126, 131
Pearson, C. G., 160
Pease-Pretty On Top, J., 60, 68
Pedersen, P. B., 5, 9, 38–39, 41–43, 187,
    196
Perez-Stable, E. J., 33, 92
Perls, I., 1
Permanent Partners (Berzon), 158
Personalismo, 94–95, 99
Peverall, J., 145
Phillips, D., 133
Phinney, J., 32, 48
Pinderhughes, E., 78–79, 85–87
Pine, G. J., 11–12
The Pinks and the Blues (Young), 135
Plas, J. M., 33
Plessy *v.* Ferguson, 75
Polish Americans, 117–118, 120
Polite, C. K., 74–75, 84
Pollard, R. Q., Jr., 29, 176–177, 180–181
Pomales, J., 33
Ponterotto, J. G., 32, 52–53, 57, 73, 75,
    86, 188–189, 192, 196–200
Pope-Davis, D. B., 32, 115, 188–189, 193
Poston, W.S.C., 49, 52–54
Posttraumatic stress disorder, 34, 43–44,
    103, 125
Pouliot, J. S., 162
Poverty
    African Americans, 74–75

Asian Americans, 162
  Latinos/Latinas, 90–91
  Native Americans, 60
  older people, 161
  Puerto Ricans, 91
  women, 129
Preli, R., 192–193, 196
Premenstrual syndrome, 130
Prichard, S., 144
Princeton University, 24
Protestant Church, 119–120
Proud Shoes (Murray), 87
Pruitt, A. S., 83
Pseudotransference, 15
Psychodrama, 116
Psychodynamic therapy, 86, 113, 118,
  120, 171
*Psychological Perspectives of Lesbian and
  Gay Male Experiences* (Garnets &
  Kimmel), 158
Puerto Ricans, 9, 90–91
  assessment devices, 33
  cuentos, 95

Q ~ R

Quintana, S. M., 198
Race-norming, 24–25
Racism, 2, 5, 12–14, 73–76, 91–92, 121,
  124
  cultural, 43
  denial, 16
Rae, D. S., 91
Rahe, R. H., 36–38
Ramirez, M., III, 33
Rasi, R. A., 158
Raspberry, W., 24
Rational-emotive therapy, 107, 144
Raven's Standard Progressive Matrices, 29
Redford, R., 101
Re-entry shock, 44–45
Refugees, 5, 34, 38, 103
  culture shock, 42–44
  test bias, 26
Regier, D. A., 91
Reich, T., 84
Reid, P. T., 124
Reis, M., 168
Remafedi, G., 153
Remotivation therapy, 171
Rendon, M. E., 175

Rennies, T. A., 120
Retirement, 167
Reynolds, A. L., 192, 197
Richard-Figueroa, K., 33
Richards, C., 54, 174
Richardson, B. L., 77, 80, 92–93
Richardson, E. H., 61, 63, 69–70
Ridley, C. R., 15–16, 190, 193, 196
Rieger, B. P., 188
Riger, A. L., 177, 183
Riggs, M., 87, 150
Riker, H. C., 169
Ritter, K. Y., 129, 149, 154
Robertson, J. M., 142, 144
Robins, L. N., 84, 129, 165
Robinson, L., 192
Robinson, T. L., 79, 81
Rodriguez-Nelson, M., 100
Rodriguez-Nogues, L., 158
Rogers, C. R., 1, 107–108, 118
Rogers-Dulan, J., 79, 178–179
Rogler, L. H., 40–42, 91, 95, 97
Rogoff, B., 25–26
Roland, J., 179, 183
Role playing, 86, 105, 128, 140, 154
Roman Catholic Church, 94, 106, 108,
  119–120
Romei, L. K., 182
Rooney, S. C., 192, 197
Roots (Margulies), 87
Rosebud Personal Opinion Survey, 33
Rosen, E. J., 117–118, 120
Rossi, E., 62
Rossi, S., 62
Rothblum, E. D., 149
Rotunno, M., 117–118
Roush, K. L., 54
Rowe, W., 32
Ruhf, L., 64
Ruiz, A. S., 49, 51, 95–96, 100–101
Ruiz, R. A., 94
Rumbaut, R., 103
Russell, D.E.H., 131
Russian Americans, 43, 117, 120
Russo, N. F., 124, 131, 133–134, 159

S

Saakvitne, K. W., 126, 131
Sabnani, H. B., 52, 191
Sabogal, F., 33, 92

Sackett, P. R., 24–25, 27
Sage, G. P. 58, 61–62, 68–69, 71
Salgado de Snyder, V. N., 30, 91
Salish Kootenai College, 67
Samoan Americans, 102, 107
Samuda, R. J., 26
Sanchez, A. R., 99
Sanchez, F., 45
Sanders, D., 58, 65, 69
Sandhu, D. S., 41–43
Sandoval, M. C., 94
Sang, B. E., 149
Santiago-Rivera, A. L., 89, 97
Satir, V., 118
Scale to Assess World Views, 30
Scarr, S., 133
Schaecher, R., 152
Schamus, J., 158
Scher, M., 144
Schnorr, D. L., 132
Schoenfeld, P., 64
Scholastic Aptitude Test, 15, 26
    Asian Americans, 111
Schwary, R. L., 122
Schwiebert, V. L., 29, 159–161, 163–169,
    171–172
The Science and Politics of I.Q. (Kamin), 14–
    15, 21
Scott, A., 45
Scott, S., 46
Scott-Blair, M., 46, 110
Scottish Americans, 115
Scott-Jones, D., 12
The Second Shift (Hochschild), 135
Sedlacek, W. E., 41–42, 200
Segregation, 75
Self-defeating personality disorder, 130
Sexism, 2, 13, 54
Sexual abuse, 125, 129, 131
    disabled people, 183–184
Sexual harassment, 19–20, 132–133
Shackford, K., 53
Shange, N., 87
Shapiro, J., 185
Shibutani, T., 3
Shintoism, 108
Shockley, W., 4
Shore, J., 68
Shrier, R., 168
Siegel, A., 84
Silverberg, R. A., 143

Simek-Morgan, K., 118
Simmons, R., 73
Sinte Gleska University, 67
Sioux Americans, 59
Sisseton Wahpeton Community College,
    67
Sjogren, E., 40
Skillings, J. H., 74
Skinner, B. F., 1
Slater, B. R., 157
Slavery, 74–75, 76, 82–83, 124
    effects on family, 77–78
Sleek, S., 117, 119–120, 148
Smart, D. W., 91–92, 99
Smart, J. F., 91–92, 99
Smyer, M. A., 164
Snyder, F., 130
Sobie, J., 45
Social Readjustment Rating Scale, 36–38
Sodowsky, G. R., 32, 189
Sohi, B. K., 58
Sontag, S., 185
Southeast Asian Americans, 26, 44, 103,
    107–108
    assessment, 34
    women, 125
Southern European Americans, 117–118
Southern University, 83
Southwest Indian Polytechnic Institute,
    67
Sparks, R., 188
Special Committee on Aging, 161
Spergel, I. A., 98
Spielberg, S., 135
Spiking, B., 145
Spirituality
    African Americans, 76–77
    Asian Americans, 108
    European Americans, 119–120
    Latinos/Latinas, 94
    Native Americans, 60–61
    Pacific Islander Americans, 108
Srole, L., 120
Stand and Deliver (Musca), 101
Standing Rock College, 67
Stanford University, 14
Starr, T., 123
State of California Department of Mental
    Health, 106–107
Stave, B. M., 117
Stearns, S. M., 154, 156–157

Steele, C., 12
Stereotypes
    Asian Americans, 108–110
    defined, 11–12
    disabled people, 177
    gender roles, 128
    Latinos/Latinas, 100
    older people, 160
    vulnerability, 12
Sternberg, T., 113
Stith, S. M., 80, 86
Stokoe, W. C., 178
Stoltz-Loike, M., 134
Stone Child Community College, 67
Stonewall riots, 147
Storytelling, 62, 70, 79, 108, 128, 140,
    144
Strickland, B. R., 124, 129
Strodtbeck, F. L., 30
Strong Hearts, Wounded Souls (Holm), 72
Strong Interest Inventory, 28
Strozier, A. L., 192, 198
Sturm, R., 165
Sudbury, M. A., 10, 181
Sue, D., 5, 16, 34, 78, 89–92, 94, 97, 100,
    103, 109, 111, 137, 186–187
Sue, D. W., 5, 7, 9, 16, 27–28, 49–50, 78,
    89–92, 94, 97, 100, 102, 109, 186–
    188, 207–212
Sue, S., 27–28, 34, 103, 109, 111, 189
Sugarman, B., 185
Suicide
    African American men, 137
    gays/lesbians, 149, 152
    Native Americans, 68
    older people, 162, 165
Suinn, R. M., 33
Suinn-Lew Asian Self-Identity Accultura-
    tion Scale, 33
Sullivan, D. M., 153
Sullivan, J. M., 144, 150
Sutherland, J. F., 117
Sutton, C. T., 60, 62–63, 69–71
Suzuki, L. A., 27, 32
Swanson, J. L., 28, 132, 137
Sweat lodges, 64, 66
Swedish Americans, 115
Sweeney, T. J., 169–172
Sweetland, R. C., 28–29
System of Multicultural Pluralistic
    Assessment, 29

T

Taffe, R. C., 189
Taffel, R., 142
Tafoya, N., 60, 66, 68
Tainter, B., 54, 174–175, 177, 182
Taiwanese Americans, 110
Tajfel, H., 48
Talking circles, 64
Tan, A., 113
Tannen, D., 126
Taoism, 104, 107–108
Tatum, B. D., 48, 50, 84
Taylor, S. E., 19
Teachers Insurance and Annuity Associa-
    tion—College Retirement Equities
    Fund, 166–167
Teen pregnancy rates
    African Americans, 74
    Native Americans, 60
Tefft, S. K., 58
Tennessee State University, 83
Terman, L., 14
Terranova, R. D., 198
Test bias, 25–30
Thai Americans, 107
*Theory of Multicultural Counseling and
    Therapy, A* (Sue et al.), 9, 187
Thomas, A., 101
Thomas, K. R., 42, 57–58
Thomas, M. B., 78
Thomason, T. C., 64–65, 69–71
Thompson, T., 138
Thomson, R. G., 185
Thousand Pieces of Gold (Yamamoto &
    Kelly), 113
Tien, L., 34
Timed tests, 26
Tokar, D. M., 132, 137
Tomes, H., 175–177, 179
Tomine, S. I., 103
Transference, 6
    clerical, 120
    color, 15
Trent, J. W., Jr., 185
Trimble, J. E., 5, 57–59, 68–71
Troiden, R. R., 55
Tucker, M. B., 120
Tugg v. Towey, 178
Turtle Mountain Community College, 67
Tuskegee Institute, 83

U

U.S. Bureau of the Census, 1, 57–58, 60,
    73–74, 89–90, 92–93, 103, 114–115
U.S. Department of Labor, 132, 182
U.S. General Accounting Office, 109
U.S. Senate Select Committee on Indian
    Affairs, 66
Uba, L., 105
Ulsh, S., 45
Undocumented workers, 43, 89, 91, 99
Unemployment
    African Americans, 74
    Native Americans, 60
United Tribes Technical College, 67
University of California–Berkeley, 24
Useem, R. H., 40

V

Vacc, N. A., 184
Valdez, L., 101
Valero, M., 45
Validation, 6, 19
Van Meter, M.J.S., 133
VanOss Marin, B., 33
Vasquez, M.J.T., 89, 93
Vernon, J., 16, 29, 176–177, 181
Vernon, M., 175
Vietnamese Americans, 9, 43, 46, 102–
    103, 106
Vigil, S., 33
Vineland Training School, 14
Violence
    against disabled people, 183–184
    against gays, 147–148, 152
    against older people, 168
    against women, 131, 142–143
Virginia State University, 83
Vision quests, 64
Vista, 4
Visual impairment, 176
Vocational counseling, 28
    Asian Americans, 110–111
    disabled people, 182
    gays/lesbians, 154
    Latinos/Latinas, 98–99
    men, 142
    Pacific Islander Americans, 110–111
    women, 131–133
Von Glinow, M. A., 132
Vontress, C. E., 5, 15, 82, 162

W

Waist-High in the World (Mairs), 185
Walker, L., 131
Walker, M., 87
Wampold, B. E., 100
Wang, W., 113
Warren, L. W., 142
Wasserstein, W., 135
Watters, E., 12
Waxman, H. M., 163
"We Would Like You to Know" (Castillo),
    88–89
Webster's Seventh New Collegiate Dictionary, 2
*Webster's Third New International Dictionary
    of the English Language*, 12
Wechsler Adult Intelligence Scale, 26
The Wedding Banquet (Hope et al.), 158
Wehrly, B., 122, 187, 191
Weinberg, G., 49, 147
Weiss, D. E., 132
Wells, K. B., 165
Welts, E. P., 117–118, 120
West Indian Americans, 75, 87
Wetzel, N. A., 117
*When I Am an Old Woman, I Shall Wear
    Purple* (Martz), 172
White Awareness (Katz), 21
White Bucks and Black-Eyed Peas (Mabry),
    56, 87
White Racial Identity Attitude Scale, 32–
    33
White, J., 23, 79
Wicherski, M., 197
Wilcox, D. W., 139–140, 142, 144
Wilk, S. L., 24–25, 27
Wilkins, R., 16
Williams, C., 23, 27, 29–30, 40–41, 43
Williams, R. M., 75
Williams, V., 33
Willms, G., 107
Wilson, J., 72
Wilson, L. L., 80, 86
Winawer-Steiner, H., 116
Wise, S. L., 189
With Silk Wings (Kim), 135
Witness (Feldman), 122
Wolf, T. J., 149
Wolfe, H. B., 123, 132, 134
Wolfe, S. M., 164
The Woman Warrior (Kingston), 113

Women of Color (Comas–Diaz & Greene),
    124, 135
Women, 3, 5, 12–13, 123–135
    acculturation, 40
    Arab, 45
    Asian Americans, 111
    counseling issues, 129–134
    cultural resources, 135
    cultural values, 126
    East Indian, 45
    histories/diversity, 123–125
    indigenous treatment methods, 126–
    129
    lesbians, 146–158
    older, 161
    violence against, 131, 142–143
Wong, D., 179
Wood, J. V., 19
Woolley, S., 158
Work ethic, 119–120
    Northern European, 115–116
World War II, 103
Worth, M., 87
Wounded Knee, 59
Wrenn, G., 15
Wright, B. A., 183

Wright, D. M., 131
Wyshak, G., 44

Y

Yale University, 24
Yamaguchi, S., 105
Yamamoto, J., 47
Yamamoto, K., 113
Yerkes, R., 14
Young, V. L., 135
Youngstrom, N., 182, 197, 200
Yung, D., 113
Yurich, J. M., 124, 137

Z

Zanuck, L. F., 173
Zanuck, R., 173
Zapata, J. T., 89–91
Zera, D., 49, 55, 152–154
Ziegler, J., 84
Zinick, G., 55
Zoot Suit (Valdez), 101
Zuckerman, M., 12, 23
Zuniga, M. E., 30, 34, 93, 95

ABOUT THE AUTHOR

Wanda M. L. Lee is a Professor of Counseling at San Francisco State University. She is an Asian American woman who earned a Ph.D. in Psychology and has two decades of experience in the field of counseling as a college counselor, private practitioner, and counselor educator. Dr. Lee teaches in a practitioner-oriented graduate program and specializes in multicultural counseling training. She has published journal articles and book chapters on the topics of new directions in multicultural counseling, ethnic and gender issues in assessment, and counseling effectiveness with Asian Americans. She was raised in Hawaii, traveled extensively around the world and in the United States, and now resides in California.